The Short Oxford History of the British Isles

General Editor: Paul Langford

The Roman Era

Edited by Peter Salway

AVAILABLE NOW

The Nineteenth Century
edited by Colin Matthew
The Twelfth and Thirteenth Centuries
edited by Barbara Harvey

IN PREPARATION, VOLUMES COVERING

From the Romans to the Vikings
From the Vikings to the Normans
The Fourteenth and Fifteenth Centuries
The Sixteenth Century
The Seventeenth Century
The Eighteenth Century
The Twentieth Century: The First Fifty Years
The British Isles: 1945–2000

Figure 1 This second-century head of the Roman god Mercury, from the cult-statue of a temple at Uley (Glos.), is in British limestone and demonstrates the high level of classical culture and craftsmanship that might sometimes be encountered in the Romano-British countryside.

The Short Oxford History of
the British Isles

General Editor: Paul Langford

The Roman Era

The British Isles:
55 BC–AD 410

Edited by Peter Salway

OXFORD
UNIVERSITY PRESS

OXFORD
UNIVERSITY PRESS

Great Clarendon Street, Oxford OX2 6DP

Oxford University Press is a department of the University of Oxford.
It furthers the University's objective of excellence in research, scholarship,
and education by publishing worldwide in

Oxford New York

Auckland Bangkok Buenos Aires Cape Town Chennai
Dar es Salaam Delhi Hong Kong Istanbul Karachi Kolkata
Kuala Lumpur Madrid Melbourne Mexico City Mumbai Nairobi
São Paulo Shanghai Singapore Taipei Tokyo Toronto

and an associated company in Berlin

Oxford is a registered trade mark of Oxford University Press
in the UK and in certain other countries

Published in the United States
by Oxford University Press Inc., New York

British Library Cataloguing in Publication Data

Data available

Library of Congress Cataloging in Publication Data

Data applied for

ISBN 0–19–873193–0 (hbk)
ISBN 0–19–873194–9 (pbk)

1 3 5 7 9 10 8 6 4 2

Typeset in Minion
by RefineCatch Limited, Bungay, Suffolk
Printed in Great Britain by
T.J. International, Padstow, Cornwall

Dis Manibus

Timothy William Potter

<small>MCMXLIV–MM</small>

General Editor's Preface

It is a truism that historical writing is itself culturally determined, reflecting intellectual fashions, political preoccupations, and moral values at the time it is written. In the case of British history this has resulted in a great diversity of perspectives both on the content of what is narrated and the geopolitical framework in which it is placed. In recent times the process of redefinition has positively accelerated under the pressure of contemporary change. Some of it has come from within Britain during a period of recurrent racial tension in England and reviving nationalism in Scotland, Wales, and Northern Ireland. But much of it also comes from beyond. There has been a powerful surge of interest in the politics of national identity in response to the break-up of some of the world's great empires, both colonial and continental. The search for new sovereignties, not least in Europe itself, has contributed to a questioning of long-standing political boundaries. Such shifting of the tectonic plates of history is to be expected but for Britain especially, with what is perceived (not very accurately) to be a long period of relative stability lasting from the late seventeenth century to the mid-twentieth century, it has had a particular resonance.

Much controversy and still more confusion arise from the lack of clarity about the subject matter that figures in insular historiography. Historians of England are often accused of ignoring the history of Britain as a whole, while using the terms as if they are synonymous. Historians of Britain are similarly charged with taking Ireland's inclusion for granted without engaging directly with it. And for those who believe they are writing more specifically the history of Ireland, of Wales, or of Scotland, there is the unending tension between so-called metropolis and periphery, and the dilemmas offered by wider contexts, not only British and Irish but European and indeed extra-European. Some of these difficulties arise from the fluctuating fortunes and changing boundaries of the British state as organized from London. But even if the rulers of what is now called England had never taken an interest in dominion beyond its borders, the economic and cultural relationships between the various parts of the British Isles would still have generated many historiographical problems.

This series is based on the premiss that whatever the complexities and ambiguities created by this state of affairs, it makes sense to offer an overview, conducted by leading scholars whose research is on the leading edge of their discipline. That overview extends to the whole of the British Isles. The expression is not uncontroversial, especially to many in Ireland, for whom the very word 'British' implies an unacceptable politics of dominion. Yet there is no other formulation that can encapsulate the shared experience of 'these islands', to use another term much employed in Ireland and increasingly heard in Britain, but rather unhelpful to other inhabitants of the planet.

In short we use the words 'British Isles' solely and simply as a geographical expression. No set agenda is implied. It would indeed be difficult to identify one that could stand scrutiny. What constitutes a concept such as 'British history' or 'four nations history', remains the subject of acute disagreement, and varies much depending on the period under discussion. The editors and contributors of this series have been asked only to convey the findings of the most authoritative scholarship, and to flavour them with their own interpretative originality and distinctiveness. In the process we hope to provide not only a stimulating digest of more than two thousand years of history, but also a sense of the intense vitality that continues to mark historical research into the past of all parts of Britain and Ireland.

Lincoln College   PAUL LANGFORD
Oxford

Foreword

It is entirely appropriate that a series on the history of the British Isles should include a volume on the Roman era, even if the balances in this volume cannot be quite the same as in those covering later periods. This is the point in time at which the Isles enter history as opposed to prehistory, the period when their past begins to be approachable through substantial written sources as well as archaeology and when for the first time we encounter named individuals and their lives. This book draws on all the branches of the two linked disciplines. Geographically, however, it is inevitable that it will contain much more on those parts of the Isles that witnessed long-term incorporation in the Roman empire than on those that were temporarily held by the Romans or not at all, because the written sources for the former is much greater and the archaeological evidence is more extensive and much easier to assign to shorter periods within the five centuries covered by this volume. Areas beyond the Roman borders are not overlooked, however, since current major topics of interest among historians and archaeologists include the effects on Rome's neighbours of their propinquity to the Roman frontier (and vice versa) and, indeed, the difficulties in defining where the empire ended and the *barbaricum* began.

Archaeological and documentary discoveries of major importance make this an appropriate time to take stock. The method adopted has been to recruit as chapter authors some of those most closely involved with discovery and analysis while also being at the forefront in conveying scholarly knowledge both to students and to the public. The General Editor has emphasized that 'The format allows historians of real quality to write what they know most about, without the impediment of footnotes and scholarly apparatus, and with a minimum of distraction from their research. I see this series as a way of conveying the authority and excitement that scholars have at their fingertips to a very wide audience.'

The Volume Editor's task has not been to impose tidiness by pretending that differences of opinion between scholars—including the contributors to this book—do not exist. 'Roman Britain' is a fast-moving subject, while also being approached from different standpoints by different scholars. The uncertainties are in many ways as interesting—or more interesting—than the certainties. There is no way in which every viewpoint current among Romano-British specialists could be represented, though the reader interested in following up specific topics will find that in many cases some extension of the range of opinion will be found in items listed in the Further Reading section, which has deliberately included a number of works whose authors fundamentally disagree with one another. The writing of history requires the application of controlled imagination to the evidence available at the time—it can never be complete—and this is critically so when the book is intended for the non-specialist. Much popular presentation through both written and broadcast media relies on catching the attention of the audience by exposing it to the proponents of the most extreme theories. This is both fundamentally unfair on the public and—in the end—unsatisfying. Balance, the Volume Editor hopes, has here been achieved by inviting contributors who apply both imagination and common sense to their material. It has thus been possible to allow them freedom to write in their own ways without serious dislocation between chapters. Some minor repetition of material between chapters will be noted: this however allows individual chapters to be read on their own. The Volume Editor's 'Conclusion' aims to round the book off by bringing together themes and debates that emerge from the earlier chapters, and by underlining some of the 'big questions' that make the subject endlessly fascinating.

Stanton Harcourt   PETER SALWAY
December 2000

Acknowledgements

The preparation of this book was sadly overshadowed by the sudden death in January 2000 of Timothy Potter, author of the first of the narrative chapters. His enormous devotion to his subject and enthusiasm for putting it over to public, student, and scholar alike comes through both in everything he wrote and in his great contributions to the British Museum. The editor of this volume can attest to his meticulous attention to detail, present as always in his chapter here, which was so near to total readiness for publication that the very slight touches that have been applied to it with the kind consent of his family and Museum colleagues created no editorial burden.

The Volume Editor and the other contributors would particularly like to thank the General Editor, Paul Langford, for the clear direction given to this series, and for unfailing helpfulness successive Commissioning Editors at the Press (Tony Morris, Ruth Parr, Andrew MacLennan, and Fiona Kinnear) and many others, including particularly Lesley Wilson and Jo Stanbridge. The Volume Editor owes a particular debt of gratitude to John Casey and Richard Hingley who stepped in at short notice as contributors, and to all the chapter authors for helpful advice on each others' drafts and for putting up with sometimes arbitrary editing of their own. The authors also wish to thank the colleagues who read parts of the text at various stages or gave other much-valued assistance, including Catherine Johns, Brian Dobson, W. S. Hanson, Richard Hingley, Sonja Jilek, and Lesley Macinnes. However, in such a collaborative work the Volume Editor in the end bears the responsibility, and hopes his colleagues will forgive any errors, omissions, or misunderstanding of their opinions that may have crept in unintentionally in the process of putting the book together.

Contents

3 The fourth century and beyond 75

P. J. Casey

4 Culture and social relations in the Roman province 107

Janet Huskinson

Conclusion   203

Peter Salway

List of Illustrations

xviii | LIST OF ILLUSTRATIONS

List of Maps

List of Contributors

DAVID J. BREEZE, Chief Inspector of Ancient Monuments, Historic Scotland; Visiting Professor, University of Durham

P. J. CASEY, Reader, Department of Archaeology, University of Durham

MICHAEL FULFORD, Professor of Archaeology and Pro-Vice-Chancellor, University of Reading

RICHARD HINGLEY, Lecturer, Department of Archaeology, University of Durham

JANET HUSKINSON, Senior Lecturer, Department of Classical Studies, The Open University

DAVID MILES, Chief Archaeologist, English Heritage

The late T. W. POTTER, Keeper of Prehistoric and Romano-British Antiquities, British Museum

PETER SALWAY, All Souls College, Oxford; Emeritus Professor, The Open University

Figure 2 Figure representing Winter on a fourth-century mosaic in a dining suite in the Chedworth (Glos.) villa. The popular Roman motif of the Four Seasons is here given a British touch by dressing the figure warmly in the *byrrus Britannicus*, a hooded cape featured (along with British beer) in the Emperor Diocletian's anti-inflation Price Edict.

Introduction

Peter Salway

What are we to make of Roman Britain? At school most of us were told that Britain was invaded twice by Julius Caesar and conquered under Claudius, and that the Romans built roads, cities, villas, baths, and Hadrian's Wall. In AD 410 'the legions were withdrawn to defend the centre of the empire against the barbarians' and 'the Romans left Britain', with hardly a trace of their society left behind, other than some rather large ruins. We probably also absorbed—particularly if we were brought up in Wales, Scotland, or Ireland—an impression that the indigenous population of these islands (or 'Celts') were free spirits devoted to liberty and high artistic achievement who universally resisted the Romans. In those parts of the islands ultimately conquered, Roman cultural imperialism replaced the magnificence of Celtic art with a dull, provincial version of classical civilization. In the rest of the Isles, Celtic art and society survived and flourished. Even within the Roman province, the Celtic world continued under the surface, since the Mediterranean culture imported by Rome was no more than a veneer, and—particularly the urban-centred aspects—was failing before the end of Roman rule. After 410, we were told, the Celts of Britain and Ireland—having become Christian—represented the forces of Western civilization against the incoming pagan Anglo-Saxons. Little by little those Saxons were converted partly by Celtic missionaries from the West and North, and partly by deliberate intervention from papal Rome, starting with the arrival of St Augustine at Canterbury in 596. From the fusion of those Celtic and Anglo-Saxon strands came the foundations of the unique structure of government and society in the British Isles.

This satisfyingly coherent picture suited both an essentially nineteenth-century liberal belief in progress and a concomitant desire to see admired British institutions (particularly parliamentary democracy) as grounded in a long but inevitable evolution from beginnings in Anglo-Saxon England. Ironically, it also suited the twentieth-century taste for the cultures of indigenous peoples as against that of colonizing Western states, and in our own time has been powerfully reinforced by post-colonial attitudes. The physical remains of Roman Britain appear as relics of an amazing and exotic interlude with no more relevance to the present than the Egypt of the Pharaohs or Minoan Crete.

More recent archaeological theory has reinforced the 'interlude' view of the Roman era in Britain. There has been a general inclination to dismiss the analysis of British prehistory dominant in the first half of the twentieth century that equated changes in the physical record with successive invasions of substantial groups of peoples from the Continent. This shift in opinion has reinforced the notion of an indigenous culture that was only superficially affected by the Claudian invasion, the one conquest of early Britain that certainly did happen. In this scenario, the indigenous culture is reckoned to have had a 'natural trajectory' that was temporarily interrupted in the part of the British Isles that came under Roman rule but developed unimpeded in Ireland and, to a lesser extent perhaps—being in part subject to Roman disturbance—in Scotland.

Some of those children whose school trips included Roman sites or museums with Romano-British displays may have begun to notice cracks in this otherwise coherent picture. To counter the popular assumption that 'the Romans' in Britain were Italians, it has become common practice to emphasize that almost all the population of Roman Britain was indigenous. Visitors to military sites are told that after the end of the first century AD local recruiting was the norm, and at Roman villas it is said that the owners were from local families that adopted Roman ways and prospered, their increasing wealth over the centuries being reflected in larger and larger houses that culminated in the great country mansions of the fourth century. It has also become a truism that even the grandest villas were essentially farms or depended on some other income-generating activity in the rural economy. The contrast between these villa people and the peasantry who occupied what used to be called 'native sites' in the countryside was not of ethnicity but wealth, class, and taste. Indeed, the realization that between the grand villa and the humble native farm there

lies a continuous range of establishments distinguished archaeologically primarily by their level of amenity and possessions reinforces
the notion that these are essentially a single people. The visitor is
correctly informed that by far the largest part of the population must
have lived in the countryside: the percipient may begin to realize that
the notion of a superficially affected society has its weaknesses.

The alleged fundamental incompatibility between British society
and Rome was particularly seen to manifest itself in the history of the
Romano-British city. It seemed to reach a peak in the first half of the
second century, as measured by evidence of vigorous economic activity and as separated out from other sorts of settlement by possession
of all or most of the public buildings and other adornments that
mark the urban centres of the classical world. Central to classical
culture was the idea of the city and of self-government through the
city—however limited that might prove in practice. However, archaeological evidence in the Romano-British cities for smaller populations in the Later Roman period, combined with reduced amounts of
imported goods seeming to indicate decreased commercial activity,
and with demonstrable decay or disuse of public buildings, all
appeared to demonstrate that the transplanted urban culture of the
Mediterranean had failed to take hold in alien soil. In some influential writing on Roman Britain in the first half of the twentieth century,
this appeared as clear evidence of inability to sustain the standards
of the Roman empire at its height. This picture has been picked up
in recent decades and developed to the extreme by some serious
archaeologists to persuade us that long before the end of Roman rule
in Britain its cities were effectively dead. It is not, however, a view that
has found universal acceptance. An understanding that cities in the
fourth and fifth centuries were *different* from those of the Early
Empire—with different but important functions derived from major
changes in society being reflected in different material remains—is
emerging from current research on other parts of the Roman world
by historians and archaeologists of the Late Roman period, which
artificial divisions in the academic world in the past between classicists on the one hand and medievalists on the other had tended to
relegate to a minor interest, particularly within Romano-British
studies.

The end of Roman Britain

The notion of incompatibility made it relatively easy to accept without serious question the idea that in 410 or thereabouts 'the Romans left Britain'. The much more complex—and much disputed—picture of what really occurred in Britain and its place in the disintegration of the western Roman empire will be examined later in this book. It is certainly now much easier to imagine in a world that has seen the sudden demise of the Soviet empire or the piecemeal collapse and reversion to primitive ethnic warfare of apparently orderly and peaceful societies such as the former Yugoslavia, with all the concomitant loss of the everyday amenities of modern living that seemed so permanent that they were unregarded. It is sufficient here just to point to the fact that from AD 212—two centuries before the end of Roman rule in Britain—almost every free inhabitant of the empire was a Roman citizen. For 'the Romans' to leave Britain—in the sense that the idea has passed into general consciousness—most of the population of England, Wales, and part of Scotland would have had to emigrate, presumably in a single mass movement. Exodus on this scale has, indeed, unhappily been seen in recent times, but understanding the implications of an accepted notion provides a very necessary freeing of the imagination to look afresh at the evidence.

Archaeology and literature

In terms of quantity, the bulk of the evidence about Roman Britain is from its material remains. Until the last few decades there was an overwhelming tendency among scholars to try to fit the archaeology to the—by contrast—fairly thin literary evidence. But a widespread reaction against interpreting the material evidence in the light of the literary accounts has led at its extreme to replacing the assessment of the usual study of Roman Britain as 'text-assisted archaeology' by the notion of it as 'text-hindered archaeology'. Some have felt that it is more 'scientific' simply to apply the techniques of prehistorians, interpreting the material evidence through methodologies derived from anthropology and other branches of the social sciences. Others have tended to favour the more extreme view that the task is simply to record, avoiding interpretation. Neither of these views withstands real scrutiny. Simple record is, of course, vital, but any form of record involves the exercise of judgement on what to record, in the light of how the information may eventually be used, however much the recorders may think themselves impartial. As far as using the ancient texts is concerned, it makes no more scientific sense to ignore the literature than for a doctor not to listen to what a patient is saying. The patient may not be able to describe his symptoms accurately nor to understand them, and may, indeed, have conscious or unconscious motives for not telling the truth, but the patient's utterances, alongside the physical symptoms, are a very important part of the evidence which the doctor must try to interpret in the light of his own training and experience. Indeed, to avoid the literary evidence ignores the fact that an enormous amount of recent work by classicists and historians has focused on reinterpreting the texts themselves and the society in which they were created. This would be true of any historical period for which texts are available, but there is an extra dimension in the case of the Roman world, as it was a culture in which very accurate use of language was ingrained. Two of the fields of activity at the centre of the life experience of members of the Roman elite (in which most of the writers of the period can be included) were the law and the type of religion in which exact adherence to prescribed ritual is critical. Most of these people will have at various stages of their careers actually practised in the courts or had to administer written law, and the same people (since there was no general ordained priesthood except among the Christians) will also have performed public and private ritual in which meticulous observation of the proper words was required. Nor was this confined only to the topmost echelons of society at Rome itself. *Mutatis mutandis* the same activities occurred throughout the empire, and at different levels of society. Even in imaginative literature the same attention to exactitude was important (to words, syntax, poetic metre, and the layout of the particular category of work). In using ancient written sources, therefore, it is always necessary to remember that the exact words, in the original languages, are the prime evidence, and that classical scholarship is the indispensable tool by which texts are established from the often fragmentary or distorted remains and meanings elucidated.

There is a very important regard in which approaching Roman Britain as essentially no different from any of the earlier periods has now been rendered out of date. We can have no quarrel with the general view that the bulk of the population was indigenous. The common assumption flowing from this that 'Romanization' was therefore a veneer that hardly affected the day-to-day lives and ways of thinking of the vast mass of the inhabitants has, however, taken a very serious knock from recent discoveries of contemporary written material that is undeniably and strikingly humdrum—in the sort of detail previously only known through the papyri of Roman Egypt—which demonstrates that in Roman Britain we are dealing with a society in which written documents and the transactions, rules, regulations, and social manners that produced them reached down to the most ephemeral aspects of daily life. The discovery at the fort of Vindolanda on the northern frontier of around 700 original contemporary documents (mostly official, semi-official, and private letters and memoranda written in ink on wooden tablets and in the region of 200 more that had been scribed in wax) is phenomenal. This is supplemented by lesser but still significant numbers from other Romano-British sites, and by substantial quantities (greater than from the whole of the rest of the empire) of inscribed lead plates from sacred sites, containing pleas to the gods, mostly to find lost or stolen objects and to bring down vengeance on those known or unknown who have allegedly wronged the depositor. We are now being given glimpses of the everyday lives of individual ordinary people, in a way and at a scale that simply does not exist for preceding or, indeed, for succeeding periods till well into the early Middle Ages.

This confirmation that life in Roman Britain had a fundamental similarity to that elsewhere in the Roman empire adds great weight to the use of *analogy* in the interpretation of evidence from Britain. From Roman Spain, for example, we know from the improbable but fortunate survival of a small number of official public notices in the form of bronze tablets the way in which—for example—mines could be leased to contractors or disputes between local communities settled. There will always have been local conditions, of course, and practice varied with time, but general principles can mostly be assumed and often detail as well. Behind this confidence lies the fundamental feature of the Roman era that makes it unique in the history of the British Isles. For three centuries the context in which the major decisions in the governing of Britain were taken was not Britain itself—or at least not Britain alone. As part of an empire that encompassed a large part of the then known world, policy was chiefly determined by what was happening in the empire at large and usually by people whose main interests were elsewhere. The most obvious are where the personal interests of an emperor or would-be emperor are at stake, such as the Claudian invasion. But these were rare—if spectacular—events. Thousands and thousands of routine decisions over the centuries of Roman rule will have had an all-pervading effect. Even on the spot in the province, all the more important decisions were taken by imperial officials on relatively short tours of duty: three years or less was not unusual. Moreover, their posting to Britain was normally only one step in a career that will have taken them to many parts of the empire, including recurrent periods in the imperial capital or with the emperor. At least under the Early Empire, the same applied to army officers down to quite junior ranks. Indeed, these were often the same individuals as the civil officials, but at different points in their careers, since a regulated and well-defined mix of military and civil posts in ascending order of responsibility and prestige was perhaps the outstanding common feature of the majority of careers in public life. It would be a mistake, however, to assume a parallel with, say, the British empire, and see these Romans as Englishmen from the motherland administering 'natives'. While their common culture—and the theatre in which at the top levels of society their aspirations and ambitions were played out—was that of metropolitan Rome, their personal backgrounds were increasingly from other parts of the empire. Though shifting as to individuals, the consistent presence of a core of people with such a cosmopolitan background at the centre of society in Roman Britain for the whole of the three hundred years is a factor which it is unwise to ignore. It is not only a matter of actual power and status, it is also of dominant *mentalité*.

The use of information about better-known parts of the classical world as one of the principal ways in which to make sense of Roman Britain has, however, not only been under fire from those who have regarded Rome's presence in Britain as superficial and therefore the relevance of evidence from elsewhere in the empire minimal. It has also been attacked by archaeologists of the Roman provinces who are more impressed by differences than similarities between them, and by classicists who regard Britain as so peripheral to their interests and so mundane as to be not worth considering. To some extent the latter was for long driven by the literary tradition in Classics already mentioned. That regarded the Latin language and literature of the second half of the first century BC and the first half of the first century AD as 'Golden', and the succeeding period as 'Silver'. Anything written later than about 120 was not 'Classical Latin' and therefore of progressively less regard. To an important extent this was driven by the primacy formerly given in the teaching of Classics to composition in the classical languages, in which the accurate employment of language and style derived from the 'best' authors was paramount. As models, therefore, Latin authors writing before the first century BC or after the early second century AD were not recommended. As guidance for the study of anything outside the narrowest vision of the Latin texts this was always unsound. It comes as a pleasing irony to discover that Britain has recently become of importance for classical philologists as the principal source of 'new' Latin, being the primary source material for the study of the language as used by ordinary people that is now emerging from the newly available contemporary documents described above.

The once-prevailing general lack of interest by scholars and teachers in the Roman world after the early second century tended to leave the study of Roman Britain—whose principal flowerings were in the second century and the fourth—out in the cold. But there was also—and sometimes still is—a parochialism that tackled the archaeology of Roman Britain as unlike anything else, with little to be learnt from the employment of analogy to enlarge and interpret the evidence on the ground. The true character of the British Isles in the Roman era will only emerge by identifying where they resembled territories and communities elsewhere, and where they differed from them.

Further new factors in the study of Roman Britain

Two further matters make this an appropriate point at which to take stock of Roman Britain. One is the 'PPG 16 factor'. The issuing of the British Government document known as *Planning Policy Guidance no. 16* has caused a revolution in the amount of excavation and other archaeological investigation undertaken in the United Kingdom, as it requires developers to bear the costs of 'mitigation' of the effects on sites of archaeological interest. In effect, this means that the archaeological potential of sites for which planning permission is sought has now to be investigated, and often excavation undertaken on a scale very rarely approached formerly. The other factor is the development of a whole range of 'high-tech' means of investigating sites and finds, some long-established but recently become much more precise, others entirely new. Tree-ring dating (dendrochronology), for example, has gradually been refined, and when applied to wooden piling supporting a major complex of Roman waterfront building in London has not only been able to date the structure to a particular year in the brief reign of the usurper Allectus (AD 293–296) but convincingly to pinpoint the commencement of construction to the spring of that year.

As the reader progresses through the chapters in this book, it will become clear that there are different opinions among the contributors on many points. This reflects the fact that the evidence available at any one time is rarely conclusive—quite apart from the fact that discoveries that require rethinking of accepted views happen all the time. It is a mark of a very lively academic discipline. Sound interpretation in the end, of course, depends on informed judgement, tempered by common sense: the choice of contributors was deliberately aimed to recruit experts actively involved in the latest research, and among them to select writers not committed to one academic extreme or another. This book aims to present a snapshot of knowledge and opinion about the Roman era in the history of the British Isles at this particularly exciting point in the evolution of the subject.

Figure 3 The Emperor Claudius overcoming Britannia. In this relief from a temple dedicated to the Imperial Family at Aphrodisias in Turkey, Claudius is portrayed in the conventional guise of a hero in classical myth.

1

The transformation of Britain: from 55 BC to AD 61

T. W. Potter

The Britain that Julius Caesar so famously invaded in 55 and 54 BC was for most Romans, and other Mediterranean peoples, dimly known, and certainly a place of no consequence: it lay much too far beyond the pale of the civilized Graeco-Roman world for that. Even the name of its inhabitants aroused confusion. Pytheas, a Greek from Massalia, modern Marseilles, who claimed to have circumnavigated the British Isles in the fourth century BC, called them *Prittanoi* (interestingly echoed by the word for a Briton in modern Welsh, *Prydain*), and it may be that it was Caesar himself who brought into wider currency the word 'British'. Admittedly, Pytheas was denounced repeatedly as a liar and a fraud by another Greek, Strabo, writing around the beginning of the first century AD; but many of Pytheas' reported observations (his actual work is lost) ring true, especially his reference to the long hours of daylight, and to Thule—a name applied erroneously by other ancient writers such as Tacitus and Ptolemy to the islands of Shetland. He irresistibly recalls the early European discoverers of America, with their often naive, and distorted, descriptions of what they saw: such is the danger of using literary sources for the writing of the history of the period. Here it should be made clear that, while the ancients did sometimes refer to the peoples north of the Alps as 'Celts', there is no justification for regarding them as some vast ethnic unity. As in Italy itself, where at least forty major languages were spoken prior to the Roman conquest, the 'Celts' must have been a diverse and complex matrix of tribes, the supposed unity of which is largely a modern supposition. The term 'Celt' needs therefore to be used with care.

The complex societies of the prehistoric British Isles

If the Graeco-Roman world viewed Britain—and Ireland (known as Hibernia)—as primitive and barbaric places, then the archaeological evidence tells a very different story. The fourth and third millennia BC saw the emergence of monumental architecture, from Stonehenge (itself perhaps a ceremonial and religious centre of international pilgrimage) to the astonishing tombs and stone circles of Orkney and Shetland; from about 1500 BC some regions witnessed the systematic parcelling out of large areas of land, with trackways and field boundaries; while the early to mid first millennium BC is characterized by a remarkable and intricately developed series of landscapes, often dominated in many parts of the British Isles by major centres that we term hill-forts. Everything points to the evolution of a highly complex and sophisticated system of tribal societies which, while displaying marked regional differences and apparently lacking in literacy, were nevertheless mediating their affairs in a far from primitive way. Wheeled vehicles had, for instance, been in use for well over a thousand years, implying a relatively advanced system of communications; and coins of the later second and first centuries BC are widely found in the South-East of England. The mechanisms behind their origin, and how they were used, remain obscure; but they are a prominent part of the archaeological record, and must reflect a fast developing world in which the gift or exchange of money played a significant role in some societies. Indeed, few prominent Britons of Caesar's day cannot have known something of the Graeco-Roman history and culture of the Mediterranean world. The foundation in 118 BC of the colony of Roman citizens at Narbo, modern Narbonne, on the southern French coast—the first such settlement in Gaul (although a fort had been established at Aquae Sextiae,

Aix-en-Provence, four years earlier)—must have been both a catalyst for change and for the further dissemination northwards of knowledge about events, traditions, and ideas in southern Europe.

Julius Caesar

A half-century or so later, in 58 BC, Julius Caesar brought his army into Gaul, where he had been given a special command, to prevent a migration of the Helvetii from what is now Switzerland. Whether meditated or not, it was to lead to his celebrated wars of conquest. It is astonishing that, by 50 BC, the whole of what is modern France and some territory to the east had come under Roman domination. Given the magnitude of the task, it is not easy to explain why he should have decided also to mount two hazardous expeditions to southern Britain. Britons had fought against him alongside some of the Gallic tribes, but this was surely an irritant rather than a *casus belli*. Nor does Caesar, an arch politician, explain his real aims, whether conquest or the mere imposition of terms. The likelihood must be that he needed dramatic victories to justify an extension of his command, agreed in 56 BC; and that his eye was already on the seizure of supreme power in the politically disintegrating world of the Late Republic. Civil war can only have seemed a matter of time, and Caesar needed his army to enforce his ambitions as, with hindsight, we might perceive them.

This is of course to read between the lines, and the matter is not uncontentious. Moreover, in the event things did not always go Caesar's way. The first expedition was held up by troubles with the Germans, and sailed only late in the summer of 55 BC. The force was extraordinarily small, with just two legions and some auxiliary (non-citizen) troops, hardly more than 10,000 men in all. Moreover, the ships transporting his cavalry were beset with contrary winds, and were never to make a landfall in Britain. Caesar had however to some extent prepared the ground by organizing a reconnaissance for a suitable place to beach his fleet, and had also sent a trusted Gallic chieftain, Commius, to Britain, to win over some of the tribal leaders. But the arrival of his force, presumably in eastern Kent, had been anticipated, resistance was strong, and a storm damaged or wrecked many of his ships four days later. Caesar presents the Romans' military achievements in the best possible light; but despite a subsequent victory, and a tally of hostages, the return to Gaul in jerry-rigged boats before the winter set in can hardly have been seen as an unqualified success.

The following year, 54 BC, a very much larger invasion force was assembled. Five legions formed the core, and the army sailed in an armada of over 800 ships. These included the private vessels of civilians, doubtless including traders, a matter of some interest as we will see. If Caesar now realized that he needed a much greater weight of arms to ensure a suitably spectacular military success, the Britons, however, had also learnt from the battles of the previous year. They placed their command in the hands of a single leader, Cassivellaunus, who may have been chieftain of a tribal grouping later known as the Catuvellauni. It is sometimes suggested that their main royal seat at this time was at Verlamion, today on the outskirts of St Albans, although Welwyn, or conceivably Wheathampstead, are more likely, since both have finds of the right sort of date, unlike Verlamion.

The Roman landing was again hindered by the weather, but this time a properly defended beachhead was constructed, to protect the disembarkation. It has never been identified on the ground—indeed, there is no unequivocal archaeological evidence for Caesar's invasions—but it makes military sense. The Roman army was not particularly experienced in this sort of ship-launched warfare, but was pragmatic, and learnt fast. The British were engaged, and routed, and then defeated en masse at an unnamed river normally identified as the Thames. Cassivellaunus, with 4,000 chariots, retreated northwards to his stronghold (*oppidum*), with his force in disarray.

It was at this point that the Trinovantes, a tribe whose territory focused upon what is modern Essex, approached Caesar. Their prince, Mandubracius, had been sent into exile in Gaul, following the murder of his father at the order of Cassivellaunus. This had driven a wedge, we can imagine, between two leading tribal groups. Following the principle of 'divide and rule' (a phrase first used by the Roman historian Tacitus), Caesar accepted the idea of restoring Mandubracius' position, in return for hostages and foodstuffs, and thus learnt of the whereabouts of Cassivellaunus' base. This was then successfully stormed. Soon afterwards, following a final battle, probably in Kent, Caesar decided to return to Gaul, where he feared—rightly, as it turned out—that a serious uprising might break out. Indeed, he may well have gleaned news of the fact that Vercingetorix, ruler of the Arverni, a tribe of the French Massif Central, might become the supreme Gallic war-leader, and thus pose a very dangerous threat to Roman success. Equally, he probably thought that he had achieved all that he could in Britain: his military reputation was, to an extent, enhanced; conditions and alliances had been imposed; and he had extracted his army from a venture which, however phlegmatic the measured tones of his carefully phrased history of the war, *de Bello Gallico*, must in reality have concealed many private anxieties. Like all cross-Channel invasions, not least the D-Day landings of 1944, the risk factor was very high, even for so formidable a general as Caesar. Whilst he was not accorded an appropriate celebration in Rome, he cannot have been unpleased with the outcome of his expeditions to what, even in the days of the Claudian Conquest, nearly a century later, was widely regarded as an island 'outside the limits of the known world', in the words of the historian Dio.

Vercingetorix (with whom Caesar's former trusted envoy, the Gaul Commius, now threw in his hand) was indeed to pose a major threat to Caesar's military achievements. It was only the dramatic siege of Alesia (Alise-Ste-Reine, to the north-west of Dijon, in east-central France) in 52 BC that finally brought Gallic opposition effectively to an end. Commius escaped to Britain, and Vercingetorix was taken to Rome where, after Caesar's triumph had been celebrated in 46 BC, he was, without remorse, strangled to death. The harsh treatment meted out generally to the Gauls, and to their leaders, cannot have gone unnoticed in Britain, and was certainly remembered, as we shall see.

Rome's impact on Britain before the Claudian Conquest

The political, social, and economic impact of Caesar's expeditions to south-east Britain, and the establishment of Rome's Gallic provinces—now just a short sail away from Britain—have, however, been generally minimized in much previous historical scholarship. The real watershed in Roman–British relations has traditionally been regarded as the outcome of the invasion ordered by Claudius in AD 43. The archaeological evidence, coupled with a new, less *colonially* influenced perception of how to think of the past, has in recent decades begun to bring about a radical reappraisal. Here, the exhibition of the national collections of Iron Age and Romano-British antiquities in the British Museum, now (since 1997) for the first time ever visually juxtaposed in conjoining galleries, strongly makes the point, in a way that words almost cannot. Whilst the impact of Rome on, in particular, architecture and literacy is extremely conspicuous in the displays of post-Conquest material, nevertheless, as the galleries make abundantly clear, the penetration of British markets by traders from the Roman world—especially Gaul—is obvious from at least one hundred years before. Indeed, at the coastal site of Hengistbury Head, near Christchurch in Dorset, Italian amphorae for the transport of wine and other goods, were arriving from about 100 BC, albeit in relatively small quantities. The real escalation in trade (and probably diplomatic gifts) began after Caesar's expeditions, and especially from the last part of the first century BC. Indeed, it is not impossible that Cassivellaunus, and other rulers such as Mandubracius, were regarded by Caesar as now having the status of 'client' kings, empowered by Rome. This can be vividly illustrated by a very rich burial from Welwyn in Hertfordshire. Although placed in a simple earth-cut pit (but perhaps once covered by a tumulus, now completely destroyed), the cremated bones of the deceased were accompanied by five Italian wine amphorae, together holding well over 100 litres; a strainer for removing the dregs; a silver drinking cup of Italian manufacture; mixing bowls; and thirty pottery vessels intended for feasting. Nail cleaners, hinting at the enhanced importance of personal appearance, were also provided, as well as a handsome set of glass gaming counters. The interment should date to around the third quarter of the first century BC, and can hardly be other than the grave of a tribal aristocrat, whose burial chamber included some gifts from foreign leaders, such as the silver cup. Interestingly, this echoes the form of burials of the elite in Gaul, as though some British rulers were now participating in a geographically much wider royal marriage network, as was to happen in later European history.

This growth in trade is not only attested archaeologically. The geographer Strabo (writing around the time that the Welwyn burial was made, in a much quoted passage) refers to the exports from Britain: grain, iron, cattle, and hides, all commodities of high importance to the Roman state; and also gold, silver, slaves, and hunting dogs. Only the inclusion of silver seems really dubious, since it occurs in Britain only in the Mendip Hills of Somerset, where it is mixed with lead: there is no evidence for its mining before the Roman Conquest, and indeed Caesar commented to the statesman Cicero on its lack. Otherwise these were acquisitions with particular appeal to a Roman aristocracy, much given to flaunting its wealth and exotic possessions. They were also greatly reliant upon a world in which slaves—perhaps three million of them in Italy alone at this time— played a fundamental role. One would like to know how many came from Britain, since there is little confirmatory evidence in the archaeological record. Nevertheless, Strabo does observe that some British leaders 'procured the friendship of Caesar Augustus by sending embassies, and by paying court to him'. Furthermore, the whole of the island was, in effect, 'Roman property' (a statement supporting the idea of client kingdoms), where the British paid heavy duties on the goods that they imported: 'ivory chains and necklaces, and amber gems, and glass vessels, and other pretty wares of that sort'.

The supercilious tone of these remarks may reflect the fact that, in a somewhat gauche way (as it would have appeared to an educated Mediterranean person), sections of the aristocracy of south-eastern Britain were in the process of rapid cultural change stimulated in particular from Gaul. To be sure, there will have been conservative elements even in the evolving societies of the South-East, perhaps supported by the priesthood of the Druids. Caesar believed that the Druidic cult, which the Romans tried several times to wipe out in Gaul, originated in Britain. Human sacrifice was said to be at the heart of its ritual, perhaps reflected by the gruesomely slain Lindow Man (whose stomach contained mistletoe, a plant associated with Druidic practices), and who was cast into a Cheshire peat bog perhaps around this time. But the Druids also played a political role, well attested in Gaul and, in all probability, in Britain too, although here the evidence is much weaker. Certainly, the Druids were fiercely opposed to Roman domination, and they were to be put to the sword at their major centre on the island of Anglesey in AD 60, although they remained strong in Ireland.

The Iceni tribe of Norfolk and east Cambridgeshire, like the

Dobunni and Durotriges of Gloucestershire, are likely to have been amongst the 'traditionalists'. When Queen Boudicca went into battle against the Romans in AD 61, she wore, according to Dio, a large gold necklace. Such ceremonial regalia had a long history in the region, as a dozen hoards containing amongst other things some 200 necktorcs, found at Snettisham in Norfolk, remind us: these were buried *c.*70 BC, over a century before Boudicca's rebellion. Imported objects in pre-Conquest contexts are very rare in this area of Britain, and—although some coinage may extend well back into the first century BC—the great majority of the hoards are very much later. Similarly, the style of other artefacts such as pottery remains insistently local. This stands very much in contrast to other areas of the South-East, where the archaeological evidence, as hinted above, points to the adoption by at least some of the elite classes of Graeco-Roman ways: in habits of eating and drinking; in dress and appearance; in the use of language and coinage; in burial customs, particularly the rite of cremation; and, to some extent, in architecture and urban planning, especially the use of rectilinear layouts. One might surmise that Caesar's invasions, coupled with the establishment of the Gallic provinces, may have been a powerful catalyst for change, particularly amongst some of the younger aristocracy of south-east England. To couch it as a 'modernizing' tendency is to deploy fashionable contemporary terminology; but it may well be a suitable way of describing some of the tensions that were emerging at this time between leaders who held to traditions firmly rooted in the past, and the more youthful aspirants, who sought power by championing new, and specifically foreign, ways.

Virtually none of the tribal names mentioned by Caesar endured into later Roman usage: the people of Kent, Cantium (but ruled by four separate kings), and the Trinovantes of Essex, are exceptions, and the Cenimagni *might* be identified with the later Iceni. However, the fact that some tribal identities do not survive into later centuries underlines the political volatility of the period. Although some of the inscribed coins imply the establishment of lineages by the use of the Latin *f(ilius)*, son, this may only have been an attempt to portray the succession as legitimate, when the truth was quite different. Nevertheless it is hardly possible to reconstruct such power struggles from either the numismatic record or the literary evidence, only snippets of which survive in the ancient sources.

Yet, we do hear of British aristocrats making overtures to Rome, and even dedicating offerings on the Capitol of the world's preeminent city. These surely reflect internal dissension in Britain and, more significantly, that Rome now had a single ruler, the Emperor Augustus. By defeating Antony and Cleopatra in 31 BC at the battle of Actium, off Corfu, Octavian, as he was then called, had brought to an end the strife of the Late Roman Republic. Caesar's adopted heir, he took the title of Augustus ('revered') in 27 BC and, if formally 'first amongst equals', was in effect master of the known world. Suppliant British aristocrats, well aware of the emperor's power, can hardly not have noticed the importance that securing his support would have on their own advancement.

The political matrix in Britain—at any rate in the South-East— had also undergone other forms of change, further encouraged, perhaps, by what some think was a sharp rise in the size of the population in the late first millennium BC. Caesar observed that the Belgae from northern Gaul (hence Belgium) had first commenced raiding and then settling in 'the maritime part' of Britain from before his time. This underlines the fact that for centuries, if not millennia (as we are reminded by the wreck of a Bronze Age boat with a surviving cargo of bronze implements, dating to c.1100 BC, from Dover waterfront), the sea had been no obstacle to cross-Channel movement. To the Gauls and the Britons it was a bridge, not a barrier. However, over the past thirty-five years or so, scholars have tended to think (unlike earlier generations) that the Belgae had left no obvious trace in the archaeological record, although the name of Roman Winchester, Venta Belgarum ('Market of the Belgae'), provides a clue. Now it can be shown that some cemeteries of cremations in south-east England, accompanied by wheel-turned pots, originated well before Caesar's invasions. One example is Westhampnett, near Chichester, where the earliest graves date to about 90 BC. Since this burial rite, and the accompanying types of vessels, can closely be paralleled in northern Gaul, a correlation with Belgic settlements seems very likely.

One definite immigrant from Gaul was Commius, the ruler of the Atrebates, a tribe based in the Pas-de-Calais. As we saw earlier, he was at first Caesar's envoy, and then threw in his lot with Vercingetorix. Two attempts by the Romans to kill him failed, and eventually, probably in 50 BC, he escaped to Britain. The town of Calleva Atrebatum, today Silchester near Reading (Berkshire), is almost certainly his foundation, and excavations have shown that, within twenty years or so of Commius' arrival in Britain, a regular pattern of right-angled streets was beginning to be laid out. This practice of 'orthogonal' planning was peculiarly Mediterranean (and especially Greek) in origin, and further illustrates how Graeco-Roman concepts were starting to permeate parts of southern Britain.

Some British coinage also demonstrates the same point. Commius himself—surely the same Commius of history—struck coins bearing his name, seemingly the first ruler in Britain to do so. Hitherto, coins had borne designs which were often abstractions from Mediterranean prototypes, a favourite feature of 'Celtic' art, although animal motifs were also popular. Thereafter, some rulers chose increasingly to imitate Roman issues. Eppillus, for example, who claimed on his coins to be a son of Commius, describes himself as REX, in Latin 'king'; others may even have employed die-cutters from the Mediterranean world. One such was Tincomarus, as coins from a recently found hoard at Alton, Hampshire, now allow us to read his name. On these, buried in the Augustan period together with a gold ring and a bracelet (perhaps diplomatic gifts probably made in Italy itself), he also claims to be a son of Commius. His name means 'big fish', which sounds appropriately Celtic; nevertheless, he is included, in a Latinized form, as Tincommius, on a lengthy list of 'kings [who] sought refuge with me [Augustus] as suppliants', one imagines in front of the emperor himself, since Augustus mentions him thus in his autobiography, known as *Res Gestae Divi Augusti*—'the achievements of the deified Augustus'.

Interpreting this coin evidence, therefore, is fraught with difficulties, especially the reconstruction of supposed dynasties. Coins were a way of conveying propaganda, not historical truths. To be described as a son of Commius—a name clearly still well-known when Frontinus wrote his *Strategemata* about military commanders' techniques some 150 years later—must have been politically important. But it would be naive to pretend that the inscribed coins inform us of historical reality. What really matters is to recognize the extent to which some did, and some did not, embrace by the design of their issues and by the use of the word *rex* the Roman world now at the door of Britain. One pro-Roman leader was Verica, also of the Atrebates. He too claimed to be a son of Commius, and is commonly identified with the 'Berikos' of Dio, who sought refuge with Claudius after being expelled from Britain shortly before 43. Some of his coins imitate issues of the Emperor Tiberius (14–37). He used the title *rex*, and sometimes featured a vine leaf: this has been seen as symbolic of embracing a taste for Italian wine as the fashionable beverage to drink. By contrast, the long-lived ruler of Catuvellauni, Cunobelinus (Shakespeare's Cymbeline), put an ear of barley on some of his coins, and we might interpret this as a piece of propaganda, championing both the quality of British beer (much later, in an edict of AD 301, to be priced at twice that produced in Egypt), and the political 'correctness' of drinking it.

Cunobelinus describes himself as the son of Tasciovanus who, according to mint marks on his coins, ruled from Verlamio(n), later the Roman town of Verulamium, close to St Albans (Hertfordshire). Tasciovanus calls himself RIGONUS, apparently the Celtic for king, and is thought to have had a lengthy reign from about 20 BC to *c*. AD 5–10. Cunobelinus, described by the historian Suetonius (*c*.70–130) as 'King of the Britons', was likewise to hold sway for several decades, down to about 40. Despite his symbolic preference for British beer, his coins sometimes use the Latin word *rex*, and also show emblems of classical mythology. Moreover, mint marks indicate that his main power base lay at Camulodunon, the 'fortress of Camulos' (a Celtic war-god), today Colchester. A few coins issued by his father, Tasciovanus, indicate the prior existence of a mint at Camulodunon; but Cunobelinus, whether by war (as the ancient sources imply) or by diplomacy, seems to have made it his principal seat.

Camulodunon was a relatively new foundation, probably originating in the latter part of the first century BC. Flanked to the north, south, and east by rivers, the western landward approaches were protected by a massive system of dykes, extending for a total of 24 km, and cutting off a peninsula of some 30 sq. km. A 'royal' complex has been recognized at Gosbecks, with rich burials, in separate enclosures, nearby at Stanway. There is also the famous Lexden tumulus, which yielded a great array of objects, including chain mail, an iron-bound chest, imported bronzes, fifteen Italian amphorae containing wine or oil, and a silver medallion of the Emperor Augustus, datable to 17 BC. This is certainly a royal interment, conceivably that of a king called Addedomarus. A ruler who adumbrated a pro-Roman stance is surely to be inferred from this assemblage.

No evidence is so far forthcoming to suggest that Camulodunon had any sort of urban-like nucleus, to match the apparent orthogonal planning of Calleva, modern Silchester. Yet, the abundance of imported goods shows that it was in close contact with the Roman world. Archaeological convention tends to apply the Latin term *oppidum*, town, to this sort of settlement, although there are many senses in which it is inappropriate, given the lack of most urban characteristics, such as a 'civic' centre. Nevertheless, such *oppida*—perhaps better termed 'royal centres'—are a conspicuous feature of the Late Iron Age in large parts of southern Britain. Mostly new foundations, they were substantial places usually in low-lying positions, protected by great dykes and banks. Rectilinear buildings, especially in timber, are being increasingly identified within them, a striking departure from the circular house plan favoured for millennia, and pottery, glass, and metalwork attest access to overseas markets.

The exception to prove the rule is Braughing-Puckeridge, in Hertfordshire. Here, no dykes and banks are known, but the artefacts nevertheless demonstrate close contact with the Roman world, especially the Gallic provinces. More particularly, they also hint at cultural change. *Mortaria*, Roman food-grinding bowls continually referred to in the cookery book from the fourth century AD known to us as 'Apicius'', are present, as are fine, imported glass vessels, both signs of a preference for Mediterranean eating and drinking practices. The animal bones indicate a taste, in Roman style, for pork (although British Iron Age aristocrats in regions like Yorkshire, had a similar preference, even if their subjects mostly ate mutton); wine was drunk, and olive oil appreciated; and stylus pens point to literacy. Indeed, a graffito on a pot-sherd from Skeleton Green, Puckeridge even reveals the presence of one Graecus, an unmistakeably classical name. We may infer either residents from the Roman world, most probably Gauls, or Britons responding to new cultural fashions—and indeed, perhaps both.

Some Britons may also now have wanted to look different. Bronze brooches, for example, turn up in Late Iron Age contexts with enormous frequency, suggesting new styles in dress. Distinctively shaped implements for preparing cosmetics (a peculiarly British type) are likewise conspicuous from the later first century BC; and handsomely decorated mirrors, the backs engraved with 'Celtic' art in characteristic curvilinear style, similarly point to an enhanced awareness of personal appearance, at any rate amongst the privileged classes. There is thus a sense in the archaeological record of significant changes in some segments of elite society, and perhaps of a rejection of many traditional values. Indeed, studies of the finds from 472 recently excavated burials at the King Harry Lane cemetery at Verlamion, which appear to have spanned the first sixty years of the first century AD, have interpreted this highly complex set of data in fascinating but diverse ways. Some conclude, for example, that these tomb groups may reflect a development from family-based individuals—with a particular power base—to a much more widely representative population that disrupted previous patterns of kinship: the idea is appealing.

As we have seen, the changes in society that we are inferring are particularly prominent in the South-East, and probably to be associated with the settlement of Belgae. It is here that cemeteries where the corpse was—in Continental fashion—cremated and buried with objects including pottery vessels (many wheel-turned), are a conspicuous feature (they are known as the Swarling-Aylesford culture, after two excavated cemeteries in Kent). Elsewhere in Britain there were similar developments. The 'brochs' of northern Scotland—tall, circular, stone-built structures, like that of Mousa on Shetland—do, for instance, suggest the emergence of new clan leaders, whose residences are formidable visual statements of power. Other fortified settlements in Scotland, known as 'duns', imply similar social change and ideology, but expressed in a rather different architectural genre. These may have been the heirs of the creators of the great prehistoric megalithic monuments; but more probably indicate the development of a new social order, although one largely untouched by the Classical world. Elsewhere, in Wales, Ireland, and northern England, modest homesteads, mainly built in wood, were however the norm. Most of these people were much more peripheral to the dynamics of change so apparent in the south-eastern part of the British Isles and in Scotland, and had less engagement with those outside their regions. Ireland, on the other hand, shows clear signs of 'royal' centres, as at Navan (Co. Armagh), and the Ráth na Ríogh ('Fort of the Kings') at Tara (Co. Meath).

Rome's intentions towards Britain

Rome's intention formally to annexe Britain properly dates to the reign of the Emperor Gaius (Caligula), 37–41. Cunobelinus had expelled a son, Adminius, who then sought refuge in Rome. The excuse for an invasion thus existed; and, in 40, an army was assembled at the Channel. But, at the last minute, Gaius—a notorious eccentric—decided to instructed his army to pick up sea shells, as a form of booty, instead of setting sail. It is an extraordinary story, perhaps reflecting both the perceived perils of the Channel crossing, and the strength of the Britons—not least the Catuvellauni, whom Cunobelinus had ruled for over thirty years.

Cunobelinus, as chance would have it, died about this time, leaving his kingdom to two sons, Caratacus and Togodumnus. How it was divided cannot be known, but it broke the stability of decades. Moreover, as we have seen, the Atrebates had thrown out their leader, Verica, who, like Adminius, sought political support in Rome (although an alternative scenario sees this as the result of Catuvellaunian aggression rather than internal discord). But Rome itself was also in turmoil. In 41, a plot launched by senators and army officers led to the assassination of the loathed, apparently deranged, Gaius, with the expectation that the Republic might be restored. Gaius, however, had an uncle, Claudius, a person portrayed in our ancient sources as deformed, half-witted, marginalized from power—and as a formidable academic, not least as reflected by his writings about the Etruscans. He was found by a soldier of the Praetorian Guard trembling behind a curtain in the Imperial Palace, and was promptly proclaimed emperor. Protected overnight by the Guard in their camp, he doubtless negotiated financially with them, so that their support was confirmed. Thus came to the throne a ridiculed scholar, but with gifts of intellect and leadership largely unrecognized by history. The conquest of Britain, although planned by a man of no military, and little political, experience is a sure sign of his thinking. He needed to make his mark, especially by seizing booty—gold, perhaps silver, slaves, and land. Britain, seemingly in political chaos, provided the perfect opportunity. Moreover, an army occupied with a clear, if challenging, external target, would provide a greatly reduced threat to an ageing, but quite clearly ambitious academic, with a thirst for power but precarious authority. Such were probably his reflections in the palace on the Palatine Hill in Rome in AD 42, the year of another attempted coup and a few months before the invasion order was issued. When Verica arrived in Rome to seek the emperor's support, it provided an entirely suitable pretext for intervention in British affairs, as Adminius had done for Gaius.

The Claudian invasion

Claudius was of course well aware that he would be following in the footsteps of the deified Julius Caesar, an association that could do him no harm in the eyes of the Roman people. But nothing was to be left to chance. The commissariat was carefully organized by the procurator (finance minister) in northern Gaul, Graecinius Laco; and the distinguished governor of the Danubian province of Pannonia, Aulus Plautius, was brought in to head a force of four legions plus auxiliary troops, an army of some 40,000 in all. At first the soldiers refused to embark, fearing the unknown, and it took the exhortations of a powerful imperial ex-slave, Narcissus, who had been sent for from Rome, before they were persuaded. 'Io Saturnalia' they cried, a humorous allusion to the annual festival of the god Saturn, when slaves dressed up in their masters' clothing.

The force was divided into three, to facilitate the landing of so many men. Where they disembarked is, however, a matter of some controversy. There is good archaeological evidence to show that Richborough, in eastern Kent, was one of them, and Chichester, in Sussex, may well have been another. Here, military-type buildings of the period have been discovered at nearby Fishbourne, where a client king, Cogidubnus (or Togidubnus: the reading in the sources is not certain) may later have resided, as we shall see. Whoever was ruling in AD 43, a pro-Roman body of Atrebates of the Hampshire region would surely have eased the path of the invading army. Caratacus and Togodumnus, the Catuvellaunian leaders of the British opposition, were soon routed, but then staged a major battle at a river crossing, probably the Medway (although not inconceivably the Arun in Hampshire). Defeat was followed by a fallback to the Thames, where

Togodumnus was killed in a skirmish. Now it was time to request the presence of Claudius, to preside over his victory.

It was to be Claudius' last journey out of Italy—he died in 54—and he spent just sixteen days in Britain. In the tradition of Hellenistic warfare in the Mediterranean he brought elephants with him, to terrify the enemy, and witnessed the fall of Camulodunon, Colchester, clearly regarded as the British capital. An inscription on a triumphal arch erected in Rome in 51 (now preserved only in fragments) records that eleven British kings surrendered, one (if the text is correctly interpreted) a ruler from Orkney, whose residence was presumably a broch. News of the Roman victory, however it was transmitted, must have spread fast, and many leaders in Britain will have deemed it politic to offer capitulation. The memory of the total destruction of Carthage and Corinth by Rome in 146 BC; the savage siege and wiping out of Numantia in Spain by Scipio Aemilianus in 133 BC; or the extinction of Vercingetorix's force and base at Alesia in 52 BC, can hardly have been forgotten. The Roman war-machine was not to be trifled with, and the more discerning Britons knew it. Furthermore, the message was backed up in other ways. The seizure and sacking of Camulodunum, and the surrender of the British kings, was re-enacted in a show in the Campus Martius in Rome; a coin was struck, showing an equestrian statue of Claudius on top of an arch, inscribed DE BRITANN[IS], to promulgate news of the conquest; another commemorative arch was built at Boulogne, to commemorate Claudius' departure to Britain and his glorious return; and a sculptural relief depicting these events was erected at Aphrodisias, as was an arch at Cyzicus. Both the last were cities in distant Asia Minor, a remarkable proof of the fame of Claudius' triumph.

Colchester, whose name was now Latinized to Camulodunum, became the site of a substantial fortress for the Twentieth Legion. There was also a fort some 3 km away at Gosbecks where, as we have seen, there may have been a royal residence: a military presence to protect or intimidate the Trinovantian ruler may have been deemed prudent. An important religious sanctuary was to grow up here in Roman times, albeit with origins prior to the Conquest, reflecting the political importance of the site. Nearby, at Stanway as mentioned above, were several enclosures containing richly furnished burials of Late Iron Age and Early Roman date. These included a remarkable set of medical instruments, echoing Roman styles but probably of

British manufacture; and also a board with glass counters, laid out for the beginning of a game, with the first pieces already moved; it is conceivably *ludus latrunculorum*, a form of 'war game'. Here is an eloquent affirmation of the extent to which Roman practices—including the employment of a British doctor trained in Roman medicine or an expatriate from the empire—were adopted by the aristocracy in this community.

From Camulodunum, the Roman army split into three, the separate detachments marching north, north-west, and west. The western army, the core of which was the Second Legion, was commanded by Vespasian who in 69 was to become emperor. It is recorded that his force fought thirty battles, took the Isle of Wight and over twenty *oppida*, and subdued two powerful tribes—probably the Durotriges of Dorset and the Dobunni of Gloucestershire/Somerset. Archaeological excavations at the hill-forts of Maiden Castle and Hod Hill, both in Dorset, have provided dramatic confirmation of the Roman assault on these great strongholds. These include a war cemetery at Maiden Castle, in which one skeleton still had in his spine a bolt from a ballista, the crossbow-like machine that acted as artillery for the Roman legion; and evidence from Hod Hill to show that the largest house, presumably that of the chieftain, was bombarded with this type of artillery, the bolt-heads from which rested where they had landed until excavated 1,900 years later.

Less is known of what befell the other two prongs of the Roman advance; but we can infer steady progress, probably along the lines of the future courses of Watling Street and Ermine Street. Meanwhile, protection of the flanks was achieved by the creation of 'client kingdoms', whose rulers were nominally independent, but controlled by Roman alliances. One such lay in the Chichester area. Here an imperfectly preserved inscription from the town itself, ancient Noviomagus ('New Market'), refers to a 'Tiberius Claudius Cogidubnus [or Togidubnus]', the three names indicating that he had been made a Roman citizen, and the *nomen* Claudius that the award had been made by the emperor himself. He is styled *Rex Magnus Britanniae*, 'Great King of Britain' and, as Tacitus implies, may well have ruled substantial parts of Hampshire and Berkshire and more than one tribe. The palace at Fishbourne (where, as noted above, there are Conquest period military buildings), is sometimes attributed to him, at least in its early form. Another client king was Prasutagus. Like

Cogidubnus, his origins are quite unclear, but history records him as King of the Iceni, of Norfolk and eastern Cambridgeshire, and as husband of Boudicca, whose role in British history will feature shortly.

The other leaders who surrendered to Claudius must likewise have pledged themselves and their subjects to support the Roman administration. Although not heard of until the year 51, one was surely Cartimandua, Queen of the Brigantes, a people that occupied a large part of northern England. It is significant that the *oppidum* at Stanwick, near Scotch Corner, was from around this time to receive relatively large quantities of Roman goods, including wine amphorae, and even building materials such as tiles, in a region that, culturally, seems otherwise to have been largely 'beyond the pale'. This may well have been Cartimandua's capital. Another may have been an anonymous aristocrat—at least in terms of the archaeological evidence—who was buried *c.* AD 50, at the site of Folly Lane, St Albans, in a conspicuous hillside position, just outside the Roman town of Verulamium. The grave, which contained some exotic objects, albeit ritually damaged, lay within an enclosure of some two hectares where, later, a large temple of Romano-British type was erected. A shrine to a respected ancestor is surely to be inferred, and the tomb of Adminius, a son formerly exiled by Cunobelinus, has been widely canvassed by modern scholars as the focus of this cult. The idea is attractive but incapable of proof on current evidence.

Establishment of military control

Despite the signs that some British leaders and their followers were to an extent acquiescent to the idea of Roman governance, the occupying forces were prudent. The true extent of a skein of forts and fortresses in south-east Britain (including bases for vexillations— legionary detachments—such as at Longthorpe, near Peterborough) remains less than defined; neverthess they were far from numerous, reflecting the belief that this part of Britain was essentially pacified. But a military *limes*, or road studded with forts as at Cirencester and probably Leicester, is known between Exeter and Lincoln, with a northern extension up to the River Humber. Called the Fosse Way and largely surviving today, its virtually straight-line course for a distance of some 320 km (together with more than 40 km, via the Ermine Street, to the Humber, a road now no more than a country track) represents an outstanding example of military planning and construction. Although the fortress at Isca Dumnoniorum, modern Exeter, was a later foundation (c.55), the first governor, Aulus Plautius, was assuredly its architect, building upon a long tradition, not least in Italy, where new roads which often bypassed older centres of urban power facilitated conquest. The Fosse Way, in essence, demarcated the territory under Roman control, with a few military bases within the conquered area, like that recently uncovered near Oxford at Alchester, to ensure this. An identical strategy was to be used in Algeria, where three fortified roads mark successive stages in territorial expansion from the coast to the edge of the Sahara Desert, over a period of some 150 years.

By about the middle of 47 when Aulus Plautius was recalled to Rome, where he was honoured with a ceremonial 'ovation', the road and its military stations had been completed, an astonishing feat. Sometimes today regarded as a 'frontier', the Fosse Way was in fact an example of a well-tried stratagem of achieving control. Moreover, it also implied that Roman territory, whether administered by the army or by suppliant British rulers, was firmly in Aulus Plautius' hands. The reality was to prove different. The new governor, Ostorius Scapula, decreed that all tribesmen, whether allies of Rome or resident within the new province, were to be disarmed. This immediately sparked off a rebellion amongst the Iceni—almost certainly in the western enclave of the central Fenland—whose principal focus lay at a 9-hectare enclosure (probably constructed for ceremonial and ritual purposes) at Stonea Camp, near March, Cambridgeshire. Whoever led the revolt is not known. It cannot have been Prasutagus, whose death set off the chain of events culminating in Boudicca's rebellion in 60/61, for he would not have remained in power; but the insurgents were rapidly crushed by storming their camp and putting them to the sword. Indeed, skeletons of this date have been found at Stonea Camp. A consequence may have been the imposition of some military control in the region, as is indicated by a newly discovered fort, almost certainly of this period, at Grandford, also near March. It lay on a road that ran from Longthorpe, west–east across the Fens, which, like the Fosse Way, was probably military in purpose.

Caratacus and Cartimandua

But Ostorius had then to face a serious escalation in warfare else-where. Caratacus, the surviving son of Cunobelinus, now sought refuge in Wales, where he began to fan the warlike spirits of these hill-peoples, especially the Silures of the south-east, and the Ordovices of central Wales. Before tackling this threat, however, Ostorius had first to quell the Deceangli of north-west Wales, and was then forced to intervene in the affairs of the Brigantes of northern England. Here, as we have seen, their ruler was the pro-Roman queen, Cartimandua whose seat may have been at Stanwick, near Scotch Corner. Some of her subjects, however, resented her pro-Roman stance, and the gov-ernor's troops had to go in to prop up the position of the invaluable diplomatic ally—a very wise move, as it was to turn out.

Now it was time to tackle the Silures and the Ordovices, both led by the charismatic Caratacus. The war appeared to require extra legion-ary support and, in 49 the fortress of the Twentieth Legion at Col-chester was therefore given up, and turned into a *colonia*. This was a town for retired legionaries, who received an allocation of land and who could both act as a reserve force, in case of emergency, and help to promote Roman ways of governance, culture, and law, especially amongst the British aristocracy, within the core area of the new province. A temple dedicated to the Emperor Claudius, a cult of widespread importance in the Roman empire as a focus of imperial loyalty, was also established here, although probably not until after his death in 54. Thus, the Twentieth Legion was now released in its entirety for active service (although vexillations had undoubtedly been in the field before this). While the exact whereabouts of the most critical battle against the Silures is unknown, the force of the experienced, highly trained, Roman army proved insuperable. Decisively defeated, Caratacus had to abandon even his family, and escaped to Brigantia. There Cartimandua, despite a prominent anti-Roman faction amongst her tribesmen, fulfilled her diplomatic obli-gations and straightaway handed him over to the Romans: the rift between Brigantian Britons who respected the old ways and those who sought to embrace a newer world began rapidly to widen.

Caratacus and his family were then taken to Rome, where he was paraded as a captured enemy, but one of great military distinction. He spoke before the Senate, reportedly remarking 'Why, with all these great possessions, do you still covet our poor huts?', and it is said that his words and demeanour so impressed the emperor that Claudius gave him a pardon. Vercingetorix had not fared so well under Julius Caesar, as the scholar-emperor will certainly have remembered: a show of clemency will surely have been seen as politically judicious.

The archaeological evidence for Ostorius' governorship depicts a spreading network of fortresses and forts, especially to the west of the Fosse Way. Assigning foundation dates and specific units (or part units) to these military establishments is a central matter for much modern scholarship, but is a detailed debate that is hardly crucial here. It is the overall picture of the way in which the stamp of authority was extended, especially beyond the South-East (where Roman traditions, as we have seen, were already well established amongst some of the aristocracy) that is so striking. When Ostorius died prematurely in 52, he and Aulus Plautius had already achieved a huge amount in a mere ten years: even lead-, and from that silver-mining in the Somerset Mendips was under way by AD 49, helping to defray the huge costs of conquest. Moreover, some urban centres other than Colchester seem to have developed during his governorship. For example, the former royal capital of Verlamion, now Latinized to Verulamium, probably acquired municipal status at this time, a *municipium* being a chartered community whose inhabitants possessed the so-called 'Latin' rights in Roman law. This was a status not far short of full Roman citizenship (and to which those who had held a magistracy, with its costly and onerous obligations, would become personally eligible). Likewise, Londinium came into existence around AD 50: timber from a wooden drain under the main east–west street has yielded a tree-ring date of AD 47. It was quite probably a new settlement (although not a *municipium*) established by overseas traders, seeking to exploit lucrative new markets from a highly advantageous position for commerce on the River Thames. Even a major Iron Age religious sanctuary on Hayling Island—and thus close to Cogidubnus' centre at Chichester—was rebuilt around this time, but in stone rather than timber, and in a Romanizing architectural style closely echoing that of some temples in Gaul.

Nevertheless when the new governor, A. Didius Gallus, arrived to take up office in 52, he was greeted with the news that a legion had been defeated by the Silures. No further details are recorded, and it may be that the battle was less calamitous than was at first feared. However, Didius' five-year governorship saw little further territorial expansion, although he was compelled again to send a legion into Brigantia. This was due to the fast escalating split between Cartimandua and her consort, Venutius, who championed the strong anti-Roman factions in this powerful tribal grouping. It was however a problem contained, rather than one that was solved, and Venutius was later to emerge centre-stage in the fight against Roman domination.

Neronian Britain

In 54 Claudius died, to be succeeded by Nero. According to the historian Suetonius, the new emperor did at some point contemplate giving up the new province; but, if early in his reign, the thought must have been relatively transient for, in 57, we hear of a new governor, Q. Veranius, pressing on into Wales, assuredly under imperial instructions. An early death denied him, however, the chance to complete the conquest of the whole region, which was left to his successor, Suetonius Paullinus. He was an appropriate appointment. An Italian from Pisaurum (modern Pésaro, on the Adriatic Sea), he had served in Mauretania Caesariensis, now north-western Algeria, where he was the first Roman to lead a force over the formidable barrier of the Atlas Mountains. He was thus well familiar both with the type of upland terrain to be found in Wales, and with the spirited and warlike nature of the peoples whom the Romans commonly encountered in such regions. Beginning his campaign in 58, by 60 the job was largely done. Only the Druids' centre on the island of Anglesey, known as Mona, where many refugees had reportedly taken sanctuary, remained to be taken. Tacitus in his *Annals of Imperial Rome* provides a famously vivid description of the scene that confronted the Roman army, as they crossed the straights between the mainland and the island. There was a 'dense armed mass. Among them were blacked-robed women, with dishevelled hair like Furies, brandishing torches. Close by stood Druids, raising their hands to heaven and screaming dreadful curses.' The Roman soldiers urged each other on, mindful that it was the

Druids' practice 'to drench their altars in the blood of prisoners'—anathema to Romans by whom the idea of *human* sacrifice was abhorred. Discipline and fortitude prevailed, and victory was won: soon, much of Mona must have been in flames.

Some possible archaeological confirmation of the cult's existence on the island may be provided by a collection of 138 items of metalwork—swords, spears, shields, horse fittings, trumpets, and even a slave chain—found in a bog at Llyn Cerrig Bach, not far from Holyhead. They represent a considerable accumulation of wealth, very possibly deposited at a Druidic sanctuary, but at an uncertain date. If not offerings, they may have been concealed for safety, not inconceivably at the time of Paullinus' attack. If so, their non-recovery as Roman booty may be connected with the news that reached the governor at this time: that the Icenian queen, Boudicca, had initiated a revolt, and on an alarming scale.

Boudicca

Boudicca, whose name has for long in accounts of British history been rendered as 'Boadicea' due to erroneous readings of ancient manuscripts in the eighteenth century, was the wife of King Prasutagus. As we have seen, they cannot have been tainted by the earlier Icenian revolt of AD 47, for their rule would otherwise hardly have been tolerated. But the site of their seat (or more probably seats, given that they were likely to have been peripatetic from one royal centre to another around the kingdom) is unknown. One may have been in the Norfolk Breckland, where a heavy concentration of Icenian coin hoards can be demonstrated, and a very extraordinary Late Iron Age and Early Roman complex has been excavated at Fison Way, Thetford. At the time of the revolt, and in its final form, this consisted of a very substantial enclosure, measuring some 220 × 175 m, the perimeter being made up of no fewer than nine concentric wooden fences: it is almost as though the interior were surrounded by an artificial grove, a traditionally 'Celtic' setting. Inside was a large and imposing central building, also made of timber, and four other wooden structures. Baked-clay moulds indicate that coins were minted there, and grave-shaped pits suggest the presence of a cemetery in which the bones have long since dissolved in the acidic subsoil. It is safe to infer that this was a major Icenian ceremonial and religious centre, although it proved to be curiously lacking in Roman imported goods, such as the wine amphorae whose contents Cartimandua and her retinue appear to have enjoyed at the *oppidum* at Stanwick. It may perhaps be that the Iceni eschewed such symbols of Roman custom, a rejection that reflected an increasing fervour for independence, despite a formal alliance with Rome.

Another royal seat surely lay in the Snettisham area of north-west Norfolk, where the hoards of regalia buried over a century before, as we saw earlier, were now enclosed within a polygonal ditch and bank. A traditionally venerated site may thus have been accorded further ceremonial recognition. So, however dimly we perceive it, the early post-Conquest landscape of the Icenian region emerges as a world that only marginally embraced Rome, and whose rulers and subjects sought liberation from Mediterranean imperialism. In short, such archaeological evidence as we have points to a tribe where thoughts of insurrection were rife.

There were many other catalysts that brought matters to a head. Prasutagus died in 60, leaving half of his kingdom to the emperor, Nero. This was a time-honoured way of ensuring that his possessions were not wholly lost to the rapacious Romans—some of whom were now choosing to call in loans made to Britons anxious to advance their political and social standing at the time of the Conquest. There was also in office an equally rapacious procurator, Decianus Catus, with the will and the power to create misery through ruthless taxation. The last straw was the rape of Boudicca's two daughters by Roman soldiers, and her own humiliation by flogging. Perhaps learning of Suetonius' devastation on Anglesey of the Druids, the upholders of the ancient religions (Boudicca herself is said to have worshipped a Celtic deity called Andraste), the Iceni rose in revolt. Gaining support from the Trinovantes of Essex, whose resentment at the insufferably arrogant behaviour of the legionary veterans at the new *colonia* of Camulodunum knew no bounds, the tribesmen marched on the city that, once a British royal centre, was now a symbolic centre of autocratic Roman domination.

The course of the revolt was given prominent—and harrowing—descriptions by ancient historians such as Tacitus and Dio. Camulodunum, which had yet to receive defences, was overwhelmed, and put to the torch. The last survivors held out for two days in the temple dedicated to Claudius and the Imperial Cult, the massive vaults of which still stand under the Norman castle in Colchester. A relieving movement by the commander of the Ninth Legion, Petillius Cerialis, was repulsed, and the Iceni and their allies then moved on to Londinium. It was by now a flourishing town, with an orderly planned street grid established shortly before 52 (on tree-ring dating), and, according to Tacitus in the context of the rebellion, an 'important centre for businessmen and merchandise'. By this time Suetonius Paullinus was back in southern England, news of the crisis having reached him on Anglesey; but Tacitus tells us that Paullinus felt unable to defend London, essentially a civilian settlement lacking any army presence, and decided to sacrifice it to the Britons. Londinium thus was ravaged, as was Verulamium too. 70,000 are said to have been massacred at the three towns, with 'no thought of taking prisoners . . . only of slaughter, the gibbet, fire, and the cross', in Tacitus' words.

Meanwhile, Suetonius moved his force, comprising the Fourteenth Legion, part of the Twentieth, and some auxiliary troops, perhaps 10,000 in all, further to the north-west. Poenius Postumus, commander of the Second Legion, based at Isca (modern Exeter), had refused to budge, a decision that was ultimately to lead to his suicide for displaying cowardice; Decianus Catus had fled to Gaul. Suetonius Paullinus and his army were, in effect, the last bastion of Roman authority. As described by Tacitus, it was a challenge that they were well able to meet. Choosing their battleground with care, their wedge formations soon drove back the tribesmen who were then trapped by the barrier of wagons, women, and children that were massed behind them. No one was spared; it was a 'glorious victory'; and Boudicca had to take her own life by poison.

The aftermath of the rebellion is properly the subject of the following chapter. Here we may note that excavations in Colchester, London, and Verulamium have all yielded ubiquitous and unambiguous evidence for the insurrection in the form of thick layers of burning and destruction. If Caesar's expeditions have apparently left no traces in the archaeological record, then Boudicca's uprising most emphatically has, even though the site of final denouement is still unknown. The terrible events of 60–61 are very much writ large both in the ancient literature, and in the ground today. Moreover,

Boudicca—as Boadicea—has become a symbolic figure in British history, as Thomas Thornycroft's evocative bronze sculpture on the Thames Embankment—a Victorian enterprise finally completed in 1902—constantly reminds one. That Boudicca's name means 'Victoria' is one of the more poignant nuances of this extraordinary saga.

The 116 years between the first arrival of Caesar and the demise of Boudicca assuredly witnessed enormous change. Britain was brought firmly within the orbit of the Mediterranean world, and the consequences are likely to have permeated, if only as ideas, throughout the British Isles. Socially, culturally, and politically, this was one of the most volatile periods of British history, with results that remain deeply embedded—not least in the physical disposition of our towns and cities, and of our roads—down to this day. Before, there had been remarkable but prehistoric achievement; now the written word—and thus the beginning of history—was to introduce a new, and very different, world.

Figure 4 The discipline of the Roman army is apparent in the cropmarks revealing a fort that housed a large auxiliary unit in the Antonine period on the River Dee at Glenlochar in south-western Scotland. The playing-card shape of rampart and ditches, the gravelled streets with central space for headquarters, commandant's house, and granaries, are unmistakeable. An annexe towards the river contained an official guesthouse (*mansio*).

2

A second start: from the defeat of Boudicca to the third century

Michael Fulford

The rebellion of Boudicca interrupted the conquest of Britain. That process was dependent not only on the situation within the province, but also on the level of commitment on the part of the emperor. The success of the Claudian invasion had been a major triumph, and surrender of the province, though considered by Nero, was not an option. However, the resources of the empire were not unlimited and, as we shall see, the conquest of Britain had to be judged against other priorities. It is clear that for most of the period up to the death of the Emperor Septimius Severus in York in 211 Rome was committed to military advance in Britain. Logically, the security of the province could only be ensured through total conquest of the island, but compromise frontier positions were adopted in the second century. The commitment to territorial expansion had a much wider impact on Britain, and on the development of society as reflected by town and rural settlement. In the third century, when Rome was much pre-occupied with the eastern frontier of the empire, there is a marked change of momentum over several decades when it is difficult to detect continuities in the archaeological record. Thus the period between Boudicca and the usurpation of Carausius and Allectus

(287–296) allows us to contrast a phase when the province was, for the most part, at the forefront of imperial interest with a time when it was more at the margin.

The sources

What we can write about Britain varies considerably with the nature of the sources, and it is important to understand that the closely phased history of military conquest—where written sources can be reasonably well knitted with a highly distinctive archaeology—cannot be matched with similar chronologies which allow us to investigate the development of civilian society. In moving from imperial politics and military campaigns that attracted the attention of historians such as Tacitus we leave behind the testimony of written sources and rely heavily on archaeology. The former provides a fairly precise chronological and geographical framework in which we can define the broad shape of the conquest of Britain in the first century and the contribution of individual governors to that process. Archaeology, on the other hand, works to a broader timeframe which reflects the inherent difficulties of achieving close dating from most sources of archaeological dating. To a limited extent the contribution of epigraphy and of dendrochronology can illuminate with a greater precision, as can the archaeological record itself in particular circumstances. The first two may be helpful in determining dates of the construction of significant buildings or defences either commemorated by inscription or underpinned by wooden piles whose growth-ring sequences can be matched against known chronologies. In the case of archaeology, the example of the destruction horizon which is reasonably comfortably assigned to Boudicca at Colchester, London, and St Albans (Verulamium) offers a clear benchmark for those cities where before and after can be compared. In contrast, however, it would be difficult to judge the more general impact of the rebellion and its aftermath on cities not so destroyed. In a rural context, the difficulty of identifying a change, which can be precisely attributable to a specific event and its aftermath, such as famine, is almost impossible to detect. For example, unless very specific, closely datable associated evidence— such as a coin with a precise *terminus post quem* or closely dated decorated sigillata (samian ware)—was associated with evidence of a farmstead destroyed by fire, it is likely that the material would allow one of two interpretations: first century AD and, probably, pre-Flavian; or, later first/early second century, determinations which relate to periods where major change in the ceramic assemblages can be seen. It is only in that kind of framework that we are able to begin to determine the nature and scale of change, whether in the development and growth of towns, or in the establishment of Romanized settlement and new agricultural practice in the countryside. However, for a large part of Britain and, particularly, in the Early Roman period, there may be no associated material from which a close chronology of settlement can be established. Thus, we need to be reconciled to a three-speed history: one of the frontiers and military campaigns, one of the urbanized zone, while the third embraces the rest of Roman Britain.

After Boudicca

Very occasionally there are links between documentary sources and the archaeological record. Thus, archaeology is a vivid witness of the effect of the Boudiccan revolt in three respects. First, in the cities of Colchester, London, and Verulamium extensive burnt deposits define the extent of the destruction, while the evidence for the date of construction of new buildings indicates a long period over which recovery took place. Second, the relative ease with which it is possible to define forts and fortresses allows us to consider the impact of the revolt on military dispositions. Third, the discovery in London of the remains of the tombstone of the procurator Julius Classicianus, sent to succeed Decianus Catus, provides important contextual information about the man who played a major role in the replacement of Suetonius Paullinus as governor. Not only does it provide strong support for believing that the procurator's office was located in London rather than Colchester by 60, but it also provides important information about Classicianus' family background, which may go some way to explaining his conciliatory stance towards the province after the rebellion. He was a Gaul, probably from near Trier, and his wife was the daughter of Julius Indus who

Figure 5 Tomb of the chief finance officer of Britain, Gaius Julius Classicianus, of equestrian rank and Gallic descent, who effectively prevented the governor Suetonius Paullinus from devastating the province in revenge for the rebellion of Boudicca. Erected in London by his wife Julia Pacata, herself daughter of a distinguished Gallic friend of Rome, it can stand for the new Romans from the provinces serving the Early Empire in senior positions. It also stands for the rebirth of the province, as it must have been one of the first monuments to be built as London rose from the Boudiccan ashes.

had played a major role in the suppression of the rebellion of Florus in 21.

This offers a vital complement to the narrative of Tacitus, who provides the names of the governors, Petronius Turpilianus and Trebellius Maximus, successively responsible for the province for the remainder of Nero's reign, but little else other than that, by implication, there was minimal military action during the rest of the 60s. With a policy directed towards containment and recovery, it would be possible to withdraw the Fourteenth Legion from Britain, probably in 66. By this time Nero's interests were focused on the East and the problem of Parthia, Rome's hostile neighbour: the priority lay elsewhere than in Britain. There is compelling evidence for the construction of new auxiliary forts after the rebellion in the South-East, inside the line of the Fosse Way. The abandonment of the Neronian legionary fortress at Usk in South Wales in favour of a reoccupation at Gloucester symbolizes the retrenchment. Elsewhere, the Second Legion appears to have remained at Exeter, while the Ninth and (till 66) the Fourteenth were concentrated at Lincoln and Wroxeter, respectively. Given our awareness of developing imperial policy in the East, and of the withdrawal of the Fourteenth, it becomes unclear whether the redeployment in the south of Britain was the result of a deliberate policy to reduce the military establishment, or of the need to extend policing in the wake of the rebellion. Equally, the slow rebuilding in the cities may reflect as much the knock-on economic impact of the slackening tempo on the frontier as a loss of confidence following the destruction.

In the same way that events within Britain were influenced by imperial needs in the East, the turbulence of the years of Roman civil war (68–9) also impacted on the province. While the influence of the legions was strong, for example in forcing the governor Trebellius Maximus to leave the province, the latter's isolation seems to have discouraged any active declaration, individually or collectively, by the legions in favour of any of the contenders for the empire. Nevertheless, some 8,000 troops from the three legions were ordered by the contender Vitellius to join his army, though the value of insularity is reflected in the decision by Vitellius to send the Fourteenth Legion, which had supported his defeated rival Otho, back to Britain. The appointment by Vitellius of Vettius Bolanus as governor appears to have been able to appease the army. However, the latter may have taken action against the Brigantes whose ousted leader, Queen Cartimandua, had appealed to Rome for help against the usurper, Venutius. In fact his period in office was too short for us to be clear on this. Nevertheless, it seems certain from the legions' relations with a governor such as Trebellius Maximus with no military experience, that their interests could not be neglected. Since it seems that the legions in Britain were not initially unanimous in their support of Vespasian, the new emperor, it was important for him to appoint a new governor who could take an active lead. Petillius Cerialis was despatched to the province with a new legion, the Second *Adiutrix*, in 71, almost certainly with the mission of moving firmly against the

Brigantes: the momentum of conquest prior to the revolt was restored.

The period between Boudicca and the elevation of Vespasian does point up both the strengths and weaknesses of our various sources. It reveals clearly that there was a balance to be struck between maintenance of the morale of the army within the province through involvement in new projects and the commitment of resources, reflected principally in legionary strength, to make such new enterprise possible. The scale of resource to be deployed at any one time was, as we have seen with events in Parthia, very much dependent on the developing ambitions of the emperor, and on ensuring the security of the empire beyond the shores of Britain. Ensuring the morale of the army seems, at this stage, to have required it to be involved in active campaigning, and it seems that a strength of four legions and their auxiliaries was the appropriate force with which to undertake offensive campaigning. As opposed to static garrisoning, this entailed a higher level of expenditure, either directly through army pay, or indirectly through the supply of food and materiel, whether through local taxation or importation from outside the province. One way or another the province as a whole was likely to benefit. Inevitably variation in sizes of the garrison and in levels of activity, reflected, for example, in the movement of supplies through the province to the frontier garrisons, would correspondingly influence the economy of the province. With the appointment of Cerialis and succeeding Flavian governors we enter a phase of high expenditure and activity in Britain, which would have done much to restore confidence. One indicator of the latter in the post-Boudicca phase would be the timing and scale of veteran settlement in the province. The decision to establish a veteran colony at Colchester within six years of the Plautian invasion had been, to a degree, a declaration of confidence in the Conquest. Correspondingly, the long interval before the establishment of new colonies at Gloucester and Lincoln at the end of the first century may in part derive from the unattractiveness of Britain as a secure place to settle, particularly in the turbulent years of the 60s and early 70s.

The Flavian advance

Under Cerialis the war was moved into Brigantia. The Ninth Legion was moved forward from Lincoln—which was then occupied by the newly arrived Second *Adiutrix*—to a new base at York. His campaigns took his armies at least as far as the line of the Solway–Tyne where dendrochronology provides a date of 72/3 for the foundation of the first fort at Carlisle. On the other hand, despite the attractiveness of the setting, archaeology does not allow us to associate more firmly than as speculation the defeat of the hostile king, Venutius, with the great *oppidum* at Stanwick in Yorkshire. Conquest of Wales and, particularly of the tribe of the Silures in the south-east was reserved for Julius Frontinus, governor of Britain from 73/4. He established a new base for the Second *Augusta* at Caerleon from *c*.75. His successor, Agricola, began his term of office in 77 with the completion of the conquest of tribes such as the Ordovices in North Wales, but the major task of his governorship seems to have been the completion of the conquest of the North. In seven campaigning seasons his armies advanced, first through Lowland Scotland to the Clyde–Forth line and, then, after two seasons of consolidation in south and south-west Scotland, through north-east Scotland as far the Moray Firth. However, only territory south-east of the Grampians was secured, with a line of auxiliary forts stretching north-east from the Clyde to Stracathro. Towards the eastern end of this line, at Inchtuthil on the Tay, a new legionary fortress was established in 83/4. The bulk of the arable land available in Britain was thus secured by the end of Agricola's governorship, but resources were inadequate to achieve the settlement of the remaining lower-lying land in north-east Scotland, and there is no evidence of serious military penetration of the Highlands.

Withdrawal from Scotland

These achievements were short-lived, as pressing problems on the Rhine and Danube frontiers required the recall of troops from Britain. In the first place, the Emperor Domitian required troops from Britain to help fight the Chatti in Germany in 85; later the invasion of Roman territory on the Danube by the Dacians demanded more substantial support and the Second *Adiutrix* was withdrawn, probably by 86 or 87, and certainly by 92. Without the appropriate level of manpower, it was impossible to maintain the forward positions, and Inchtuthil was abandoned before the completion of the fortress. The Dacians remained a major problem, and it is likely that the Emperor Trajan required reinforcements from Britain to assist in his campaigns in Dacia in 101–2 and 105–6. In the early years of Trajan's reign the network of forts in Scotland was gradually abandoned so that, by or soon after 105, for most of its length the frontier lay along the Stanegate, the east–west Roman road that connected at Corbridge and Carlisle the main routes northwards into Scotland. Given our understanding of the wider imperial scene, it is uncertain whether the destruction levels, which have been identified at a number of lowland forts in Scotland, are attributable to enemy action or a deliberate policy of demolition.

The territory given up by 105 was substantial, but the implication of the decisions of Domitian, in the first instance, and then Trajan, is that such a loss was not considered significant. Strategically, in terms of the line of the frontier to be adopted, the Stanegate was presumably considered as, or more effective than earlier arrangements, while the economic value of the lost land was, equally, not rated. Nevertheless, no emperor could afford the humiliation of abandoning Britain. As we have seen with Nero's removal of the Fourteenth Legion in 66, there was scope to make significant changes to the size of the military establishment without seriously risking the security of the province. At the same time the forces in Britain represented a reserve, reasonably remote from the heart of imperial affairs, which could be drawn on in time of crisis elsewhere in the empire. However, whereas the reassessment by Vespasian of the general political and military situation after the Civil War effectively limited the period without a fourth legion for a period of only some five years (66–71), the decision to remove the Second *Adiutrix* was, effectively, never reversed. Indeed there is persuasive evidence for the removal of the Ninth *Hispana* between 108 and the early 120s, thus reducing the military establishment to two legions and associated auxiliaries. These decisions, with their associated resource implications, were not without consequence for Britain. It is appropriate now to consider the impact of the Conquest on the natives and the lands within the frontier zone.

Urban development

The destruction levels associated with the Boudiccan revolt provides a horizon with which to compare developments before and after that event in the three cities of Colchester, London, and Verulamium. Elsewhere there is very little to go on to assess the nature and character of urban development before the Flavians. In the first place we could turn to the other towns (as they eventually turned out) of Canterbury and Silchester, apparently unaffected by the revolt but which, like Colchester and Verulamium, have produced significant evidence of late pre-Roman Iron Age settlement. At Silchester there is convincing evidence of a major pre-Flavian courtyard building in the centre of the town and on the same orientation as the street grid. However, that coincidence does not, of itself, secure a similar, early date for the street grid, as there is more compelling evidence, in the nature of the relationship of the succeeding timber forum-basilica to the road leading into the town from London, to suggest that the street grid as it largely survived through the Roman period originated in the Flavian period rather than earlier. Excavations of the amphitheatre provide the possibility, but not the certainty, of a pre-, or early Flavian date for that monument, as does the skewed relationship of the town baths to the street grid. However, although not associated with the fabric of any particular building, a number of tiles stamped with Nero's name indicate the presence of a substantial masonry building somewhere in the town. In contrast, at Canterbury there is evidence for the continuity of occupation of a substantial settlement originating in the Late Iron Age, but of no other major developments before the later first century.

Beyond this group of towns there is even less substantive evidence. At Chichester, where evidence for a nucleated late Iron Age *oppidum* remains elusive, a pre-Flavian dedication to Neptune and Minerva by a guild of metalworkers (*collegium fabrorum*) points to the construction of a classical-style temple under the direction of the client king, Tiberius Claudius Cogidubnus, while a second dedication to Nero points to a further, but unspecified development. At Fishbourne a mile west of the focus of the subsequent town of Noviomagus, excavation has revealed the impressive remains of a major villa, the so-called 'proto-palace', beneath the extensive remains of the Flavian palace which is attributed to the client king. How these various elements related to each other and to the development, or not, of an associated town, is at present obscure. Perhaps relevant as a comparison with the developments at Chichester is the building of the temple dedicated to Sulis Minerva and its associated thermal baths at Bath. Architectural considerations, rather than independent dating evidence, suggest that this temple and thermal complex may have originated in the reign of Nero. Although a substantial settlement developed around it, there is no evidence for the subsequent promotion of a community to the status of *civitas* capital or *municipium*.

What all these strands of evidence suggest is that, in the Claudio-Neronian period, there was no concerted policy towards the development of an urban structure within the province. What is striking about the period is the variety of achievement, ranging from a situation of apparent continuity at Canterbury, to evidence of some radical replanning in relation to the Late Iron Age grid at Silchester, and of rapid development of Roman timber-framed shops and workshops within a street grid extending over some 20 hectares (50 acres) at Verulamium. Apart from the establishment of Colchester as a *colonia* following the departure of the Twentieth Legion to the West in about 49, such developments as there are appear to result from largely local initiatives, though involvement of the emperor at Silchester should not be overlooked. The development of London is a further example of the difficulty of disentangling the local from more overarching policies towards the province. On the one hand, the decision to develop the major port of the province at London could only have been sanctioned at a high level, since it would affect both the use of Richborough as the major port of entry to the province, and the future of Colchester, as the first planned city of Britannia. The recognition of the role of London as the main supply base for the conquest of Wales and the North is further indicated by the location there of the office of the procurator. The burial of Classicianus in London indicates that this decision had certainly been taken by the immediate aftermath of the rebellion, but it could have happened earlier. Indeed the decision to press forward in Wales and the reloca-

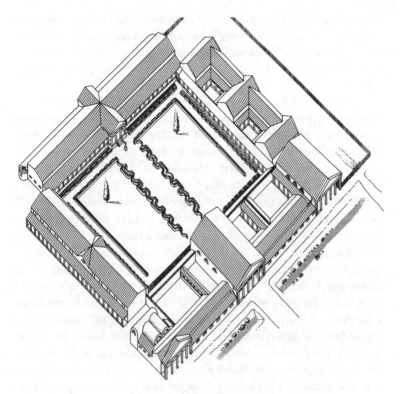

Figure 6 Reconstruction of the palatial villa at Fishbourne, near Chichester, in about 80. The enclosed Mediterranean plan makes it unlike other villas in Britain but rather closer to the official residences of commanding officers in military bases. Approached through parkland (*right*), the great entrance hall gave a view across the formal courtyard garden to the principal reception rooms. The private apartments (*left*) adjoined the baths; and suites for guests, relatives, and staff were arranged round smaller courts.

tion of the Twentieth could well have provided the context for a decision to develop London in 49. Yet all of these considerations belie the apparent informality of the settlement implied by Tacitus' description of it as a centre of merchants and goods, and demonstrated by the evidence of rapid ribbon development along the roads leading away from the settlement, particularly to the west. Although there is a core of a planned street grid, with its origins pre-dating the Boudiccan destruction, east of the Walbrook which articulates with the bridge across the river, there is no sense otherwise that the subsequent development of the city was contained within a planned framework. Indeed the strength of early road alignments both east and west of the Walbrook was such that they overrode considerations of conformity with the later grid and survived through the Roman period.

If, then, it is difficult to see a pattern in the development of towns in Britain before the Flavian period, thereafter there is a greater sense of coherence which embraces both existing cities and new developments. Although the problems of arriving at a close chronology remain as intractable as ever, it is possible to make a case for the laying out of the street grids of a large number of towns in the later first century. Such a process would have been necessitated by the task of constructing roads across the province and the need to articulate these locally with town grids: traffic would then have to be able to pass through the towns. Towns which show evidence of such investment in the Flavian, or Flavio-Trajanic period include Canterbury, Chichester, Winchester, Dorchester, Cirencester, Exeter, Leicester, and Caistor-by-Norwich. In addition, at Silchester a case can be made for something of a fresh start with the construction of a new timber forum-basilica articulating with the street grid and the main approach from London, while at Verulamium the inscription recording the completion of the forum-basilica in 79 demonstrates a renewed confidence in that city. If we are to suppose that one element in the variation among the urban developments with which we associate a pre-Flavian date is a reflection of choice on the part of the native British elites, then the broad consistency in arrangements across the province in the Flavian period implies other agencies and processes. Given the incoherence in the nature and extent of urban developments in the pre-Flavian period in the South-East, arguably the richest part of the province in the first century, the synchronization and, to a degree, standardization of provision right across the Flavian province is all the more remarkable, if it, too, is to be attributed solely to native enterprise. It is important to emphasize that standardization of provision. At the lowest level it embraces a regular street grid, one of the criteria for distinguishing a *civitas* capital, *colonia*, or *municipium* from other towns. Then there is the provision of forum-basilica and public baths. Although these have not been located in every *civitas* capital, because later developments have obscured their location, none has produced clearly negative evidence from the central locations where they are to be expected. Such regularity of location within the city grid cannot be claimed for *mansiones* (post-houses) or temples, though the latter are certainly found in most of the towns which have been reasonably well explored. If our sample of extensively explored towns is rather small, the general similarities in the provision of amenities between, say, Silchester from the later first century onwards, and the relatively remote Caerwent, which develops from the early second century, are striking. Wroxeter, in the north-west Midlands, whose establishment also dates from the second century could also be included. The consistency in the architecture of town baths and the forum-basilica has also aroused comment. A good illustration of this is provided by the similarity through time of the Flavian timber basilica at Silchester with its equivalents in masonry of the early second century at Caerwent and Wroxeter, and then with the successor building in masonry of Hadrianic-Antonine date at Silchester itself. Further resemblances can be seen in a number of other forum-basilicas which have so far only been partially explored. If the design parallel with military headquarters buildings (*principia*) is not, of itself, important, the consistency in approach to the provision of the principal public building of the town does suggest implementation of a provincial policy. A firm contrast has to be drawn between pre-Flavian developments which highlight individual initiative, exemplified, for example, by the construction of temples, and the process of establishing an urban network from the early 70s onwards.

Figure 7 The impetus given to civic regeneration by the visit to Britain of the Emperor Hadrian in 122 lies behind this splendid dedication inscription dated 128/9 for the forum at Wroxeter, the capital of the *civitas* of the Cornovii. The unfinished Flavian city centre was swept away, to be replaced by an entirely new forum and baths.

In attempting to distinguish between local and provincial initiatives in the development of the Roman province, it is important to pause and consider who was making the running in the new province. The implication of the pace and character of urban development is that, outside the sphere of the client kingdom of Cogidubnus, the initiative was in the hands of the provincial authorities. Sadly we have precious little firm evidence in the form of dedicatory inscriptions to go on to distinguish between the response of a native aristocracy and that of newcomers. The latter might have come as merchants or as entrepreneurs to set up new businesses. In respect of the latter we have the evidence of the *tria nomina* denoting Roman citizenship of C. Attius Marinus stamped on the *mortaria* (mixing bowls) produced first at Colchester and then in the Verulamium region. The association of technologies new to Britain with named Romans is one clue to help reconstruct the society of Roman Britain. Some of these individuals may first have served in the army, which is likely to have been a major source of new settlement in the province. We have no figures, but can reflect on the opportunities presented by a province which was the setting for so much imperial activity. That there was a continued demand to settle in Britain is evidenced by the foundation of two new colonies at Gloucester and Lincoln at the end of the first century AD. Since it is unlikely that Colchester would have had the capacity to absorb a significant number of new settlers by the early 70s, it could be suggested that veterans were going elsewhere other than to the *colonia*. Given the character of the development of the Flavian *civitates*, it is not unreasonable to suppose a veteran involvement. The completion of this phase of city foundations at the end of the century may have occasioned the need for new colonies as a measure to absorb a continuing stream of veterans. By the time the *civitas* capitals attributed to Hadrian had been established, recruits to the army were being increasingly drawn from within Britain itself. While there has been a recent presumption in favour of the contribution of native aristocracies to the development of the province, we should remind ourselves of the range and variety of evidence to suggest the deep involvement of newcomers.

Infrastructure and the economy

While we might choose to associate developments across Britain with renewed confidence in the province, and the prosecution of the conquest with Vespasian's initiative, necessity was certainly a co-partner. In considering how the conquest of southern Britain was achieved, it is acknowledged that there is considerable direct and proxy evidence for the early importation of foodstuffs and supplies generally: hence the logic of the decision to encourage the development of London. Whatever the potential of Britain for maintaining the Roman army establishment in the province unaided, sheer practicalities would have militated against this until a network of communications, at least, had been developed across the province. Inequable and corrupt treatment was bound to occur: another problem whose resolution is attributed by Tacitus to Agricola (but illustrative of the basic reforms required in the 80s). Appropriate administrative systems also needed to be in place to manage the arrangements for taxation that were necessary to achieve the appropriate level of support for the Roman military and civilian infrastructure. While the start of such a task might have been the responsibility of a governor like Trebellius Maximus whom Tacitus describes as having no military experience, the transfer of the Fourteenth Legion out of Britain in 66 would have reduced the urgency of developing the provincial infrastructure. The impetus of the new policy of advance and the return of a fourth legion with Cerialis in 71 provided the context for putting in place the administrative infrastructure necessary for the province. The decision to pursue the conquest of the North introduced the additional strain of developing extended lines of communication to support an army remote from the heart of the province. While Tacitus attributes to Agricola the policy of encouraging 'Romanization' by his 'giving private encouragement and official assistance to the building of temples, fora and private houses . . . so that the Britons were gradually led on to the amenities that make vice agreeable—arcades, baths, and sumptuous banquets', it is not only archaeologically impossible to define consistently a chronology of building that can be associated with a very limited period of years, but there is also the evidence for work starting on the construction of the Verulamium forum-basilica several years before 79. The resources required to deliver a combination of projects of road building, laying out of street grids, the provision of forums, basilicas, public baths, etc. were not such as to lead to a rapid execution. It is not surprising, therefore that we see evidence for such key projects still being undertaken among the cities listed above into the middle decades of the second century.

What evidence then do we have for how the province worked in the later first century? In the absence so far of a greater insight into the development of the circulation of Roman coinage within the province, we have the proxy evidence of artefacts such as pottery to give insight into distribution networks, and the level of integration of different parts of the province. Until the later first century the production of Romanized pottery, for example in the sandy wares which become typical of subsequent production, was extremely limited. Up to then continuity in production means it is difficult to distinguish between pottery manufactured before and after the Conquest across lowland Britain. One of the earliest industries established in Britain which achieves more than a local distribution is that at Brockley Hill on Watling Street between London and St Albans. Verulamium-region *mortaria* with their distinctive potters' stamps are found distributed widely throughout the province, with examples found on the frontier zone in the north from the Flavian period onwards. Overland transport via the developing road network seems to account best for the pattern, and the success of the industry can be partly explained by the proximity to London and access to the principal route to the North. Potters were attracted to the industry from Colchester where the *colonia* had sustained limited pottery production at this time. Complementing the pattern of Verulamium-region products in the later first century is that of the imported North Gaulish *mortaria* whose findspots are more concentrated to the West and South Wales as well as to the North. Rather than an extensive use of different ports, importation appears almost exclusively confined to Richborough and London, with distribution thereafter by road. The flow of goods through and out of London is pivotal to this and to the underpinning of the Verulamium-region pattern. The wide range of imported goods, which are represented in the archaeological record from London, emphasize the latter's continuing importance as a port in the Flavian period.

This centralized pattern brings sharply into focus the degree of integration of the rest of the civil zone of the province and how much London might have acted as a collecting point for grain and other commodities required at the frontier. Were there sufficiently robust systems in place in the first centre to assure both effective collection from the *civitas*, and transport to collection points like London for delivery onward to the army? With the probable exception of the developing adjacent cities of the South-East—Colchester, Verulamium, Silchester, and Canterbury, there is no hard evidence to support the existence of such arrangements. One possible explanation would be that the very development of the provincial infrastructure, of the cities and the associated road network, demanded the greater part of the surplus that was locally available. The evidence from the countryside lends some support to this picture, for it is not until the late first century we begin to see a pattern of small Romanized farmsteads emerging in the South-East. Around Verulamium a number of such villas develop, such as Park Street, Boxmoor, Gadebridge Park, and Gorhambury close to the city itself, with some showing continuity of occupation of site from the Late Iron Age. The typical plan consists of a rectangular range of mortared brick and stone, subdivided into three or four rooms; where present, bathhouses are detached in separate accommodation. Simple tessellated floors and the use of painted wall plaster are attested. The skills needed for the construction and decoration of these buildings imply specialists and thus the ability to raise the cash to pay them. Although comparable examples can be found in the South and South-East, nowhere else in the South exhibits such a clear articulation of town and country. Indeed there is reasonable evidence from Kent to argue that the influence of Watling Street and the river valleys of the Darenth and Medway, rather than the *civitas* capital at Canterbury, best accounts for the distribution of villas. Much of the precocious development around Verulamium can also be attributed, as we have seen above, to the generating economic power of Watling Street which facilitated the flow of goods to the North. While the area of southern Britain which saw the most vigorous development in the first and second centuries is also that in which the more precocious Romanizing took place in the pre-Conquest period, we should not assume the latter provides the explanation. It is not unreasonable to suppose that outsiders built and occupied the first villas, rather than that they were an *ex vacuo* introduction on the part of native farmers, and in so doing the incomers provided a model for others. Close parallels can be found across the Channel in Gallia Belgica. We should also note that there are also some exceptional developments in the later first century, of which the sumptuous villa at Fishbourne, immediately to the west of Chichester, is the best known example. Isolated examples occur elsewhere in the South such as at Angmering in Sussex, Eccles in Kent, and Rivenhall in Essex.

Early Roman burial evidence reinforces the pattern of new settlement in the countryside with parallel Romanizing developments concentrated in an arc around London which embraces Colchester, Verulamium, and Canterbury. While in part this can be explained by a continuation of developments already in place from the Late pre-Roman Iron Age, that continuation was undoubtedly and emphatically influenced by the organization of the infrastructure of the province in the first century AD. Central to this was London's role as the principal port of entry for the supply of the army, and its logistical support in the advance to the West and North.

Military consolidation

The military retrenchment under Trajan is reflected in the pattern of inward trade into the province and the slow development of the urban centres beyond the south-eastern core. Consolidation of conquest is marked by the construction of permanent fortresses at Caerleon, Chester, and York with inscriptions showing the projects well advanced during the reign of Trajan. If this and the associated work on auxiliary forts were the principal task for the army in the absence of further advance, new projects would be required to follow on. That there was no enduring commitment to a garrison strength of three legions is indicated by the evidence pointing to the withdrawal of the Ninth Legion in the latter part of Trajan's reign. Thus, Hadrian's decision to construct a permanent linear barrier, stretching 80 miles between the Tyne and the Solway just to the north of the Stanegate, makes every sense in a context where thought of total conquest of the island requiring a strength of at least four legions and their equivalents had been implicitly—if not explicitly—abandoned a generation earlier. This was the great new project for an army which was otherwise insufficiently strong to make—and secure—further territorial advances.

A sense of the need to mark physically the division between Romans and barbarians, and to monumentalize that frontier seems a more convincing explanation than military necessity. In truth we are unlikely to be able to assess the potential threat from the north, but the presence of regular gateways at every mile through the barrier seems to imply that assuring security was not paramount. Nevertheless, Hadrian's biographer refers to difficulties in Britain at the beginning of his reign, and coins struck in 119 commemorate a victory in the province. This contrasts with the evidence emerging from the writing tablets found at Vindolanda on the Stanegate. Dating from the closing years of the first, and opening years of the second century, these reveal the complexities of maintaining a garrison on the northern frontier. There are few references to fighting or campaigning; in one instance the natives are referred to dismissively as 'Brittunculi'. Other documents reveal a garrison under strength with detachments deployed at Corbridge and London, a picture hardly consistent with a unit at full strength and on full alert to face a dangerous and numerous enemy. The correspondence of the fort commander's wife gives no hint of anxiety or insecurity. While circumstances had undoubtedly changed in the period before Hadrian's decision to build the Wall, our understanding of the densities of native settlement in the north and the likely scale of the opposition are also not commensurate with the scale of the mural barrier. That the idea of constructing a linear frontier in Britain was not wholly determined by circumstances within the province is demonstrated by developments elsewhere. It may be appropriate to think in terms of a policy where territory not otherwise delimited by natural barriers such as the sea or rivers was closed by a continuous mural arrangement. A close parallel is provided by Upper Germany where such a linear frontier had been developing between the Main and the Danube from the reign of Domitian. Whether we shall gain further insight into the factors which influenced decision-making, it is implicit from the subsequent decision to advance the frontier to the line of the Antonine Wall that there were balances to be struck. A more lightly manned and shorter linear barrier could, potentially, release troops to garrison a more extensive territory such as the Lowlands of Scotland by a looser disposition of forts.

The construction of the frontier was a formidable undertaking, and we cannot now determine how long the process took. The epigraphic record is rich. It reveals that the project involved all the British legions—the Second *Augusta*, Twentieth *Valeria Victrix*, and Sixth *Victrix*, the last brought to the province by the new governor, A. Platorius Nepos, as a replacement for the Ninth *Hispana*. Numerous auxiliary regiments are attested in the project as well. The final scheme involved a continuous wall with fortlets ('milecastles') at every mile and intervening turrets, while auxiliary forts were evenly distributed on the wall at intervals of 8–10 miles. There is much uncertainty about how permeable the barrier was intended to be: the provision of gates at the milecastles and the eventual disposition of the garrisons on the Wall themselves argue that policy was forward looking into the North. On the other hand, the secondary construction of the Vallum (the ditch with flanking ramparts behind the line of the curtain wall) suggests security issues with the tribes to the south, or the need to define a 'military zone'. The secondary blocking of some milecastle gates could also be read in different ways: insufficient manpower available to garrison the fortlets or increasing threat from the tribes to the north.

Economic integration

Whereas we can detect changes to the original scheme in the ground plan of the Wall and its associated installations, the very state of the surviving monument prevents us from appreciating the finished state of the project and, indeed, whether it was, in any sense, finished. Calculations about the resources required for the project can only be speculative, but the timing would have been critical in terms of the delivery and volume of materials and supplies. As with a forward campaign such as Agricola's, much could be drawn on from elsewhere in the province or beyond. Although the stone and ballast were a local resource, transport, tools, food, and animals would need to have been drawn from a wide catchment. With these factors in mind we can, perhaps, see evidence for the full integration of the *civitates* into a provincial system. Examples of Romanized farms can be seen across the province in the second century, while pottery production and distribution of a Romanized repertoire, generally a helpful indicator of trade and market development, is also more evenly distributed across the *civitates*. Distinctive industries take shape in the second century: in the West, in Dorset, and the Severn Valley; in the Midlands, in Hartshill-Mancetter, the Nene Valley, and Oxfordshire; and in the South-East in the Alice Holt Forest, Colchester, and the Thames Estuary. Given the assumed level of expenditure on both the garrison itself and its enterprises on the northern frontier, it is likely that the state was the principal agency behind these developments among the *civitates*. Nevertheless, imported goods continued to flow into the province, sigillata from the region of Lezoux in Central Gaul and also the Rhineland, olive oil from the estates along the Guadal-quivir in Baetica (southern Spain), and wine, now principally from Gaul and the Rhineland, transported in barrels, or amphoras from Narbonnensis. Both Central Gaulish sigillata and the olive-oil carrying amphoras are very widely represented in the archaeological record of settlement across the *civitates* in the second century. A major development of the early second century is the greater exploitation of western and eastern coastal sea-routes as a means of transport to and from the northern frontier. Just as the distribution of pottery shows the vitality of overland routes within the province, with products of Midland industries such as Hartshill-Mancetter and the Nene Valley regularly found on military sites up to and including Hadrian's Wall, so it also demonstrates a comparable movement around the coasts which engages the south and north of the province. To the west, black-burnished cooking wares from south-east Dorset are found across the South-West Peninsula and the Bristol Channel in Wales and the northern frontier, and comparable cooking wares from sources in the Thames Estuary as well as more specialized wares from Colchester are found up the East Coast, with concentrations on Hadrian's Wall (and the Antonine Wall). At the same time on the eastern seaboard, we see epigraphic evidence of the fleet (the *classis Britannica*) with bases in the South at Dover, for example, or in the Weald, but also engaged in construction work on Hadrian's Wall. If we see this combination of land and sea-moved pottery as tracers of a more broadly based trade with and supply to the garrisons of Wales and the North, it seems to represent an involvement of the entire 'civil' province in sustaining the military establishment. The combination of all our sources reinforces the view of integration and an evenness of development across the *civitates* that had been established by the late first century.

Confidence engendered by the new arrangements for the frontier encouraged the foundation of new *civitates* as symbolized by the construction of towns westwards at Caerwent and Carmarthen, and northwards at Wroxeter, Aldborough, and Brough-on-Humber. Of these only Wroxeter may have developed to a size comparable to that of towns in the South and South-East. Otherwise further development is confined to the already established centres of the lowland zone of Britain. Certain areas, excluding Wales and the North where military occupation is attested, remained undeveloped. The South-Western Peninsula as a whole, for example, seems to have been almost unaffected by Romanized forms of settlement. Even the foundation of the *civitas* capital at Exeter seems to have had little impact on its immediate hinterland. In the North the legionary fortresses at Chester and York remain as virtual islands linked to each other and the northern frontier by a network of forts along the principal lines of communication. As in the South-West where, on general environmental grounds, development might reasonably have been expected, productive landscapes like the Cheshire Plain remain virtually devoid of Romanized settlement. Thus, a sharp contrast can be drawn between the environs of the fortress at Chester and those at Caerleon, where not only a small, but vigorous urban community developed close by at Caerwent, but the adjacent productive lands of Glamorgan supported several villa estates. No such 'satellite' town emerged near Chester. Equally, the development of Aldborough, in the 'shadow' of the legionary fortress at York, was not paralleled by developments in the countryside comparable with those in South Wales.

In drawing attention to areas of the province where, on prima facie environmental grounds, such as access to good soils, Romanizing developments might have been expected, we should equally consider areas where positive development was taking place in relatively hostile circumstances. The settlement of the East Anglian Fenland provides one such example. In an environment prone to both freshwater and marine flooding, there is astonishing evidence for settlement developing from the late first/early second century. That these alluvia were still subject to a tidal regime is demonstrated by the inland distribution of salt-making debris of Early Roman date. Although there is some evidence for localized schemes of drainage and regularized land allotment, there is no hint of any overall scheme of land division. It is difficult not to associate the scale of building at Stonea Grange without some official involvement, and the Stonea development as a whole hints at a role in the supervision or management of the Fenland landscape at large. The expansion of settlement in this region contrasts with the evidence for the abandonment of settlements with origins earlier in the pre-Roman Iron Age elsewhere in the south of Britain. While this process could be related to a rationalization of the countryside in association with the development of villas and towns drawing off peasantry from the countryside, it seems unlikely that such a process would have left yet more surplus to colonize the Fenland. One possibility could be that the population of the province was being steadily increased through the settlement of captives from successive wars on the frontier, as well as through the settlement of retired soldiers and other incomers to the province. The former might be destined to exploit marginal, but potentially productive land, the latter to create their estates among and out of native farms in established arable lands across the province. Even within those otherwise productive arable landscapes of southern Britain, we can identify marginal landscapes which were aggressively developed in the Roman period. On the dry chalk uplands of Salisbury Plain, for example, we see the beginning of the intensive development in the second century of substantial peasant villages like Chisenbury Warren in a way which has no parallel in the pre-Roman Iron Age. The organized nature of the settlements suggests a relationship with larger estates, perhaps controlled from villas in the river valleys. Like the settlement of the wetlands, that of the waterless chalk uplands suggests a control of displaced populations either from within the province, or from native populations from beyond the frontier.

Civic projects and their completion

As far as the general development of the towns is concerned, the second century saw the completion of the big building projects. The latest civic centre projects, including forums and public baths, at Caistor-by-Norwich, Leicester, or even Silchester all seem to be under way by the second quarter of the century. In London there was a major redevelopment of the forum-basilica in the early second century, but the scale of public building, such as the so-called Governor's Palace, or the Huggin Hill baths was of a different order to that evidenced in the *civitates*. The city's role in the administration of the province was highlighted by the construction of a fort for a garrison in the north-west quarter. Extensive waterfronts were constructed, principally along the north bank of the Thames. While London seems to distinguish itself as different from the *coloniae* and *civitas* capitals, there is little to separate one *civitas* capital from another, though in the second century there may be a case for seeing the *coloniae* as a distinct group, not least because of their early provision with defences in stone. Development in the towns was not simply confined to public building. We also can see examples of timber-frame town houses, particularly as revealed by excavation at Verulamium, developing in the second century. Like their villa counterparts in the countryside these houses reveal evidence to indicate a sophisticated urban community. The nature of their decoration, whether by painted plaster on walls or ceilings, or by tessellated and mosaic floors, compares well with that from the countryside. Alongside the residential occupation there is also evidence for the presence of shops and workshops within the towns, particularly along the principal streets. These tend to be related to food preparation or consumption or to specialized crafts, while the 'heavier' industries, such as pottery production, were situated in the countryside.

With religious activity there is a move away from expression in traditional classical forms, so that the temple of Sulis Minerva at Bath and that of the deified Claudius at Colchester remain the exceptions rather than the norm. While there is evidence for a multiplicity of cults and dedications to Roman, Celtic, or hybrid deities, these are associated with a simple architectural form consisting for the most part of a small, rectangular cella (shrine) surrounded by an ambulatory to give the so-called 'double-square' plan. The latter is found widely distributed in town and country from the late first/early second century onwards. Temples of this kind are found frequently across Gaul and the Rhine provinces.

Smaller towns and villages

In parallel with the development of the *civitas* capitals and the chartered towns we should also note the growth of smaller nucleated settlements, for the most part distributed along the principal roads of the province. Although commonly referred to as 'small towns' these communities probably emerge as settlements around the *mansiones* and other establishments connected with the operation of the *cursus publicus* (the Imperial Post). Excavation at Chelmsford, which some might argue was intended to be the *civitas* capital of the Trinovantes, suggests development from the late first century AD onwards, although several others are likely to have been on the site of earlier forts, themselves influenced by the presence of native settlements. The more significant of these settlements were provided with defences at the end of the second or the beginning of the third century. Apart from their role in servicing the *cursus publicus*, no evidence has emerged for any other 'public' function. There is no evidence for regular street grids; often the main road acts as the principal determinant of plan with evidence of 'strip buildings' (shops or shops-cum-workshops) aligned along it and lanes leading off at right angles. Equally there is no evidence for forum-basilica or public baths. Although little is known about this category of settlement in general, there is very little indeed to associate with the Early Roman period. Nevertheless, there appears to be very limited evidence for the emergence of private housing comparable to that found in the larger towns. Besides that role, attested or presumed, in relation to the *cursus publicus*, we can associate specialized functions with certain sites. Outstanding among these is Bath (Aquae Sulis) with its spa and associated temple dedicated to Sulis Minerva, but the specialized pottery industries associated with Water Newton (Durobrivae) and Mancetter (Manduessedum) were also significant within the province. Off the major roads, settlement of this kind was much more limited, and is accounted for by special factors such as specialized industries. Thus, a substantial settlement associated with lead-mining developed at Charterhouse-on-Mendip, as it did at Weston-under-Penyard in relation to iron-making, and at Droitwich where salt was extracted. Roads serving these centres were subsidiary to the main network.

The wealth of the province

Mineral extraction was a defining imperial exploitative process of the province, but it is difficult to assess its overall importance, not least because it is so difficult to trace evidence of the product. Some gold was extracted from mines at Dolaucothi in south-western Wales from the Flavian period onwards, but probably the most valuable mineral mined in quantity was lead, in which silver might be present in quantities worth extracting. One indication of its importance is the incidence of lead pigs or ingots, many stamped with the emperor's name or that of a lessee, which have been found across Britain. We know that this metal was being quarried from the Mendips as early as 49, while extraction from the Flintshire mines of North Wales had begun by 74, and from Yorkshire by 81. No doubt the high silver content of Mendip lead was an important factor in its early exploitation, but we have no means of assessing either the total output of lead or of the amount of silver extracted from it by cupellation. Copper, from mines in Shropshire, North Wales, and on Anglesey, and tin from Cornwall were also extracted, but far fewer examples of stamped and datable ingots survive. Equally, no centres like that at Charterhouse-on-Mendip are associated with either of these metals. Production on a completely different scale, but equally difficult to quantify, was that of iron, a metal required in bulk for a whole range of military and civil requirements. It was extracted from a variety of sources, especially from the Weald between the first and the third centuries, where numerous smelting sites are recorded. In the absence of stamped ingots as a measure of output, there is evidence to associate some iron-making in the Weald with the *classis Britannica* (the Channel fleet). Several bloomery sites—where an intermediate stage in the production of iron was carried out—have produced examples of tiles stamped 'CLBR'. Since we noted earlier the involvement of the British fleet in the construction of Hadrian's Wall, part of the rationale may have been in the supply of materials including iron (and probably timber) from the South.

By the middle of the second century, the structures were in place to ensure a consistent administrative regime for taxation and justice across much of the province. In this respect little was to change during the remainder of the Roman administration of Britain. In parallel, and insofar as this activity can be quantified, the exploitation of minerals—by law the property of the emperor—appears to have peaked in the second century. Despite this, we have a hint from the historian Appian that the province still cost more than it brought in to the imperial coffers. Working out what these costs might have been is extremely difficult, but, as material evidence of a level of continuing subsidy of the province, there is the incidence of finds of imported commodities like wine and olive oil, as well as of manufactured goods like Gaulish sigillatas. Perhaps less in volume than the scale of pre-Flavian imports, these are nevertheless found widely across the province, in no way limited in their distributions to the military garrisons. Given the demands of supporting the army and the infrastructure of fortresses, forts, roads, towns, *mansiones*, etc., etc., it seems unlikely that further surplus was available for export to pay for the range of imported goods and commodities in the archaeological record. Certainly there is no evidence for any significant export (apart from, perhaps, imperial property in the form of metals) in the first and second centuries. More plausible is that such imported items served as payments in kind for goods and services delivered across the province over and above those paid for out of the taxes levied in the province.

Antonine Scotland

Imperial confidence in the province as is so clearly expressed by the range of evidence described above was also undoubtedly coloured by a perception that arrangements could still be improved upon. Hadrian had attempted to rationalize the northern frontier with a monument which would also reflect well on himself and the empire, but his successor, Antoninus Pius, set about establishing a radical, alternative policy. Just as Hadrian may have used achievement in Britain as a way of promoting his own image, so Antoninus Pius' decision to advance the frontier to the line running between the inner estuaries of the Forth and Clyde may have been similarly motivated. A significant conquest of territory in the north of Britain, accompanied by the construction of a shorter, but hopefully more effective mural barrier, would have been seen as a major triumph at the start of his reign. Since coins commemorating victory in Britain were struck in 142 or 143, it seems that the policy was initiated at the outset of the new reign. Construction work at Corbridge in 139 and 140 is interpreted as evidence of the necessary preparations for the advance into the Lowlands by the new governor, Lollius Urbicus. Although the successful advance was undoubtedly to the credit of Antoninus Pius, as the specific reference by his biographer to the war against the Britons and the construction of the new turf wall implies, it is possible that the decision was heavily influenced by the legionary commanders in Britain. A generation had passed since Hadrian's initiative, and a new project for the army in Britain may urgently have been required to sustain morale. Once again, all three legions as well as auxiliaries were involved in the project.

Writers have also considered that the new, shorter frontier system represented an advance on its predecessor, in that it required a relatively small garrison, perhaps only 60 per cent of the strength necessary to man Hadrian's Wall. On the other hand, additional forces were required to police the Lowlands and maintain lines of communication. Whatever savings might have been made in relation to the manning of the frontier itself, they were likely to have been more than offset by the new establishments in the Lowlands and the outpost forts to the north of the Antonine Wall. In debating the reasons for the change in policy with the accession of the new emperor, some weight has been attached to the prestige which would accrue to the new emperor in the wake of success, but military considerations and the need to control the Selgovae and, perhaps, the Novantae, may have given further legitimacy to the scheme and there is some support for this in a difficult passage of the second-century writer Pausanias which refers to aggression on the part of the Brigantes against a subject of Rome. This reminds us how difficult it is to assess the military situation without the benefit of written commentary, even if from the perspective of Rome!

More persuasive evidence of threats to the security of the North is provided by coin issues of 154–5 which show Britannia subdued. An inscription from the Tyne records the arrival of reinforcements from the German armies during the governorship of Julius Verus, who is certainly attested elsewhere in Britain in 158. Although it now seems as if the Antonine Wall continued to be manned, there were significant changes both in terms of structure and garrison in southern Scotland during the brief overall period during which the Antonine Wall was held. This seems to imply that the scale of the threat in the North required the temporary withdrawal from garrison of considerable numbers of troops. It is assumed that the problem lay within northern England and southern Scotland and that the resolution of the problem required withdrawal from Lowland Scotland. This probably happened early in the reign of Marcus Aurelius, although, on the basis of coin evidence, there may have been some limited continuity of occupation of certain forts in Scotland into the 170s. The differential representation of sigillata on the two walls makes it reasonably clear that they were never held in force together, so that the Antonine reoccupation of Hadrian's Wall and the reconstruction in stone of the western section originally built of turf is likely to belong to the 160s and later. The change of policy is perhaps to be associated with the governor Calpurnius Agricola or his predecessor M. Statius Priscus Licinius Italicus.

As with most changes of policy on the northern frontier, the possibility of confidently distinguishing between internal drivers, such as rebellion among the Pennine tribes, and external factors is difficult. In the case of the withdrawal early in the reign of Marcus Aurelius, we should not overlook the problems the latter faced on the Danube in confronting the power of the Marcomanni and the Sarmatians. A certain strategic redeployment of resources away from Britain, such as to make the maintenance of the Antonine Wall untenable, may have been necessary. A reduction in manpower, after all, had been the principal reason for retrenchment in the North under Trajan. Just as that weakening of the military establishment may have been seized upon by native tribes at the beginning of Hadrian's reign, native resistance seems to have increased after the abandonment of the Antonine Wall. Dio reports that the greatest war of Commodus' reign was fought in Britain and there is some correlation, albeit difficult to date precisely, in the archaeological record. Dio records that the tribes 'crossed the wall that separated them from the Roman garrison and killed a general', and there are Late Antonine destruction deposits at Rudchester, and at Halton and Corbridge along the line of Dere Street. Ulpius Marcellus appears to have restored the situation, but without re-establishing the Antonine Wall. At the same time he appears to have provoked unrest among the troops, but the issues do not seem to have been resolved until after a successor, Pertinax, had been appointed in 185.

Mutiny, civil war, and their aftermath

That the British garrison felt neglected, requiring a greater commitment from the emperor, is not only evidenced by the group of mutinous soldiers who went to Rome to air their grievances in 185, but by a more significant event which followed the deaths of Commodus in 192 and then Pertinax (now emperor) in 193. With the support of his three legions, and a further legion from Spain, the new governor of Britain, Clodius Albinus, already declared *Caesar* (junior emperor) by his rival Septimius Severus, fought against the latter for control of the empire. Proclaimed *Augustus* (senior emperor) in 196, he crossed to Gaul with an army and was defeated by Severus at Lyon the following spring. Although the enterprise may have been fuelled by naked ambition, it remains a possibility that discontent among the army remained an issue. We should recall that a significant period had elapsed since the Antonine advance and the subsequent retrenchment of the 160s. To take an army to the Continent was a clear sign to it that its influence mattered in the settlement of imperial affairs at the very highest level. This action was reciprocated by Severus in due course when he arrived in person in 208 to lead an army into Scotland against the northern British tribes. Before this, inscriptions from northern forts show evidence of investment through rebuilding from 197 in the hinterland, from 205 on the wall itself, and from 205–7 at Risingham beyond the wall. This action on the part of governors Virius Lupus and Alfenus Senecio may have been sufficient for the moment to restore confidence in the garrison without the personal intervention of Severus. It was also paralleled by a treaty with the barbarians where peace was bought. Under Lupus' governorship we hear of such a settlement with the Maeatae of Lowland Scotland who had been acting in concert with the Highland Caledonii. This is the first mention of the former as a tribal grouping, and of their involvement with the Caledonii. However, such concerted action on the part of the barbarians may already have been a factor earlier in the troubles of Commodus' reign.

Town defences and their context

Evidence that the situation on the northern frontier affected more than the military situation is evidenced by the widespread building of defences around the majority of both major and minor towns in the late second or early third century. As with the close dating of destruction events in northern forts at the end of the second century, similar problems surround the dating of the urban defences. These were constructed with ramparts of earth, clay, and gravel derived from associated defensive ditches, giving the impression of projects conducted with urgency. Calculations of the manpower required to construct them support a rapid execution with completion in a matter of weeks or a few months. Although for the most part the layers sealed by the construction of the rampart only give a Late Antonine *terminus post quem*, it is likely that the projects were initiated in response to a province-wide situation. Various possibilities have been canvassed—including protection against northern barbarians in the reign of Commodus, or as a safeguard in the absence of Clodius Albinus' army in 196—and given the difficulties of dating, all are possible. The group has no counterpart of defence in earthwork in adjacent Gaul or Germany. If we accept construction before *c.*200, it is likely that the subsequent combination of actions associated with the reign of Severus restored confidence throughout the province.

Peace and retrenchment

The military intervention which ended with Severus' death in York in 211 was sufficient to restore peace in Britain through the remainder of the third century. Although the disposition of forts and marching camps suggests that total conquest had not been in the emperor's mind, we cannot exclude this possibility. Certainly all the forces in the province were used, and a combination of fleets drawn from Germany, Moesia, and Pannonia appears to have worked with the Classis Britannica. There were associated major supply bases at South Shields at the mouth of the Tyne and at Corbridge. The parallel with the

Agricolan campaigns is very close, not least in the establishment of a legionary base at Carpow on the Tay, perhaps for part of the Sixth Legion. Following the death of Severus, his son Caracalla concluded peace with the Maeatae and the Caledonii in 212. Reorganization was not solely confined to the North: at some point the province was divided into Britannia Superior and Britannia Inferior, probably with the aim of dividing responsibility for the garrison in order to avoid a repetition of the events of 196–7. Although we cannot be certain of the boundary between the two, the evidence of Dio points to Chester and Caerleon being assigned to Superior, and York to Inferior. An inscription assigns Lincoln also to Inferior.

With the conclusion of the Severan campaign, we move into a period when there is almost no written source for the province. On its own this might be taken to signify that Britain no longer had such an important role to play in imperial affairs: that events in the East, for example, had overshadowed the West. If Britain had been among the priorities for imperial expenditure up to the time of Severus, only taking second place when crises intervened elsewhere, then from the settlement of Caracalla the province(s) appear to have become a backwater in terms of military activity. If some of the discontent apparent in the army in the reign of Commodus and immediately after had been a reflection of a scaling down of activity out of proportion to the size of the garrison, resolution might be achieved by a reduction to achieve a 'peacetime' establishment. How and when this was accomplished is not clear, but there is general agreement that the Late Roman military establishment in Britain was a fraction, perhaps a third, of its second-century strength. The epigraphic record commemorating the construction or repair of buildings within forts, or of forts themselves is particularly weak after about 225. Indicators of change include a marked decline of trade flow into Britain, best evidenced by the decline and virtual cessation in the importation of sigillata and of olive oil from Baetica, and a slackening in the inward flow of money such that low-denomination coins minted in the second quarter of the third century are extremely rare as site finds. Within the British provinces, it is difficult to recognize characteristics of consumer goods such as pottery which are third-century as such. However, production dating from the later second century or the later third can by contrast be readily identified. This hiatus in material culture and of the circulation of low-value coinage, both critical to the dating of archaeological deposits, has led some inter-pretations of site histories to argue for gaps in occupation in the third century. In reality, the nature of the archaeological record at this time makes it difficult to argue a *positive* case for continuity of occupation at a particular site.

Urban change

Notwithstanding that Britain was no longer central to imperial affairs after Severus, there are important developments to consider. In the first place it is clear that London continued to be regarded as an important centre, where it was appropriate for successive governors to make their mark, despite the evidence for the abandonment of buildings and their burial beneath soil horizons in the later second century. In the first place, the city was defended with a stone wall built of Kentish Greensand, which enclosed an area of 130 hectares (330 acres). Initially constructed between 190 and 230, this work was only completed with the construction of the riverside wall in the third quarter of the third century. London is conspicuous as the only city other than the *coloniae* to be provided for in this way. Prior to the completion of the city wall there had been major investment into the timber riverside wharf on the north bank in the second quarter of the century. Within the city, notable monuments include a splendid arch and a screen of gods of late second or early third century date. Although the presence of Severus in Britain may have precipitated some of the building of the public monuments, it is possible that an elevation of the city to *colonia* may have provided another context. There is no certain evidence of this, but we should note that York, the location of the Sixth Legion, is attested as *colonia* by 235, and was presumably the principal city of Britannia Inferior.

Other cities in the province show evidence for the gradual replacement of timber buildings in stone. This process has been well documented in Verulamium where a steady rebuilding of town houses in stone takes place after an extensive fire in 155 and extends into the third century. A sense that there was now a more residential character to a town like Verulamium is given weight by the treatment of the street frontage. A dense-packed row of timber-framed shops fronting on to Watling Street was replaced in the third century—after a long interval when the plot remained undeveloped—by three separate shops or workshops built in masonry. At Verulamium, as elsewhere among the *civitas* capitals, third-century developments were concentrated within the perimeter of the hastily constructed defences of the end of the second century. In the countryside we can document changes to existing villas from the later second century, but there is little evidence for new building between the later second century and the later third. While this may be a reflection of the difficulties of the dating evidence described above, there is a sense that the relative lack of activity in town and country is a correlate of the decline in economic activity discussed above.

Military developments on the coasts of the South and East

The exceptional investment in the waterfront in London reminds us that the construction of new fortifications along the east and south coasts of Britain can be assigned to a period between the late second century and the late third. Initially these may have had a role in the supply system of the Severan campaigns, and this may have been the case for the earliest attested forts at Brancaster in Norfolk and Reculver in Kent. After Severus it is possible that these were linked with London to assist in the supply of the Rhine frontier. In support of this, one of the latest deposits from the London waterfront with massive quantities of imported goods includes a very high proportion of samian ware and other goods from Eastern Gaul and the Rhineland. More developed forts, typically with massive walls and projecting D-shaped towers, appear to belong to the late third century. This group includes Burgh Castle in Suffolk, Bradwell in Essex, Richborough, Dover and Lympne in Kent, Pevensey in Sussex, and Portchester in Hampshire. These have been seen as a gradually evolving response to piracy and incursion by barbarian groups which had become a major threat to the security of Gaul and Germany in the course of the third century. The later group of forts is closely linked to the usurpation of Carausius in 286. Appointed to rid the Channel coasts of barbarian raiders, he had usurped power in Britain where he ruled as emperor until his murder at the hands of his finance minister, Allectus, who succeeded him in 294. Control of Britain was eventually wrested back by Constantius I ('Chlorus') in 296, with a cross-Channel invasion in which divisions of his fleet played very important parts. While it is possible that the completion of the coastal forts was to secure the coasts from raiders and pirates, the massiveness and character of their construction is typical of the new kind of Late Roman fortification designed to withstand sophisticated siege. An alternative—and the recently-established Allectan date of Pevensey adds weight—is that they were part of a scheme to defend Britain from reconquest by the central forces of Rome. Little else is known of the usurpation. A milestone of Carausius from near Carlisle suggests that his power extended across both provinces, and this is supported by the widespread diffusion of the coinage of both Allectus and Carausius in Britain and, to a lesser extent, in north-west Gaul. For a period it seems as if Carausius' power included part of north-west Gaul, and some of his earliest coinage was probably minted in Rouen.

The end of the third century

The recovery of Britain by Constantius symbolizes the beginning of a period of new development and prosperity for Britain. This is evidenced in a variety of ways, such as by new building in towns within existing defensive circuits freshly refurbished in stone in the later third century, and by new villas in the countryside. At the same time the emergence of new, or the renaissance of existing industries is registered in the countryside from the later third century onwards.

Figure 8 The continuing importance in the fourth century of Caerwent on the Severn, founded as the *civitas* capital of the Silures of South Wales, is clear from the updating of the town wall with massive external towers.

3

The fourth century and beyond

P. J. Casey

In a notable encomium on the state of Britain, the Labour politician Aneurin Bevan said that an island made mainly of coal and surrounded by seas full of fish could neither freeze nor starve and therefore must, by implication, be able in the last analysis to survive, were it not that some organizational genius had contrived to produce a shortage of both commodities at the same time. In the event neither coal nor fish now play a very large part in the economy of the island, but the truth of the overall sentiment is more than the reality of the parts as events in the period 1939–45 proved.

Extending the concept of insular political survival back to the Roman period, we are faced by the need to explain the apparently inexplicable. How could Britain, rich in well exploited natural resources, administered by diligent authority, disposing of what was for its time a formidable military force, a coherent element of a still vast empire, disintegrate into a series of petty Germanic and native kingdoms, chiefdoms, and principalities in little more than a couple of decades? How not merely was political power transferred but the very structure of society transformed, the language changed, religious institutions swept away, and the material basis of life irrevocably altered?

Any number of explanations have been offered, all of which, in the last analysis, boil down to more or less sophisticated versions of the nineteenth-century concept of the 'white man's burden'. Historians of the age of British imperialism saw the withdrawal of a specific, specialized Roman authority and administration as leaving behind an under-prepared native population who had had little or no participation in government for the three centuries of occupation and were soon adrift in a welter of localized political problems; incapable of resisting aggression from overseas, incapable of maintaining even the most primitively industrialized society. Post-imperialists advance the same argument with a new emphasis by which the revival of indigenous social institutions, no matter how fallible, is seen as a positive and profitable response to attempts at enforced Romanization. Thus non-integration is recognized as a social positive out of which, but for the intervention of Anglo-Saxon raiders and settlers, a uniquely insular society would have evolved, possibly something akin to pre-Norman Ireland. Neither view commends itself very strongly to the present author.

Fourth-century Britain

Britain began its last century of Roman rule in exactly the same manner as it had entered the previous century, with intense imperial activity in the island: armies led by the emperor in person fought in the North (Constantius I, like Septimius Severus a century earlier), and the civil administration of the island underwent fundamental changes resulting in the division of the province into smaller units of regional government. Just as in the first decade of the third, the early years of the fourth century saw the death of an emperor at York whilst campaigning in Britain (Constantius, again like Severus) and the dissolution of the preordained arrangements for the imperial succession by the son of the deceased ruler (Constantine, unconstitutionally proclaimed in 306, bears comparison with Caracalla's seizure of sole power from his colleague and brother Geta in 211). As in the previous century early promise of dynastic stability was replaced by a succession of rulers, civil wars, changes of civil and military allegiance, and fundamental changes in the structure of the army necessitated by the calls for manpower occasioned by internal and external warfare.

If such parallels had been evident to the inhabitants of Britain, they would have known that no matter how threatening the current crisis might seem stability would eventually be restored, the forces of the

Roman state would prevail over external enemies, and the fundamental stability of the institutions of the state would survive any damage inflicted by the ambition, incompetence, or folly of individual rulers. Rome and its empire were eternal, victory was eternal. To Christians the emperor, whether himself of their faith or pagan, was the vice-regent of god on earth; to pagans he was the appointed representative of Jupiter Best and Greatest under whose benevolent care the empire had been created and under whose benign concern it had been protected by generations of Roman heroes, many of whom were emperors raised to divine status in death. The empire was founded on a shared faith more fundamental than any division between Christianity and paganism. Further, authors of the period acknowledge the symbolic importance of Britain as in some manner empowering the empire as a whole. Britain, beyond the formal geographical boundaries of the civilized world, conquered with difficulty, inhabited some said by brutes, was yet held by Rome and thus symbolized the tenacity of Roman power and the right of the empire to govern more civilized areas. Britain was the Falkland Islands or Gibraltar of the Roman world.

Thus, the spirit of the age in antiquity is in direct conflict with modern perceptions of the period. Historians, with hindsight, see an uncontrolled descent into anarchy. Contemporaries like the Christian apologist Orosius saw, even in the darkest moments of the collapse of authority in Britain, an opportunity for the divinely inspired renewal which had characterized response to crisis from the earliest days of the Roman state. And there were plenty of opportunities to express optimism in Late Roman Britain, since each crisis, except the last, was met with military success and the injection of fresh resources into the island. Public expressions of official joy and public celebration, what the Romans called 'gaudium', followed thick upon each other.

The chronology of events following the defeat of Allectus (see Chapter 2 above) inevitably revolves around military episodes, since these were of primary concern to contemporary historians. Other events or trends can be detected by archaeological means, though on a diminished scale of chronological exactitude. The careful study of artefacts such as pottery, glass, and especially coins contributes information which the historians chose to ignore or knew nothing about. But in the main the lives of the ordinary inhabitants of Britain, their thoughts and feelings about the events in which they were passive participants are lost to us. At best we can conjecture from what seems to be the common stock of human reactions to good fortune or adversity and in doing so clothe what we conjecture in a spurious reality by describing it in the technical language of sociology, economics, or philosophy.

The defeat of the regime established with brilliant initial success by Carausius and continued by Allectus for three years in the face of mounting imperial preparation for the reconquest of Britain coincided with a number of changes in the administrative structure of the empire which now had to be implemented in Britain. But the first concern of the restored authority would have been to re-establish a loyal military and civil administration. In the North the garrisons of Hadrian's Wall remained in post, unaffected by the largely naval events of the previous decade of revolt. In the Pennines the protection of key east–west communication routes were probably put into the hands of new forces, though the evidence is not very strong. Of changes in the personnel of the civil administration we know nothing. The official line, propagated in celebratory speeches commissioned by the victorious emperors, was that Allectus' chief supporters had, conveniently, perished with him on the battlefield and that in any event his military support had been largely barbarian and mercenary rather than regular Roman forces. Whereas later revolts were followed by inquisition and retribution, the decision appears to have been to get on with implementing administrative reforms by cooperation rather than by provoking further resistance.

The Tetrarchy

The empire into which Britain was reintegrated was very different from the one from which it had been abducted by rebellion. At the highest administrative level the Emperor Diocletian had split the empire into an eastern and a western bloc, each with an emperor designated *Augustus*. Ruling the former directly himself, he appointed a colleague, Maximian, to the West. Each emperor was supported by a designated heir apparent, or *Caesar* (in the beginning Constantius I in the West and Galerius in the East). This scheme of government by a college of four is known to historians as the Tetrarchy. Further administrative division was imposed. Individual provinces were split into smaller units, each with a governor or *praeses*. Groups of provinces constituted larger administrative entities or dioceses under the oversight of a new official, the *vicarius*, or governor-general. Groups of dioceses were themselves amalgamated into prefectures supervised by a Praetorian Prefect.

In this scheme Britain was divided into four provinces. Probably originally called Britannia Prima, Britannia Secunda, Flavia Caesariensis, and Galeria Caesariensis. They are later attested, after civil war had rendered the last of these names, that of the Emperor Galerius, unsavoury, as Prima, Secunda, Flavia, and Maxima Caesariensis, the latter taking its name from the title Constantinus Maximus, used by Constantine the Great after 314. The boundaries of the provinces cannot be established with topographic certainty but a reasonable conjecture is that Prima comprised Wales and the West, Secunda the North from the Humber to the Wall, Flavia Caesariensis the Midlands, and Maxima Caesariensis the South-East. However some scholars would prefer to identify York with Flavia Caesariensis on the grounds that the Flavian (i.e Constantinian) dynasty owed much to events which took place there, and some to identify Britannia Prima with the Midlands. Each province had an administrative capital: York for the North, Lincoln for the Midlands, Cirencester for the West, and London for the South-East. A fifth province was created later in the century.

The *vicarius* established his office in London, which also housed the diocesan treasury and, until its closure in 324, an imperial mint. In the event, conflict with the *praeses* of Britannia Maxima seems inevitable and that particular post of *praeses* might have been regarded as an unenviable one or reserved for less talented candidates. A number of high officials who served in Britain later entered the Christian priesthood, though whether this is indicative of their natural goodness or the expiation of past wrongdoing is not known.

The reason for these empire-wide changes can be found in the full implementation of a taxation system geared to meet the needs of the army and administration by which the bulk of dues were paid in produce and manufactured articles rather than cash. Under this system the Praetorian Prefect estimated the material needs of his prefecture on a five-year consumption cycle. Productive capacity of provincial land was estimated and a tax burden assigned similarly manufacturing capacity was estimated and the production of special needs, army uniforms for instance, were allocated to communities. Crises could be met by imposing extraordinary levies. Smaller administrative units met the need for closer financial supervision and the allocation of specific impositions on specific population groups.

Regionalism

The long-term effects of this system have been seen as detrimental to the development of the empire as a whole; in Britain the reverse may be true. The smaller provinces increased the number of people with direct access to top-tier imperial administrators, thus the regional power structure was certainly enhanced and may have led to the creation of the class of magnates who make a hazy appearance in the post-Roman period as kings or regional leaders in the war against the Saxons. Regional economic development also probably benefited from having closed markets, protected by the existence of inter-provincial customs duties. Certainly to judge by the development of the pottery industry smaller enterprises closed down and each province produced a major centre of production which dominated the regional market. Overseas trade, certainly in cereals and probably in wool also, appears to have flourished, and the pre-existing situation largely reversed to an export-led economy rather than one dependent on imports. The insular isolation of the Carausian decade laid a foundation of self-sufficiency which could be exploited in the wider context of reunification with the empire.

The regionalism of the economy produced other tangible effects. Apart from the new administrative capitals, the traditional tribal-based cities inherited from the earliest Roman attempts to administer Britain through its existing native elite lost their political and economic roles. Attempts by the state to maintain these historic centres largely failed for although, as we shall see, many towns were fortified or re-fortified in the period under review, individuals failed to maintain existing privately-funded structures or to invest in new building programmes. On the other hand, minor towns—really extended roadside villages without elaborate administrative buildings—appear to have taken on a new lease of life as local market places, distributing the enhanced produce of the countryside or acting as collection centres for the unwieldy tax-render in kind or cattle.

Economic events in the third century, which saw a collapse of the currency system throughout the empire, laid the foundation of rural expansion in the fourth century. With hyperinflation characterizing the financial system from about the middle to nearly the end of the century, producers of primary products, effectively foodstuffs, benefited. Such negotiable wealth as was available would have drained into the possession of larger scale, self-sufficient agricultural producers. At the same time land may have been cheap as smallholders, still dependants on urban industrial products, fell under the burden of inflationary pressures and concomitantly increasing rents. Opportunities to buy out—or reduce to tenantry—smaller agriculturists may account for the phenomenon of the growth of palatial villas in the fourth century.

The army

Whilst Britain may have embarked on the post-Allectan period with a wholesome economy and entered a period of stable provincial administration, there was no let up in the central role which it had played in imperial politics in the previous half century. Archaeological evidence points to the changing role of the army. Already the need of the briefly-independent Gallic Empire for troops on the Continent had been met by the deployment of elements drawn from the frontier army and the legionary garrisons. Economies of manpower had been achieved by cutting down the size of frontier units and stationing mobile units in forts near enough to the northern frontier to intervene and at the same time well placed to guard the communication routes between the east and west of the island. Evidence, notably from the fort at Piercebridge (Co. Durham), indicates that these fundamental military changes pre-date any arrangements contemplated by Constantius I after the recovery of the island.

All this notwithstanding, a decade after the recovery of Britain a crisis arose of sufficient gravity to bring Constantius, the reconqueror of Britain by now raised to emperor of the West from the rank of *Caesar*, on an expedition to fight the Picts. This previously unknown people were to become central to military affairs in Britain until the middle of the fifth century. Located, in the historical period, on the east coast of Scotland, the Picts appear to have superseded other named tribes, such as the Caledonians, and to have established a political and military hegemony of sufficient coherence to present a recurring threat to Roman Britain. The name itself presents a problem, since it may be nothing more than an epithet bestowed by Roman sources (i.e *Picti*, or Painted People) on an already existing tribe or confederation which was adopted, at a later date, by these peoples themselves, rather as the Welsh (the *Cymru*) adopted the name (*Wealas*) conferred on them by the Saxons.

Details of the campaign are scarce, though Scotland is the likeliest location of operations, and success was achieved after brief intervention. Perhaps more important than the war itself is the aftermath. Held as a political surety in the court of the eastern emperor, Galerius, Constantius' son Constantine managed, by various subterfuges, to cross Europe and join his father's campaign. On the death of the parent at York in 305, the son was proclaimed emperor by the army at the instigation of a mysterious Germanic king, Crocus, who was presumably leading a contingent of his people as part of Constantius' forces.

Constantinian Britain

Constantine's elevation was completely unconstitutional and eventually brought about the demise of Diocletian's scheme for a regulated succession through pre-ordained *Caesars* serving co-equal eastern and western *Augusti*. Constantine spent the next two decades fighting a series of civil wars which saw him rise from pagan usurper at York to Christian emperor (known to history as Constantine the Great) ruling the whole empire from the new imperial capital, Constantinople.

For approximately ten years Britain played a central, but hazy, role in political affairs. Although based on the western imperial city of Trier, Constantine paid at least three visits to Britain between 307 and 314, each visit attested by the issue of special coins by the London mint as elements of the long-established rituals of an imperial state visit. Of these visits that of 312 has independent literary confirmation and traceable archaeological consequences and that of 314 coincides with Constantine adopting the title *Britannicus Maximus* in a style normally associated with the conclusion of successful provincial warfare.

Faced by a rival in the West in the shape of Maxentius, the usurping son of the retired emperor Maximian, Constantine had gathered forces, and in a swift strike in 312 invaded Italy, the base of his opponent's power. Rapidly progressing down the peninsula, Constantine met Maxentius in decisive battle at the Milvian Bridge on the outskirts of Rome. Vouchsafed, according to his own testimony, a Christian vision immediately before the conflict, Constantine became undisputed master of the western Roman empire and the first Christian emperor. Of the troops which took part in this campaign we can be assured that a significant number were drawn from Britain. Specifically, there is evidence that the garrisons of the forts stationed north of Hadrian's Wall were withdrawn, and that thereafter a permanent Roman military presence north of the Wall did not figure in Roman strategic planning. Elsewhere the Constantinian regroupment of forces in Britain is less easy to perceive. A cavalry unit which appeared to be named in honour of Crispus—the *equites Crispiani* stationed later in the century at Danum (Doncaster)—is now known to take its name from a military site in the Balkans rather than from Constantine's son Crispus.

On the whole the period in Britain does not seem to have benefited from any sort of extensive imperial building programme, though some cities had their defences refurbished, a notable example being Caerwent in South Wales where stone walls were erected for the first time. In contrast private building, especially the enhancement of country properties, is characteristic of the Constantinian period, with surplus wealth going into the creation of richly decorated houses. Especially visible is the patronage of mosaicists which reached a sufficient extent as to maintain a number of distinct regional schools of workers. Of these schools, that centred on the estates of the Wessex region is notable both for the ambitious size of the floors and the eclectic nature of their designs, with mingled pagan mythology and Christian piety seemingly expressing the uncertain theological grasp of a class coming to terms with the need to express loyalty to the new imperial house and its extraordinary change in religion.

Changes brought about by Constantine's military interventions in Britain may have created the situation which brought his son Constans, now western emperor, on a hasty visit to Britain in the winter of 342–3. It is a misfortune that the text of the history of Ammianus Marcellinus, which introduces this episode, is defective, and that only allusive back references survive. As far as can be reconstructed a problem had arisen involving a body called the *areani*, or in some versions, the *arcani*. The function and history of this body is described by the contemporary historian Ammianus as:

a class of men established in early times. . . . [which] had gradually become corrupted, and consequently he [Constans] had removed them from their posts. For they were clearly convicted of having been led by the receipt, or promise, of great booty at various times to betray to the savages what was going on among us. For it was their duty to hasten about hither and thither over long spaces, to provide information to our generals of the clashes of rebellion among neighbouring peoples.

We do not know where these operations took place, though most scholars assume that it was beyond Hadrian's Wall. Given the withdrawal of outpost garrisons, it is not unlikely that some sort of intelligence operations were mounted in Scotland. Their nature may be judged by later references to *arcani* in the reign of the Emperor Justinian (527–65), where they are merchants paid an imperial retainer to spy on and report upon the activities of the Persian empire as they travelled to and fro on their business. There is no reason why the earlier members of this corps in Britain may have been anything more than cross-border traders, either Romano-British or natives of Caledonia. Like Justinian's *arcani* they may have ceased to be loyal because their pay had been withheld. In any event their activity, or lack of, was sufficiently serious to bring the emperor from Gaul to Britain in a season when normally land campaigning would not be contemplated and seaborne operations be impossible. Attempts to associate the visit with restructuring and improving the coastal forts of Britain have not survived archaeological scrutiny. The fort at Pevensey, long notorious for the deliberate planting of misleading archaeological evidence, appears to date to the last quarter of the third century (see Chapter 2 above) and can no longer be associated with Constans.

Civil war and its aftermath

Constans' visit demonstrates the centrality of British affairs in the politics of the western empire, and this position is emphasized by Britain's participation in one of the most disastrous civil wars ever embarked upon by Roman forces. In 350 a conspiracy in Gaul resulted in the overthrow and death of Constans and the creation of a usurping imperial regime lead by Magnentius, with his brother Decentius as co-ruler. The revolt was well supported in Britain, and one major programme of building work can confidently be attributed to the period on the basis of stratified coin evidence: the reinforcement of the defensive walls of towns in Britain with external towers. The provision of sophisticated defences has implications for their manning, since the towers were specifically designed to house powerful catapult artillery, such as would require the employment of specialist gunners and maintenance crews. Little is known about the internal politics of this regime, though it had sufficient military backing to successfully occupy Italy and to drive as far east as the Balkan provinces. Temporary success was assisted by the preoccupation with the eastern army and the Emperor Constantius II (eastern colleague and brother of the deceased Constans) with events on the eastern frontier, where warfare with Persia was endemic. In 351 the contending armies met at Mursa in the Balkans, where after huge losses on both sides the western forces were forced to withdraw. Two years were to pass before the eastern forces had regained sufficient strength to move west, force the suicide of Magnentius and Decentius, and reunify the empire once more.

The aftermath of revolt was dramatic. Always suspicious to the point of paranoia, Constantius struck at the roots of conspiracy. To Britain a commission of inquiry, with plenipotentiary power, was despatched under Paul the Notary. This official, effectively the head of the civil service, was employed to weed out army officers who had been loyal to Magnentius. The adherence of the army of Britain to the usurper seems to have been widespread, and Paul's pursuit of rebels appears to have got out of hand to the extent that Martinus, presumably the *vicarius* of Britain, attempted to bring the affair to an end. Paul immediately indicted Martinus as a conspirator. In a dramatic confrontation the governor attempted to murder the emperor's legate but, failing to do so, committed suicide. Since accusation and guilt were inextricably linked, a large, but unknown, element of the officer corps of the army of Britain was executed, exiled, or banished from public life. The extent to which civilians were involved in these events is unclear, and attempts by archaeologists to link structural changes in villas with the fate of individuals lack conviction.

Constantius' political problems reached as far as Britain but had their origins in events which had followed upon the death of his father, Constantine the Great, in 337, when a long-standing family feud resulted in the slaughter of the late emperor's stepmother. Only the two half-brothers Constantius Gallus and Julian now survived of the male members of Constantine's close family. Lacking an heir and needing a member of Constantine's family to secure the loyalty of the army, Constantius first promoted Gallus to *Caesar*, then executed him. But the recovery of Gaul demanded the presence of an imperial figurehead, and Julian was despatched in 355 to fill the position under the strict control of Lupicinus, the commander of the western armies. Every effort was taken to circumscribe the activities of the *Caesar*, to the extent that draconian financial laws were enacted which led to serious monetary supply crisis in Gaul and Britain, the effects of which lasted for nearly a decade.

Contrary to expectation, or imperial desire, Julian turned out to be a brilliant military commander and skilled administrator who out-witted his keeper, Lupicinus. Unconvinced by the examples of prac-tical Christianity exhibited in the treatment of his family, Julian was a fervent pagan. His practical policies included reforming the taxation system of Gaul, which would have included Britain as a component of the Prefecture of the Gauls. He consolidated the Rhine frontier, expelled and defeated the Franks who had been originally introduced into northern Gaul in order to subvert the regime of Magnentius, revivified the corn trade between Britain and Gaul and, finally, in 360 led the inevitable revolt against Constantius. Elements of the army which might have been loyal to Constantius together with their commander Lupicinus were sent to Britain in mid-winter to deal with incursions by the Scots and Picts, who were accused of breaking a treaty. Whether this was a real threat or not is open to doubt. The season was not one in which seaborne Scots, from Ireland, were likely to be ranging abroad, nor does the climate of the northern frontier, the scene of the alleged incidents, favour traditional stock raiding, there being little profit in the few beasts the agricultural system could afford to overwinter. More significantly, no sooner was Lupicinus in Britain than all communication with the island was cut off and the general and his forces were isolated for three months whilst the serious business of establishing a viable regime in Gaul was undertaken. The death of Constantius prevented a repetition of the calamitous events of the Battle of Mursa a decade earlier. Julian himself died in battle with the Persians in 363 and was succeeded, after the very brief reign of Jovian, by Valentinian I who immediately promoted his brother, Valens, to rule the eastern provinces of the empire.

The 'Barbarian Conspiracy'

The new reign ushered in one of the best recorded but, nevertheless, enigmatic episodes in Romano-British history, the so-called 'Barbarian Conspiracy'. Virtually everything known about the mid-fourth century in Britain depends on the text of the historian Ammianus Marcellinus. His seductive narrative gives a vivid account of the invasion of Britain in 367 by an unprecedented confederation of barbarian forces. Three peoples were involved, the Scots from Ireland, the Picts from eastern Scotland, and the Attacotti, a people of unknown but presumably northern origin. All seem to have been capable of long-range naval action. At the same time the Saxons attacked Gaul. The narrative of events is worth recounting in detail, since the archaeological interpretation of the text has established a chronology of events in the second half of the century which is still used, erroneously, as an authoritative basis for British historical studies.

No explanation is offered as to the nature of the conspiracy, the mechanism of inter-tribal diplomacy which brought about concerted action, the manner in which attack was timed, the way in which areas of activity were apportioned to the participants. In reality, there was probably no coordination and a series of unrelated attacks by a number of tribes a conspiracy only in Roman eyes. Nonetheless the two senior generals in Britain were involved. Nectaridus, the commander of the Saxon Shore forces, was killed, and Fullofaudes, commander of the garrison troops in the North of Britain and on

Hadrian's Wall, was strategically outwitted, his garrisons bypassed and isolated from events. At the same time the *arcani* betrayed their trust, failing to warn of impending hostile activity. After some delay Theodosius, a general with the rank of commander in the elite field army (*comes*, or Count), was despatched to Britain with a number of crack regiments. Almost all of the military activity took place in the region of London, and involved not only the eventual destruction of bands of barbarian raiders, but also a crisis in the Roman army itself characterized by serious desertion by garrison forces, who seem to have participated in looting and brigandage. At the same time political exiles in Britain, led by one Valentinus, a highly placed exile from the Balkan provinces, attempted to raise a revolt. Political and military order was restored, and an unknown area recovered from enemy control was given independent provincial status and named 'Valentia' in honour of the emperor Valentinian. Troops from the Balkans were probably transferred to Britain to stiffen the garrison. Of the trio of attackers, the Attacotti appear to have suffered the worst, since units recruited from the tribe appear in the Late Roman army list: normally at this period such units would be assembled from enemies who had surrendered en masse. There are no similar units of Picts or Scots.

The archaeology of this episode is difficult to establish. There are no coin hoards which can be dated to this period of trouble, though fourth-century hoards are very common in Britain. The claimed reinforcement of city defences ascribed to this period had, as we have seen, taken place two decades earlier. A series of watchtowers, erected on the high cliffs of the Yorkshire coast, can now be attributed to a defensive scheme initiated by the usurping emperor Magnus Maximus some decade and a half later. The creation of tribal allies in the Lowlands of Scotland in coordination with the abandonment of the outpost forts of Hadrian's Wall loses credibility now that it is known that these forts were denuded by Constantine the Great.

Little remains of this episode apart from the narrative of Ammianus, and he was writing in the reign of Count Theodosius' son, the Emperor Theodosius I ('Theodosius the Great'). Count Theodosius had been executed by Valentinian on a later posting. Ammianus does not say why: his account of events in Britain may be seen in the light of the need skate over a period of particular sensitivity in a manner such as to preserve the reputations of an ambitious historian and of an executed imperial parent in a difficult political climate. Beneath the story of barbarian attack may lay a more serious narrative of incipient civil war in Britain, with the conspiracy of the political exiles being more of a threat than that of the Picts, Scots, and Attacotti.

Whatever the truth of the event, archaeologists and historians have taken the episode as a watershed in the chronicle of Roman Britain, seeing little other than a steady decline for the next half century and an inevitable end of Roman administration. This dystopian view is engendered by wisdom after the event which was not shared by contemporaries. Ammianus claims that Count Theodosius left the provinces of Britain 'dancing for joy', though we should beware of the use of authorial hyperbole. An independent authority, writing in Italy at about the same time, could claim that, as a result of successful Roman naval activity, the Saxons had been sent packing, that the Irish pirates dared not leave their lairs, and that the Rhine had been swept clear of intruders.

Magnus Maximus

When further problems did arise in Britain, they were the result of imperial events not domestic. In 378 a large part of the eastern army was destroyed in Thrace at the Battle of Adrianople, together with the Emperor Valens himself. Ill-treatment of Gothic settlers had caused them to revolt, and in pitched battle they were victorious. The losses to the eastern army were made up with some drafts from the West, but manpower was short and a dangerous, even fatal, new tactic was introduced, the wholesale hire of barbarian armies under their own leaders to fight Roman wars. In theory such armies of so-called *foederati* (foreign forces serving under the conditions of a temporary treaty of friendship) returned to their homelands after the campaign for which they had been contracted. In fact the successful ones stayed put, eventually forming their own kingdoms within the decaying structure of the empire.

In 383 Magnus Maximus raised a revolt in Britain which succeeded in the five years of its duration in spreading the power of the usurper's regime from Britain to the Balkans. Maximus appears to have served in Britain with Count Theodosius; and, though his subsequent career is unrecorded, he may have held one of the key military posts in the island, as *dux Britanniarum*, commanding the bulk of the provincial garrisons, or 'Count of the Saxon Shore', commanding the coastal defence forces. On the other hand, many aspirants to power in the fourth century were drawn from the middle-ranking officer corps, representing the concerns of career professionals rather than political nominees.

Maximus, for reasons connected with much later nationalism, acquired mythic status in mediaeval Welsh historical and romantic literature. The belief that these sources enshrined a historical tradition going back to Roman times has served to obscure the details of the revolt and of its consequences. In short there is nothing to connect Maximus to Wales: archaeological evidence shows that forts alleged to have been stripped of their troops by the usurper continued to be occupied later than the overthrow of the regime. Gildas, the sixth-century author of a work of religious polemic which enshrines a version of the end of Roman Britain, claimed that Maximus stripped Britain of its troops, who never returned. As we shall see, this claim is very far from the truth; indeed both literary and numismatic evidence shows that Maximus actually returned to Britain, probably in 384, and conducted a successful campaign against the Picts. It was after this episode that signal stations were erected on the Yorkshire coast to give warning of Pictish fleets heading south to raid the rich areas of Lincolnshire and East Anglia. It is probably in conjunction with these watchtowers that a new naval tactic was devised. This involved the deployment of squadrons of warships at strategic points which put to sea to intercept raiders that had been detected by another fleet consisting of swift, oared vessels. Both the ships and crews were camouflaged, the ships and their rigging being painted sea green; the crews wearing similarly coloured uniforms.

The regime of Maximus ended with his defeat in Italy in 388 by the Emperor Theodosius; no doubt subsequent reprisals against the usurper's administrators spread as far as Britain. But ever the victim of imperial politics, the island was again involved in serious revolt only a few years after the death of Maximus. In the manner of Late Roman politics the instigator of the new troubles, Arbogastes, had been instrumental in bringing down Maximus. Following the suppression of that revolt, Theodosius I had appointed Valentinian II as ruler in the West and promoted Arbogastes to be *magister militum*, effectively commander-in-chief of the western army, with the specific task of controlling the activities of the young western emperor and in practice governing on behalf of his eastern colleague. Valentinian made urgent but unsuccessful attempts to rid himself of his minister and master. In August 392 Valentinian was found hanged; whether this was suicide or assassination is not clear, though the former is likely. Whatever the truth, Arbogastes now had a dead emperor on his hands and an eastern emperor who saw the death of his puppet as an assault on the foundations of the imperial institution itself. Arbogastes, of barbarian Frankish origins and thus constitutionally excluded from holding imperial power, had no choice but to rebel and appoint his own nominee emperor. He chose an obscure pagan civil servant, Eugenius, and set about recruiting forces to oppose Theodosius. Both sides lacked resources: the East had still not recovered from the losses of Adrianople. Theodosius recruited Gothic mercenaries, led by Alaric (who was later to be a major player on the imperial stage, and incidentally in the events surrounding the end of Roman rule in Britain). Arbogastes enrolled troops from his Frankish kin.

In Britain the demands of a new civil war can be traced in Wales, where the remaining forts were abandoned at this time. In a document drawn up shortly after these events, the *Notitia Dignitatum*, no Welsh military sites are listed. Similarly absent are a number of forts situated west of the Pennines. Finally coin issues later than the date of the revolt are absent from both Welsh sites and those on the western seaboard. Evidence for Irish settlement in both North and South Wales suggests that the Roman administrative grip had been relaxed, at least in the rural areas. The fate of the two major towns in Wales, Carmarthen in the west and Caerwent in the south needs to be examined. The latter has already yielded results. Beyond the western extension of later Saxon penetration, Caerwent has produced quantities of very late Roman metalwork, possibly associated with the presence of soldiers, a cemetery which was still in use in the eighth century, and a fictitious mediaeval life of the local holy man, of St Tathan—which, whatever its date of compilation—shows a lingering awareness of Roman bathing practices. A further hint of late *Romanitas* may be found in the persistence in use of a Roman system of land measurement for several hundred years after the collapse of Roman administration.

Britain at the end of the fourth century

It may have been as a consequence of Britain's involvement in revolts—with the subsequent depletion of the garrisons of the island, coupled with the reputation of uneasy loyalty enjoyed by their officers—that a small mobile army was posted to Britain at the end of the fourth century. This elite force consisted of nine regiments, six of cavalry and three of infantry. If precedent established elsewhere was followed, the units would have been stationed in or near towns or in regions where their needs for supplies and equipment could be met. Their relationship with the rural and urban population can only be conjectured. Other provinces, especially in North Africa where we have detailed knowledge, suffered various abuses at the hands of such army corps. Venal commanders kept the units under strength whilst collecting the pay of fictitious soldiers and refused to meet the challenge of hostile forces. If the precedent of other provinces was followed in Britain, larger landowners would have had recourse to two strategies to protect their interests. On the one hand, suitable arrangements could be evolved to use the army to protect economic and social interests against any stirrings of the peasant community. On the other, landowners with sufficient resources could, with the connivance of the administration, recruit their own protective forces. These so-called *bucellarii*, literally 'bread eaters' (i.e. armed followers, dependent for their food and keep) feature in the history of a number of provinces in the later fourth century and the fifth to the extent that they were later formally incorporated into the imperial army. The occurrence of weapons and items of metalwork fashionable in army circles of the period on civil sites may be indicative of the presence of, if not actual private armies, at least some sort of armed bands, possibly composed of ex-soldiers.

Before discussing the very last years of formal Roman control of Britain and the aftermath of its decline, it would be as well to review the physical and economic state of the country at this critical moment in its history. As far as official administrative matters went, the island enjoyed regular government, provincial officials were appointed, the *vicarius* still coordinated the affairs of his diocese. Soldiers occupied forts that had been established in the earliest days of Roman rule in the island, or others which had been established in the third century to protect the coastal regions. Well-fortified cities bound the country in a network of administrative centres, minor towns occupied economically strategic positions on the still maintained road system. Industrially, Britain maintained its indigenous pottery industry, minerals such as silver-rich lead deposits were exploited. Agriculture seems to have flourished, the importing of exotica such as expensive table glass continued. Far from being isolated, Britain was so far integrated into the empire that even the small-change coinage used throughout the island was regularly shipped in bulk from the distant mints of Rome and Aquileia into the first decade of the fifth century.

But in many important aspects the official view obscured a more complex reality that has been brought to light by archaeology. We have already discussed the attrition of the military forces in Britain, and time and time again the excavation of forts, which had garrisons once counted in the hundreds, reveals structural changes which offer accommodation to only a fraction of the original complement. The legions, once each numbering nearly six thousand soldiers, were a shadow of their former strength. From Chester the Twentieth Legion disappears completely from the army list, at York, the base of the Sixth Legion, excavation reveals wide-scale underuse of areas of the legionary fortress. Most graphically the Second Legion *Augusta*, which had played a leading role in the invasion in 43 and had occupied a fortress at Caerleon in South Wales which covered 22.5 hectares (fifty-six acres), was relocated to the coastal fort at Richborough with an allocated space of barely 2 hectares (five acres). In North Wales, barely half of the 2.2 hectare fort at Caernarfon—which served as a bulwark against Irish pirates—was occupied; the rest being given over to rubbish dumps and industrial activity. On the northern frontier the picture is more complex; some sites such as Housesteads on Hadrian's Wall suggest very diminished levels of occupancy, whilst nearby sites such as the fort at South Shields appear to have been maintained at a higher level.

In the past archaeologists have attempted to fill the ranks of the depleted military by invoking the presence of settlements of armed foreigners, placed by the authorities in strategic locations to resist armed incursions by their own kinfolk. No credence is now given to the presence of such settlers, whose allegedly distinctive pottery, so-called Romano-Saxon ware, is now known to have its origins in the regional products of the mid-second century. Similarly, decorative buckles and belt fittings attributed to barbarian use and taste are now firmly fixed in the context of the Late Roman army's regular equipment.

In towns matters are very complex. Late Roman legal sources suggest that the urban elite systematically attempted to withdraw from their administrative obligations by absenting themselves on their country estates, even stripping their town houses of statuary and architectural ornament to grace their rural retreats. It is clear that throughout the empire the sense of social obligation declined in the fourth century; public buildings were not maintained and major towns such as London, Silchester, and Wroxeter all show both administrative structures and social amenities, such as public baths, were either demolished or allowed to fall into decay. In contrast many towns show that very extensive and well-regulated cemeteries were maintained on their outskirts, suggesting that there is a discrepancy between the structural evidence and the size of urban population.

Religion

Similar ambiguity attaches to the problem of religion in the fourth century. The impact of Christianity on the population of Britain is questionable. It is clear that there were established bishoprics in the four provinces of the Constantinian period, and ecclesiastics attended international church conferences. But this evidence gives no indication of the actual adherence to Christian practices by the population and the most assiduous attempts to identify actual churches, the private chapel in the villa of Lullingstone in Kent aside, has produced no more than three structures which are architecturally suitable for church use. Equally these buildings could serve as pagan structures or even non-religious functions. It is curious that the best candidate for church status, an apsed building in the centre of Silchester, appears to convert to industrial activity just when Christianity reached an imperial apogee in the middle of the fourth century. Portable witnesses of faith are not uncommon, Christograms (monograms of the Greek letters Chi and Rho, the first letters of 'Christ') appear on wellheads and walls, on tiles, pots, and items of jewellery. The Christogram also appears on items of silver plate, spoons being particularly graced with such symbols, a fact that has been interpreted as evidence of widespread baptism among the upper classes. Equally evident is the continued production of objects of pagan reverence.

If churches are hard to find, the fate of pagan temples and shrines is less difficult to plot. Some share the fate of other urban buildings and appear to be neglected, possibly reflecting the absence of their patrons rather than an actual rejection of the faith, others continue in use for as long as objects with attributable dates are found with them. The very late *floruit* of paganism elsewhere in the ostensibly Christian empire, especially in Gaul, and the continued promotion of pagans to high office as late as the sixth century in the eastern empire are perhaps better indications of the actual situation in Britain than any overnight conversion. Attempts to use burial evidence as an index of adherence to Christianity has also been critically received. The conjecture that east facing burial, with few or no grave goods, denotes a Christian occupant of a grave is contradicted by such funeral rites as the decapitation of the corpse or the provision of a new pair of boots in which to make the journey to the afterlife. Archaeologically, the fourth century suggests a period of changing faith, in the sense that organized religion appears to be less subject to observance but that private devotion—of all cults—remained at a high level. In short, the last century of Roman Britain may coincide with a spiritual shift within existing institutions rather than a revolution of faith.

In the agricultural landscape there were also changes in the fourth century. Economies of scale had been achieved through acquisition and expansion. The countryside changed, or was changing, from a pattern of use established in the pre-Roman period of small fields to one of broad acres. Intensive cereal, cattle, and especially sheep production dominated the industry. Climatic change towards a wetter, cooler regime induced the introduction of sturdier, quicker ripening grains. Increased yields encouraged the development of more efficient agricultural tools such as the large scythe. Storage facilities were expanded or redundant living quarters made over to new uses.

All this productivity resulted in very great wealth flowing into

Britain in the second half of the fourth century. The evidence for this wealth is to be found in the extraordinary number of hoards of gold and silver coins and precious-metal vessels found in contexts dating to the very end of the century or the beginning of the next. If we divorce the material from the immediate context of its deposit, we may consider where it came from originally and what it signified in terms of wealth. The distribution of the material is also significant: no finds are made west of the Pennines, and, though this may reflect later problems experienced in these areas, the arc of wealth stretches from Cleveland in the North to the Mendips and beyond in the South. The association between Roman wealth and the areas which are much later identified with the creation of wealth by the mediaeval wool trade must, in the last analysis, be regarded as fortuitous. Nonetheless, the coincidence is suggestive, especially when taken in conjunction with the increasing evidence from osteological studies of the dominance of elderly sheep in rural contexts in the Roman period— of animals, that is, maintained for the fleece rather than for eating. In the context of levels of daily living standards, the few available studies of burials suggest that a high level of nutrition was available to all classes until the end of the Roman period.

The end of Roman rule

The fifty years between the re-establishment of legitimate imperial rule in 393 and the middle of the following century saw the extinction of Roman control in Britain, the establishment of regional rulers who formed a confederation of some sort under a high king, the arrival of Saxon mercenaries employed to repel raids by Pictish aggressors, and the loss of a significant part of southern Britain to Saxon control when the mercenaries sought to establish independent domains.

The details accompanying these events are obscure to the point of near unintelligibility. Archaeological evidence, both positive and negative, is ambiguous at best; a limited coherence can only be achieved by discreet use of the contemporary and later literary evidence, though consideration of the nature of this evidence forms an academic industry in its own right. These sources range from contemporary accounts of events in Britain in the work of the Christian apologist Orosius to the account of Zosimus, the late fifth-century eastern historian. From about the middle of the fifth century survives a chronicle, the so-called *Gallic Chronicle of 452*, which has entries devoted to Britain, and from the mid-sixth century the *De Excidio et Conquestu Britanniae* (The Decline and Conquest of Britain) of Gildas. The latter is a garbled but just intelligible account of Late Roman Britain serving as an introduction to a work excoriating the rulers of the western parts of Britain in the writer's own day. From a later age comes the work of Nennius, a ninth-century scholar working in Wales, who brought together surviving elements of the Celtic historiographic tradition of the loss of Britain to the Saxons in a work known as the *Historia Brittonum*. The work of Bede, derived from Orosius and some Saxon sources, adds little to the earlier accounts. The *Anglo-Saxon Chronicle*, a work still under composition after the Norman Conquest, embodies accounts and memories of Saxon military success in southern Britain in the fifth and sixth centuries. Less full but nonetheless interesting sources include the works of the poet Claudian, the chronicles of Hydatius and Theophanes, the *Life of Saint Germanus*, and the works of the sixth-century Byzantine historian, Procopius.

The drama starts in 406 with two separate events which eventually coalesced: a revolt in Britain, and the invasion of Gaul by German tribes, the Alans, Sueves, and Vandals, who had been pushed up against the Rhine frontier by the western movement of even more aggressive eastern peoples, the Huns. By the end of 406 Britain had created no less than three usurpers. Two were quickly disposed of, whilst the third led an ill-fated expedition to the Continent leaving, after his death, the island bereft both of imperial administrators and an effective army. The third of these island emperors, Constantine, was created to meet the problem raised by the Germanic invasion of Gaul that threatened to cut Britain off from communication with the rest of the empire. The other rulers, Marcus and Gratian came to power before this turn of events and must, therefore, represent a reaction to an existing, but unknown, situation. Marcus, a soldier, failing to assuage the army was killed and replaced by Gratian. This ruler is described as a *municeps* or town councillor. As we have seen, this position was held on a hereditary basis, with the rich contriving to avoid the burdens imposed by the status. Thus the title *municeps* may equally well describe a landowner as a rich resident of a town. In any event after a few months Gratian went the way of Marcus, and in a wilful gesture the army appointed as emperor a Christian soldier named Flavius Claudius Constantinus, allegedly on the grounds that he had a lucky name. Given his later actions, it is more likely that Constantine III was a well-respected officer with military skills. Nevertheless, he renamed his two sons auspiciously Julian and Constans, thus appealing both to pagan and Christian sentiment as well as to the military reputation of the dynasty of Constantine the Great with whom he clearly sought identity. His son Constans he proclaimed co-emperor in 408, a clear indication of the intention to found a dynasty.

It was a meteorological disaster which brought Roman rule in Britain to an end. In December 406 the Rhine froze over and the assembled Alans, Sueves, and Vandals crossed the frontier barrier and entered Gaul. As in other Continental wars the military authorities in Britain feared the loss of the coast of Belgium and France, a loss which would cut Britain off from the empire. Constantine, elevated to deal with this crisis, embarked for Gaul taking with him the provincial mobile field army. Quickly establishing himself in Gaul— though with little success in stemming the flood of migrants—after a brief period of imperial recognition he found himself at war with the legitimate emperor, Honorius, son and successor in the West of Theodosius the Great. Extending his rule to Spain, Constantine set up his capital in Arles in southern Gaul. Here he was besieged in 411, surrendering to Honorius after taking the precaution of being ordained as a priest. Despite the expected protection of ecclesiastical status, he and his son Constans were killed en route to Rome as captives.

Constantine's defeat left Britain without effective imperial government, though even before the defeat of the usurper loyalists had sought the intervention of the legitimate emperor in the affairs of the island. Further, both the historian Zosimus and the *Gallic Chronicle* record a barbarian attack on Britain in 410 which was repulsed by the exertions of the islanders themselves. The Chronicle ascribes the attack to Saxons, Zosimus speaks of 'barbarians from across the Rhine'. He adds further that in common with other provinces in Gaul under attack at the same time, Britain expelled its Roman governors, in other words the administration of the usurper Constantine who was by now a broken force harried by troops loyal to Honorius. Clearly an attempt was being made to change sides before imperial retribution could be levied. To this end an appeal was directed to Honorius which, in effect, asked for reincorporation into the fabric of the legitimate empire. And why not? The entire episode of Constantine's elevation had been designed to maintain Britain as an active element of the empire at large rather than an attempt at independence. Honorius' rescript (written answer) told the Britons to undertake their own defence, which as we have seen they did with success. It was this success, and no doubt the creation of leaders thrown up by the need to wage war against the invaders, which accounts for the failure of Britain to rejoin the empire after the defeat of Constantine. In the brief interval between the appeal to Honorius and the recovery of Spain and Gaul by the imperial forces something had changed in Britain. Procopius, writing more than a century later records that 'The Romans were no longer able to recover Britain, which from that time on continued to be ruled by tyrants [i.e. usurpers]'. Independent success in battle had changed the complexion of British politics, the intervention of an imperial army had not been required to secure victory; the house could stand without what had hitherto been regarded as its very foundation. Further, independence meant exemption from the imperial taxation system, the imposition of curial (town council) duties, and the whole business of state intervention in the affairs of regional power brokers. And no reprisals against those who had initially enthusiastically endorsed Constantine.

The *Gallic Chronicle of 452* records that in 441 Britain was in the hands of the Saxons. Clearly this is not the whole story, since a century of warfare was to pass before such a claim had any geographical reality. Nevertheless a chronicler compiling his work in the south of Gaul, with which southern Britain still had contacts as late as the mid-fifth century, considered the reality of the situation to be that the Saxons had sufficient grip on sufficient territory as to constitute an independent polity. Complementary evidence for contacts with Gaul is to be found in the hoard of Roman gold and silver coins found at Patching, near Worthing in Sussex. The hoard contains Visigothic copies of imperial coins as well as regular issues, the latest dated item is a coin of the Emperor Majorian (455–61). Significantly, the find was made within 3 miles distance from the mid-fifth century Anglo-Saxon cemetery at Highdown, Sussex.

Whether this dominance was won by warfare or by politics is a crux in the conflicting views of the end of Roman Britain. Scholars, observing how completely and quickly Roman institutions such as the law, the church, and the Latin language were extinguished in Britain as compared with other provinces which came under barbarian domination, seek explanations in the nature of the relationship of Rome with the indigenous population over the centuries of rule. Perhaps, it is argued, the Roman way of life made very little impact on the bulk of the population, who retained their language, their familial and tribal ties; in short, in Roman terms, there was very little to survive. Thus once the elite lost contact with Rome, entered a spiral of cultural and economic decline, and were extinguished by the warfare in which they took a leading role, the bulk of the population, hardly visible at the best of times, simply exchanged one set of rulers for another.

The half-century before this stage was reached is full of detail in the literary sources outlined above. As we have noted, the interpretation of these texts constitutes a separate academic industry, but a narrative thread can be established which represents at least some aspects of events. First, we have some evidence for the continuity of ordered urban life, evidence which has been increasingly substantiated by archaeological evidence from sites as diverse as Verulamium (St Albans), Wroxeter, Silchester, Colchester, and Caerwent. When, in 429, Germanus, the bishop of Auxerre and subsequently saint, came to Britain from Gaul to cope with the spread of Pelagianism (a heretical doctrine fiercely contested by the Church), he was met, probably at Verulamium, by the leading men of the city. Later the bishop, a retired army officer—possibly even a former commander of the defences of the coast of northern Gaul and thus familiar with adjacent parts of Britain—led the Britons in a successful attack on marauding Saxons.

Germanus was sent to Britain by Pope Celestine at the behest of his adviser Palladius, who urged the need to re-establish Roman control over the Church in Britain, possibly in conjunction with an imperial policy for the recovery of Western Gaul and Britain. A little later Palladius himself was appointed to a bishopric, and sent to Ireland to minister to—and possibly ransom—enslaved Christian Britons abducted by Irish raiders. Among the captives was St Patrick, who later converted the pagan Irish masters of these slaves. Patrick's story, recounted in his two biographical works, is a graphic account of Late Roman rural Britain and the threat to life and liberty posed by piratical raiders. Probably living in the west of Britain, Patrick was abducted from his father's country estate by Irish raiders and sold into slavery in the west of Ireland. Despite the fact that his father was a landowner, town councillor, and clergyman we hear of no attempt to rescue or ransom the captive. Rather, Patrick escaped after five year's servitude, made his way to Gaul, took holy orders, and returned to Ireland to undertake his missionary work.

The saint's story is unique in that its details survive and the day-to-day life of a single captive can be reconstructed, and from it can be reconstructed the context for the occurrence of Late Roman artefacts in Ireland that had their origins in Britain. This material consists of hoards of coins and silverware either looted from Britain or paid over to raiders, or potential raiders, as blood money. Thanks offerings for successful raids may be found in the coins buried at the foot of the stones which ring the great prehistoric tomb at New Grange, a monument already two millennia old when made the scene of offerings snatched from Britain.

The Britain which Germanus visited was not that which Constantine had left three decades earlier. The failure to restore imperial administration led to the creation of an unknown number of insular rulers, probably regional magnates already in control of *bucellarii*. These rulers seem to have formed a confederation which by 425 was under a high king whose name is given by Nennius as Vortigern and who is described by Gildas as *tyrannus superbus* ('The Great Tyrant', or usurper). The fact that this ruler has a Celtic name may suggest a studied rejection of Roman administrative practices. On the other hand, the Celtic is a near version of the Latin, and may be a descriptive term coined by Nennius for a someone with a perfectly respectable Roman name, a name which Gildas (in normal Roman manner) cannot bring himself to repeat because the disaster brought on the island by this ruler had rendered his name inauspicious. The inadequate sources certainly give Vortigern a Roman ancestry, his father being Vitalis and his grandfather Vitalinus.

It was Vortigern who, it is claimed, brought into south-east Britain Saxon mercenaries under the leadership of the brothers Hengist and Horsa; these he settled on the Isle of Thanet in the Thames estuary. Whether the brothers really existed—their names mean 'horse' and 'mare'—or whether they are simply an attempt to clothe events with personalities by later historians is irrelevant to what happened. It is

Gildas who gives a detailed account of why Saxons, so recently the attackers of Britain, should have been sought as allies. 'The old enemy' the Picts were attacking in what sounds like a concerted maritime campaign intended less for looting than for settlement. Tactically, the Saxons, a maritime people themselves, were well able to cope with the Picts whose threat quickly faded. However, in a move reminiscent of the ill-treatment meted out to the Goths which led to their revolt and defeat of the Roman army at Adrianople, the Saxon mercenaries were kept short of their scale rations and allowances, at this period reckoned as being worth five *solidi* (the standard gold coin of the period) a year for ordinary soldiers. They revolted and brought in reinforcements from their homeland: henceforth, their progress was unstoppable.

Germanus' visit was in the context of a renewed imperial preoccupation with Britain. A chance reference in Nennius sets the context. In discussing Vortigern he indicates that in 428 the ruler was concerned with two problems: the threat of the Picts and the threat of the Romans. The latter threat has largely been ignored but it was real. At this period the effective ruler of the West, the *magister militum* Aetius, appears to have been following a well-planned strategy to reoccupy the lost western provinces of Gaul and Britain. This plan was thwarted by the high politics of the empire when his rival Boniface allowed the Vandals, now settled in Spain, to cross to undefended North Africa where they established a kingdom from which they mounted attacks on Sicily and Rome itself. Aetius was forced to withdraw from the north-west to protect the very heartland of the empire; Britain slipped out of Roman strategic consciousness. His actions did not go unremarked in Britain: an appeal for intervention against the Saxons, when it had become clear that it was better to be a province of Rome than an island subjected to the depredations of an out-of-control mercenary army, went unanswered, and Britain entered a century of conflict. For Gildas this reached standstill only with the Battle of Mount Badon, when Ambrosius Aurelianus, thought to be the latest of a line of regional petty rulers of Roman descent, brought Saxon advance westward to a temporary halt.

The archaeological evidence for these events is exiguous. Early Saxon cemeteries and settlements have been identified in south-east England at sites such as Mucking in Essex, but most burial and settlement evidence relates to a period one or two generations later than the initial phase of settlement. Nor is the archaeological evidence unambiguous: the context of Saxons as invaders has completely obscured the relationships which must have existed between Briton and Saxon even in times of conflict. Thus all Saxon objects are interpreted as indicative of the presence of the invaders, and intercommunal trade, which must surely have taken place, is entirely ignored.

In the extreme North, where Saxon penetration did not take place before the end of the fifth century, a picture of Roman continuity in the context of the remaining military installations is beginning to appear. Studies of the environment indicate that the agricultural landscape of the frontier area was maintained as it had been in the Roman period until the middle of the sixth century. At the same a number of forts, both on and near Hadrian's Wall, show signs of major structural work which dates later than the latest datable Roman artefacts on the sites. Forts such as Piercebridge, in County Durham, where the defensive ditches were refurbished later than 402, South Shields, on the Tyne, where a complex series of refortifications can be associated with fifth- and sixth-century activity, Malton in North Yorkshire where supplementary defences are designed to thwart river-borne raiders, and Housesteads, Birdoswald, and Vindolanda on or near the Wall, all point to a continuity of use after the formal dismantling of the Roman military command structure. No doubt throughout the former military zone small pockets of soldiers, their families and descendants maintained themselves as best they could for perhaps a century and a half. Such a situation would not be unprecedented, being attested in both Gaul and Switzerland where attenuated garrisons left behind by events struggled to retain their identity. Eventually the Romans of the North and the Saxon, or Anglian, incomers coalesced to form a force which succeeded, where Rome had failed, in creating a firm frontier with Scotland.

In the final analysis, the politics and strategic moves added up to very little. It was ownership of the land which determined who would win the support of the silent population: better to eat as a Saxon than starve as a Roman. Writing in c.380—and thus in the lifetime of people to whom the latest events outlined above would form the background of existence—the orator Themistius (who had a distinguished public career at Constantinople) had said:

All other occupations need agriculture. Those engaged in skilled occupations and other pursuits, as well as men who have power and men who acquire a royal sceptre, put their hopes for their reign or their power . . . in the blessings of agriculture . . . the interests of those who nourish the whole community take precedence over the whole military establishment . . . if the fruits of agriculture are inadequate, then nothing is left to sustain life. (trans. R. J. Penella)

Figure 9 The 'Venus mosaic', a detail from the principal mosaic of the villa at Rudston (Yorks.): naive art, incompetence, or a non-classical way of looking at classical themes?

4

Culture and social relations in the Roman province

Janet Huskinson

In its broadest sense 'culture' may be defined as values shared within a particular social group. These are represented through various means such as the arts, religious cults, and lifestyles, which not only reflect the society's values, but also help to shape them. The Roman province of Britain is a place in which these connections between culture and social relations can be seen with particular clarity, despite some inevitable gaps in our knowledge. One reason for this must be that in the overall cultural history of the British Isles this was a particularly formative period: it has been said that 'Rome took Britain from pre-history'. Another reason is that in the course of this development Roman Britain contained, in effect, a number of different 'micro societies' which each demonstrate culture and social relations in their own particular terms: inhabitants of early, post-Conquest towns, Roman military personnel in Britain, the wealthy elite in the fourth-century country estates are all examples of different social groups in Roman Britain which have their own particular stories to tell. Put together they show just how variegated was the culture of the province of Britain, and how closely related to its different social groups and to their development across the centuries. The aim of this chapter is to trace some of these connections, looking closely at some particular strata in Romano-British society through primary source material.

Perceptions of Roman Britain

But before looking more closely at these sources, we should pause to consider changing perspectives in the study of Roman Britain and its culture. This is not just a matter of antiquarian interest, but is vital for understanding the kind of judgements that have been passed on it, which—over the last century or so—have altered considerably. A case in point is the evaluation of Romano-British art. In the past, like most Roman provincial art it tended to be judged in terms of the art of metropolitan Rome, and this in turn was compared to the styles and forms of classical Greece which were taken as the benchmark of excellence. This hierarchy of standards led to some negative judgements about the art of Roman Britain which have been proved hard to shift: the most famous perhaps is the much quoted remark by the philosopher and historian R. G. Collingwood: 'The Roman models themselves were poor enough; the empire was not an age of good taste; but there is perhaps no province where local attempts to reproduce them failed so dismally as they failed in Britain.' Even in the 1960s when Roman art was beginning to be valued more positively, the yardstick by which Romano-British art was measured tended to remain that of Roman Italy or Gaul. But the current interest in looking at the art of any culture in its social context has opened up a new approach to the art of Roman Britain. Questions about who produced it, for whom, how, and why, allow it to be evaluated in terms of its own society and in the context of its own cultural values, rather than those of imperial Rome or classical Greece.

Such new perspectives are not confined to art. In the post-colonial period of the later twentieth century, the focus on Romano-British culture shifted away from imperialist Rome and the supposed benefits of empire to look more at the local people, the 'colonized' Britons. Related to this has been an interest in trying to chart the 'Romanization' of Britain. Although this term was invented by modern scholars to describe the process whereby Roman culture spread within a subjugated territory, it is actually quite problematic to use as a tool for interpreting the ancient source material. One reason is that scholars use the term in different ways, some to describe a one-way move in which Roman culture prevailed over the indigenous (whether deliberately imposed or not), and others a two-way process in which the cultures interacted on each other. But there is a second, much more substantial problem attached to the term, since (however used) it implies that there was a homogeneous and identifiable 'Roman' culture to be part of the process; and bound up with this is a sense that this was superior (in strength and quality) to the indigenous culture it encountered. Increasingly, though, this view of Roman culture is becoming outmoded: there is greater awareness of its diversity, and of the diversity of the local responses it met. So there is now a question mark hanging over the usefulness of the concept of Romanization with its absolute tones as a model for assessing cultural change in the Roman empire; but even so, it can still provide an effective entry point into considering the situation in Britain.

Sources

Important literary sources for Britain exist in the works of Roman writers, notably historians such as Tacitus. But although they may reveal how Britain and its inhabitants appeared to people writing from the centre of empire, they reflect the agenda of Rome itself: for example, the passionate pleas for liberty attributed to British leaders like Calgacus and Boudicca by Tacitus and Cassius Dio actually articulated a Roman rhetoric of dissent from the empire, and cannot count as a 'British' source. In fact, there are no first-hand records in ancient literature of the British experience of participation in the empire. On the other hand, the material sources are plentiful: buildings, art, inscriptions, and objects all offer insights into life as lived in the province itself. Britain has yielded some amazing archaeological discoveries which contribute to our understanding of culture and society. A roll-call of major finds since the Second World War includes the wooden writing tablets from Vindolanda, the Hinton St Mary mosaic, and 'treasures' from Mildenhall, Hoxne, Thetford, and Water Newton.

Most of these examples provide evidence for what may be termed 'high culture' in Roman Britain, since they were generated by powerful and wealthy people. But material sources can also throw valuable light on the everyday culture of less exclusive social groups who are so often 'invisible' in the written historical record: for instance, they can help to trace the lives of local rural communities or of women and children through evidence of their housing or objects that they used. They can also give important general insights into aspects of culture in Roman Britain: one of these is literacy and its social role. Evidence from the early days of Roman occupation shows the importance of the written word in the institutions that they had brought with them. This is clear, for example, in the inscriptions on funerary monuments (such as the soldiers' gravestones at Colchester (Figure 10) or the great tomb (Figure 5) of Julius Classicianus in London), and in the writing tablets from Vindolanda (which will be discussed in greater detail later). Evidence from the following centuries shows an expansion of contexts, ranging from official stamps and communications and inscriptions on public monuments to its use in the decoration of domestic objects and floor mosaics: Britain too became part of the literate culture of the Roman empire. Or did it? There are degrees of literacy, and it is likely to be the case that only a small proportion of the population of the province was ever fully literate. For the rest, though, and particularly in towns, there was the experience of being part of a culture and society in which the literacy had a defining role.

The question of literacy, and possible experiences of it, is a good illustration of the importance of considering evidence in context, in this case particularly of different social groups. Time and place are other important factors. Accurate dating can be difficult, especially where objects have been found outside a datable context, so that discussion and revision of dates from time to time is all very much part of the process of working with these material sources. Geographical location should also be taken into account. In particular, it is important to consider the culture of Britain in the context of the empire as a whole, and also to look at the parts of the British Isles which lay outside the province yet were affected by 'Romanization'. This chapter will concentrate on three important periods in the cultural history of the province of Britain, which together show variation across time, place, and community, particularly as represented through the arts.

Turning Britain into 'the form of a province'

This first section looks at cultural changes that occurred at two places—Camulodunum (the modern Colchester) and Verulamium (St Albans)—in the twenty years or so between Claudius' invasion in 43 and Boudicca's revolt in 60/61. The central question to be considered is how far the arrival of the Romans may have changed the culture of these two settlements (see also Chapters 1 and 2 above). There are ancient primary sources, literary and archaeological, that can point to some answers.

In the period before the Claudian invasion Britain appears to have been a relatively settled society with a developing agriculture and economy which could sustain an elite from which the various tribal 'kings' or 'chiefs' were drawn. Its warrior traditions, which had been a major factor in inter-tribal relations, remained an important way of symbolizing power and social standing. The invasion inevitably had a decisive impact on all this. It altered some existing social structures and introduced others, and in doing so set up some new relationships between different social groups. In his description of how 'little by little' the Romans reduced post-Conquest Britain 'into the usual form of a province', Tacitus identified military prowess, new settlements, and the strategic use of existing social networks as playing a critical role in what historians would now describe as the Romanization of Britain. Writing of his father-in-law Agricola's policy during his first year as governor, he gives further insights into how cultural change was deliberately exploited as an effective means of settling the Britons: new amenities, civic buildings, and houses were used in a policy of persuasion, reinforced by a natural competitiveness which led people to imitate the lifestyle of their social superiors. How far can such elements be found at Camulodunum and Verulamium?

Before the Roman Conquest in 43, Camulodunum was an important local centre for the powerful tribes of the Catuvellauni and Trinovantes, and the site of their local mint (see Chapter 1 above). This made it an immediate objective of the Roman invading force, and it is not surprising that after its capture Claudius set about overstamping it with symbols of Roman control. In the years immediately after the Conquest, two units of the Roman army were kept stationed there, the Twentieth Legion and auxiliaries from Thrace, each with its own base. Coincidentally, each of these is represented by a surviving tombstone: that of M. Favonius Facilis, a centurion of the legion, and that of Longinus, an auxiliary cavalryman (Figure 10). But once the legion was transferred to fight in Wales, the site of its fortress was converted into a *colonia* to accommodate Roman veteran soldiers (see Chapter 1 above).

The establishment of 'colonies' of this kind was a strategy that Romans had often used to reinforce their presence in conquered territories and to provide for their veteran soldiers at the same time. Most of the colonists had been legionary soldiers and so already had Roman citizenship. They enjoyed this status within their colony which had its own administration and set of laws; and they also received a grant of land to farm in the surrounding territory, which often meant that—as happened at Colchester—locals were dispossessed. Some of the latter may have moved into the new city, since we know that at the time of Boudicca's capture of Colchester a decade later there was a 'fifth column' in the form of *incolae* (a general term covering residents without citizen rights).

The archaeological evidence shows how the legionary fortress at Colchester was converted into the *colonia* over several years. Some military buildings survived in use as they were (at least up to the time when the whole site was destroyed in Boudicca's rebellion), but various barracks and centurions' quarters were converted into houses. Parts of the old defences were levelled to provide more space for the large public buildings: there was the great Temple of Claudius, a theatre, and an arch, and Tacitus also refers to a council chamber and a statue of Victory. Imposing as it was, the *colonia* must have been a constant reminder to the Britons of Roman rule and military dominance. The Temple of the Deified Claudius (probably built after the emperor's death in 54) added to this message, since it was the centre of the imperial cult in Britain, huge and classical in design. The bronze portrait head of Claudius, now in the British Museum, may have belonged to an equestrian statue from its precincts. So here in the *colonia* a small version of Rome was re-created, with Roman citizens, its own set of Roman laws and administrative structures, Roman-style buildings and facilities, and in the imperial cult the presence of the emperor himself. Even some 'Roman' foodstuffs were available: preserved in the layer of burned debris that resulted from

Figure 10 Longinus, a sergeant in the First Thracian Cavalry, was buried at Colchester far from his birthplace in Bulgaria, but the lavish monument (originally richly painted) that his heirs could afford underlines the gains that service in Roman auxiliary units could bring. It is ironic that he is shown riding down a barbarian enemy, as his memorial was desecrated almost certainly in the Boudiccan rebellion.

the destruction of the town by Boudicca were dates and figs presumably imported from the Mediterranean.

However, at Colchester there is also some interesting and important archaeological evidence to suggest that the establishment of the colony did not entirely disrupt existing customs and practices of some sectors of the local British community, however much deprivation and resentment it caused for others. The Roman authorities seem to have acted with some sensitivity towards the religious centre at Gosbecks and later allowed developments of the local sanctuary, while elite British burials seem to have continued at Stanway after the establishment of the *colonia*, up to the time of the Boudiccan revolt (see Chapter 1 above). Indeed, the occurrence of a surgical kit and an inkpot there suggests the possible presence of a professional class already before the Conquest, including Roman-educated Britons and even some Roman expatriates.

However we choose to interpret the evidence for the cultural and social relationship between Romans and Britons in post-Conquest Colchester—as suggesting positive coexistence or reluctant collaboration—in fact this relationship was interrupted in 60/61 by the devastating uprising of the Iceni against Roman rule, led by Boudicca, the widow of their ruler. They soon found support amongst the Trinovantes around Colchester. In the event, the inhabitants of the colony (many of whom had gathered for protection in the Temple of Claudius) were killed, and the town burned down. For the Romans it was humiliating: their culture was eradicated by fire, looting, and destruction. Statues were attacked, including, quite possibly, the bronze image of Claudius; even the tombstones of Roman soldiers were attacked, to judge from the fate apparently suffered by those mentioned earlier.

Another Romanized town attacked by Boudicca and the Iceni was Verulamium. As a British settlement it seems to have shared many features with Camulodunum, but its development in the period between the Conquest and the revolt reflects a different Roman strategy towards acculturation: rather than imposing a very 'Roman' settlement at Verulamium they appear to have worked within the existing local cultural framework.

In its pre-Roman days the British settlement of Verlamion was an important centre for the Catuvellauni. Like Colchester it was a widespread site containing several small centres with evidence of religious, agricultural and metalworking activities, a local mint, and some high-status cremation burials with grave-goods imported as luxuries. After the Roman Conquest, it was briefly occupied by the Roman army. It seems to have been the site of a small fort, and lay on Watling Street, the Roman road that linked London and the Midlands. But while the legionary fortress at Colchester was turned into a *colonia* after the troops had moved further into Britain, the settlement here was soon developed as a *civitas* capital after the army left. The Roman objective here, as with other *civitates*, was to create a stable and flourishing local society managed by the members of its own elite, who would in turn be motivated by what they had personally gained from Roman culture to give it their further support. This is very much the policy of persuasion which Tacitus described: it operated by winning over the local elites through 'carrots' rather than 'sticks', and allowing them to display the perceived benefits of Roman rule to lower orders of society. So what did its new status as a Roman *civitas* capital bring to Verulamium, which as we have seen was already a flourishing place of some standing?

One innovation was the rectilinear town plan which was laid out during the reign of Claudius when the town was given a defensive wall and ditch. Another is to be found in various new buildings erected in the town: a public bathhouse (which survived the Boudiccan revolt) introduced a Roman-style amenity, while the design and structure of a timber building on Watling Street has suggested the possible influence of Roman technical expertise. By the time of its destruction by Boudicca, Verulamium may indeed have been fairly Romanized in its culture. When Tacitus calls it a *municipium* he may not have been strictly accurate. If Verulamium had actually acquired this status by 60/61, it would have been rather speedy promotion (but see Chapter 1 above), yet the use of the term does point towards a 'Roman' identity for the town. On the other hand, there is evidence to suggest that Romanization did not exclude the continuation of certain British traditions, at least amongst the local elite. As at Colchester, the remains have been found of an important burial dated after the Conquest. So imposing was this cremation burial found at Folly Lane, St Albans, that it is thought to be of a local chief who must have died around 50. The grave-goods include many Roman-style luxury items (silver vessels, amphoras, a Roman-style couch, for instance), as well as a coat of iron mail armour of the type worn by

Celtic auxiliary troops. One possible explanation for this collection of goods is that he had served in the Roman army or commanded an auxiliary unit of his own people attached to it. Just how far this burial reflects a highly exceptional situation—rather than some regular, tolerant relationship—is difficult to tell.

Cultural change: acceptance and resistance

If we try to sum up the changes that occurred in this highly formative period for the culture of Roman Britain, it is clear that social and political factors played an important part. Roman authorities may have imposed major aspects of their culture on Britons in some localities, but in other cases they seem not to have forced the issue but to have allowed emulation to do its work, and to have tolerated certain customs of the British elite, at least up to the time of the Boudiccan revolt. This was also a highly important period for the history of the arts in Britain. Romans introduced artistic forms and skills new to the island, monumental inscriptions, stone sculpture, building techniques and mosaics were all here to stay, at least for the centuries of Roman occupation. Not only did these new arts link Britain with the other provinces of the empire and with its predominant Graeco-Roman culture, but they also offered its people new modes of self-identification and expression.

Yet the British elite may well have feared that such innovations would lead to the obliteration of their traditional culture, which could explain the ferocity with which Boudicca destroyed these particular settlements. But the fact was that the revolt failed in the long run to destroy their Romanized lifestyles: both towns were reconstructed and came to flourish in the second century, enjoying the kinds of facilities and artistic goods which marked out 'Roman' towns across the empire. This can be illustrated with examples from Verulamium. As early as 85, a rich grave was endowed with items that were typical of a wealthy Romanized life: a set of samian-ware dishes, imported glass, and a bronze tripod. Mosaics first appear in the houses there from 150; and around the middle of the second century (after the fire which destroyed much of the town in 155) its theatre was built.

Communities on the northern frontier

Relations between the Roman military and local civilians are also the theme of this part of the chapter, but the setting moves to some rather distinctive communities which developed in the frontier areas of northern Britain between the late first and early third centuries AD. Frontier zones often have rather different cultures from the central area of their territory, being, by definition, places 'at the edge' with different patterns of settlement and communication. A strong military presence at the frontier may bring to it the institutional traditions of the army as well as the culture of individual soldiers and civilians who work at the camps; and along the frontier-line military and civilian, incomers and natives interact in ways which may not happen elsewhere.

All these elements may be found in the frontier area of northern Britain, which also constituted the northern limit of the whole Roman empire. For much of this time, its boundary ran between the Tyne and Solway Firth (first with the so-called 'Stanegate' line of forts developing from the mid 80s, and then from 122 on with Hadrian's Wall), but for a period from about 140 to the 160s, when the Antonine Wall was in occupation, it was moved northwards to the Forth–Clyde corridor (see Chapters 2 above, and 6 below). Away from the immediate frontier, rural life must have gone on scarcely touched by the Roman presence, although unfortunately so little evidence for it has survived. In contrast, communities along the frontier had a much more diverse and changing culture, for which there is a wide range of documentation. They include military forts occupied by 'Roman' soldiers, themselves drawn from various parts of the empire, and civilian settlements (*vici*) which grew up around the forts and main roads (and which in some cases later developed into more regular towns). In many respects these communities are atypical of Roman Britain as a whole, yet they are an integral part of it and show with particular clarity how different social groups came to draw on elements of each other's culture. They are also a reminder that the province of Britain was very much part of the wider Roman empire and its cultural pluralism.

A major factor in this is the presence of the Roman army, which we shall consider first. Some vivid evidence for life in a fort in northern Britain comes from Vindolanda, which was situated on the 'Stanegate' road between Carlisle and Corbridge. Exceptional conditions there have preserved many fragments of wooden writing tablets and leatherware which would otherwise have perished. Together they give an insight into aspects of military culture, on both the institutional and personal level, for the early part of our period before the building of Hadrian's Wall. Amongst the tablets are fragments of military documents which record various activities at the fort, including rather a dismissive comment on the fighting style of the 'Brittunculi' ('wretched Britons', if that term is correctly interpreted), and fascinating correspondence between several high-ranking soldiers and officials. Some of the most interesting material relates to Flavius Cerialis, prefect of the Ninth Cohort of Batavians (soldiers from the Low Countries) which was stationed at Vindolanda around 100. The form of his name suggests that he was a second-generation Roman citizen, but his rank, his connections with other Roman administrators and soldiers across Britain, the lifestyle he apparently enjoyed in the *praetorium* (the commander's house), and the level of literacy displayed in the letters all show him to be thoroughly integrated into the culture of the wider Roman world. This seems also true for his wife, Sulpicia Lepidina who had accompanied him to this rather isolated site, probably with their children. The now-famous birthday invitation which she received from an officer's wife at a nearby fort gives an insight into the social life that they were able to make for themselves at this outpost of empire (Figure 26), while a fragmentary tablet which includes a line from Virgil's *Aeneid* suggests that the children of the *praetorium* may have used this great Roman epic for writing-exercises, as happened across the Roman world. The picture derived from these writing tablets is confirmed by other material evidence from Vindolanda. Army officers and their families stationed there on the edge of Roman territory were still able to share in some of the luxuries enjoyed by the well-to-do across the empire, with their fine pottery (samian ware) and leather shoes imported from Italy (one bearing the name of the manufacturer, Lucius Aebutius Thales, son of Titus).

As an institution, the army represented Roman imperial culture as well as its power: its forts, for instance, with their regular design replicated across the empire, are an immediate reminder of this.

Just as military roads and structures strode unswervingly across the British countryside generally ignoring the particularities of terrain— witness the positions of 'milecastles' on Hadrian's Wall as at Poltross Burn (no. 48) and Castle Nick (no. 39)—so the Roman army in northern Britain seems to have carried on its particular customs and practices as if it were anywhere else in the empire. Outside the fort at Maryport in Cumbria, for example, a series of altars to Jupiter 'Best and Greatest' (*Optimus Maximus*) was erected by commanders of the First Cohort of Spaniards, the First Cohort of Dalmatians, and the First Cohort of Baetasians, all of whom at one time or another were stationed there. Military building work was also recorded in terms which are paralleled across the empire. Some of the most attractive examples of this practice provide a striking illustration of this imperial perspective: a unique series of distance slabs erected by the Second, Sixth, and Twentieth Legions commemorates the construction of the Antonine Wall in central Scotland in the early 140s. This achievement is celebrated in terms, both verbal and visual, which belong totally to the Roman vocabulary of imperial triumph. There are personifications of Victory (Figure 11), of the *Virtus Augusti* (Valour of the Emperor), figures of Mars, and a scene of official sacrifice. Nowhere is there any reference to the immediate local context, and defeated captives are depicted only generically. So here, on the very edge of the Roman world, these monuments symbolize Roman power through the use of conventional imperial iconography. If they did have a message for the local inhabitants who saw them, it was of a culture which was alien, and apparently concerned with them only as objects of conquest.

Yet if the institution of the army seems uncompromisingly and exclusively Roman in its culture, the picture that emerges from evidence about its individual personnel is much more varied. Soldiers garrisoned at the northern frontier of Britain could certainly enjoy many important aspects of mainstream Roman material culture: for instance, the evidence from Vindolanda showed what was available there to officers like Flavius Cerialis, while at other forts such as Chesters and Bearsden there were Roman-style baths for soldiers to use. In their religious cults they brought their own gods to worship, as soldiers did right across the empire (see also Chapter 6 below). Some of these were traditional Graeco-Roman deities, such as Mars, Mercury, and Fortuna, while others were of Middle

Figure 11 Stone 'Distance-Slab' from Old Kilpatrick on the Clyde, marking the western end of the Antonine Wall. Erected to the glory of the Emperor Antoninus Pius (as announced in the pediment), it records the building of 4,411 feet of the wall by a detachment (*vexillatio*) of the Twentieth Legion *Valeria Victrix*, whose regimental badge—a boar—is depicted below. The unit's details are inscribed in the laurel wreath which the winged personification of Victory displays with her right hand while she holds the palm branch of triumph in her left. She reclines with her elbow on a globe, able now to rest after the worldwide dominion she has bestowed on Roman arms.

Eastern origin. Mithras was worshipped in special temples (Mithraea) that have been identified at several sites along or near to Hadrian's Wall: a popular god with soldiers throughout the Roman world, here he received many dedications from relatively senior army officers. Other deities were apparently brought by soldiers from their homelands: at Housesteads self-styled 'Germans, citizens of Twenthe and from the unit of Frisians' dedicated altars to Mars Thincsus and the two Alaisiagae; and at Carvoran soldiers in the First Cohort of Hamians from Syria made dedications to their native goddesses Hammia and Syria, and to Jupiter of Heliopolis (Baalbek).

Dedications like these to the gods of their homelands show that for many soldiers serving in this area their place of origin still remained an important part of their cultural identity. They record it in inscriptions alongside their status and identity within the Roman army. This, of course, had been the case on the tombstone of Longinus at Colchester noted earlier, but there the fact of his own Thracian origin, mentioned in the epitaph, was overwhelmed in the visual image of him as a thoroughly Roman soldier (Figure 10). Occasionally they commemorate connections with Rome itself: a dedication to Mithras from Carrawburgh Mithraeum made by Aulus Cluentius Habitus from Larinum, prefect of the First Cohort of Batavians, is worded to leave readers in no doubt that he is a direct descendant of the man of the same name immortalized by being defended in court by the statesman and author Cicero in 66 BC, and therefore part of Roman literature and history. But most inscriptions are not so detailed or grandiose. One of the simplest is on an altar to Fortuna Conservatrix (Fortune the Preserver) found in the bathhouse at Chesters which records that Venenus, a German, set it up.

Many of these inscriptions, then, link their dedicants with two potentially different cultures, that of the Roman army and of their homeland. Some also link them with local British culture, for at various places along the Wall Roman soldiers set up dedications to local deities. At Benwell, near the eastern end, the god Antenociticus (Figure 12) had a small temple outside the Roman fort that was found to contain three votive altars set up by soldiers. The background to one of these seems particularly unusual, in that it seems to show local religion touching on the politics of Rome itself. Here an officer serving as commander of an auxiliary regiment (a post ordinarily occupied by a person of equestrian rank) thanks the god for personal promotion to senatorial rank and for being designated as a *quaestor* (a senior Roman civil magistrate) while still in this post. The god Cocidius is recorded in numerous dedications, and may have had a shrine at Bewcastle, where silver plaques dedicated to him were found in the fort's headquarters building (Figure 13). Sometimes linked with Mars, he was honoured by various senior officers, by soldiers of all the legions, and by the cohort at the fort of Birdoswald. It may at first seem surprising to find that so many of these dedications to local

Figure 12 The head of the cult-statue, from the shrine of the local god Antenociticus at Benwell on Hadrian's Wall whose devotees included senior army officers, displays what artists from the Celtic tradition could do when working in the Roman-introduced medium of stone figurative sculpture.

gods were made by men of senior status in the Roman military hierarchy, but it should be remembered that to Romans there was nothing particularly untoward about adopting local gods in this way. It could be justified on one level as good pragmatic sense to negotiate with whatever effective religious powers there were in a locality, and on a more symbolic plane it was a way of appropriating local deities and linking them in with Roman culture. In another dedication at Benwell, the centurion Aelius Vibius gave Antenociticus equal status with 'the Deities of the Emperors' (in fact putting him first), thus drawing this otherwise-unknown local god into the world of Roman official religion.

Turning now to look for the local British element in the culture of these frontier communities, we find that evidence is relatively scarce. What is more it almost all comes from sites which are essentially 'Roman' rather than 'native' (see also Chapter 6 below). Civilian settlements (*vici*) grew up around forts such as Housesteads and

Figure 13 Silver plaque of the local god Cocidius found discarded in third-century rubbish under the fourth-century floor of the strongroom of the fort at Bewcastle, a western outpost fort of Hadrian's Wall. He is portrayed in a shrine, with spear in one hand and shield in the other. Gold and silver votive plaques deposited by worshippers are found in both pagan and Christian contexts in Roman Britain.

Vindolanda, but most surviving evidence for them comes from the later third century. Their populations must have been fairly mixed, with some retired soldiers living alongside Britons who may have moved in from the surrounding country to find a more prosperous existence servicing the army. Some were probably involved in small-scale industry and others in working on nearby land.

For the intangible aspects of local British culture—their values or beliefs—first-hand evidence is virtually non-existent, apart from a few images of native deities such as the *genii cucullati* (local gods shown wearing a hooded cloak) depicted on a relief from the *vicus* at Housesteads, or of one of the Mother Goddesses from Bewcastle. But it is one thing to recognize the names and images of local gods and another to understand the social context of their cult. This is where it becomes useful to look back at some of the Roman material from the area to see if it can shed any light on British attitudes. Potentially useful in this respect are those religious dedications made by Roman soldiers which also record local deities: not only can they can fill an important gap in our understanding of cross-cultural influences between Romans and local inhabitants, but they may also suggest something about the site and nature of particular local cults. We can deduce, for instance, from the distribution of dedications that the cult of Cocidius centred on an area around the western end of the Wall, and—as just noted—that his qualities were associated with those of Mars. And we can tell that Coventina (whether originally a local goddess or not) was regarded as particularly important by her devotees, since inscribed material found at her well at Carrawburgh gives her the epithets *sancta* and *Augusta*, unique for goddesses in Britain.

But material like this poses a knotty problem in using it as a way of pursuing local, 'British' culture. For although it may represent deities who are essentially British (as opposed to Graeco-Roman), it does so through media which are unquestionably derived from Rome, such as Latin inscriptions or Graeco-Roman artististic iconography. This raises the question of just how far these 'Roman' means may shape, distort, or conceal the original local features—and how are we to tell? Just as ethnic identity was suppressed by Roman in the tombstone of the Thracian soldier Longinus from Colchester, so a similiar deliberately Romanizing tendency might be at work in some of these more classical images. A case in point is a relief showing Brigantia from the fort at Birrens, Dumfriesshire. Personifying this part of northern Britain, she is represented here in completely classical terms with attributes of Minerva, Victory, and Juno Caelestis in an image devoid of any local element. Indeed, it has been argued from this sculpture and from the series of dedications to Brigantia which were primarily non-British that her cult was a Roman creation, rather than a British tradition. The head and limbs which survive from the cult statue of Antenociticus from the Benwell shrine (Figure 12) show an interesting and effective combination of classical and non-classical features. This could be interpreted as reflecting the adoption of a classical model for the representation of the god as a young man (and indeed by a cult statue in the first place), which was then given a 'local treatment' in the rather patterned delineation of features like the eyes and hair, and in the addition of a Celtic torc (only part of which now survives). Here then perhaps it might be said that Roman art provided the essential artistic form for this local god to take, which was enhanced by local artists according to their own particular styles and values. On the other hand some images of local deities seem to owe little to classical iconography or style: vivid examples of this are a head of the so-called 'horned god' from Netherby, the figure of Cocidius on silver plaques from Bewcastle (Figure 13), and the various *genii cucullati*.

Cultural values

This matter of different artistic traditions introduces some other questions about evidence for different cultural values, British or Roman. Should the use of a markedly non-classical style (which may for instance, ignore the classical niceties of proportion and scale in a figure, or suggest its volumes through patterned surfaces rather than by modelling) be taken as an indication of a 'local' subject or 'local' ideology? Can it be read in a positive way, or does it perhaps suggest a local failure to get to grips with Romanization? Issues like these, and some of their underlying assumptions, were touched upon in the introduction to this chapter where the evaluation of Romano-British art was discussed, and they will recur in the next section in connection with the art that decorated Roman villas in the fourth century. They are important because they seem to hold a key to understanding more of what is at stake in provincial Roman art, yet they are undoubtedly complex. For instance, the line of argument that seeks to link 'local' style with a locally significant subject would fit the obviously non-classical examples of the Netherby head, the Cocidius figure, and the *genii cucullati* cited earlier; it would also fit the sculptor's treatment of the Antenociticus head. Outside the area of religious art it would tie in with the figures of civilians found on funerary reliefs from places like Corbridge and Carlisle. But the argument is quite subverted by the fact that this non-classical style is also found on images made for and used by the Roman army, as on dedication slabs at the forts at Risingham and High Rochester and the gravestone of the cavalryman M. Aurelius Victor from Chesters. They may reproduce essential features of classical iconography for the gods or soldiers, but show little regard for classical rules of proportion or perspective. Perhaps some were made by local masons, but the fact remains that they would have been viewed by officials and soldiers in the Roman army. What links can then be argued between the style and the cultural values of the social group for whom they were made? This then is the problem: artistic style can be a useful pointer to the intrinsic cultural values of a society (and is a specially valuable one when there are few other sources of first-hand evidence), but understanding how these connections work in a context as multicultural as these frontier communities is very difficult. There seem to be no hard and fast answers, but it remains useful to be aware of the full range of artistic styles and the contexts in which they appear.

Trying to ascertain the 'local' element in the cultural life of this area has introduced some thorny problems of methodology, but they must be confronted for what they might be able to add to the total picture. As it has emerged, this picture is made up of various elements: the contribution of local people which may have been quite limited at the time (and of which so little direct evidence survives), the official culture of Rome conveyed primarily through the institution of the army, and the much more variegated experiences of individual soldiers, derived from their own different backgrounds and different reactions to the opportunities of their present location.

The town of Corbridge makes a good conclusion to this section because it seems to have turned—in various complicated phases, as yet not fully understood—from military base into flourishing town. Like Carlisle to the west, it had long stood on a major north–south route which acquired critical importance at various times when the army was on Scottish campaigns. It seems that the fort at Corbridge ceased to be active in the 160s when soldiers were withdrawn from the Antonine Wall back to Hadrian's Wall. After that, the settlement began its development into what was to become a fairly substantial town. The evidence suggests that early third-century Corbridge enjoyed a multicultural life in which many of the different elements discussed in this section of the chapter played a part. The army retained a small presence, and some of the buildings erected at this time may have been for military supplies. 'Old' Roman traditions were still honoured, notably in the temple built to 'Eternal Rome', with its pedimental sculpture showing the Roman wolf suckling Romulus and Remus, but there are also reliefs from temples apparently dedicated to oriental deities such as Jupiter Dolichenus and to Sol, and altars inscribed to deities from Tyre. A fragmentary tombstone recording a man called Barates from Palmyra (in modern Syria) is particularly interesting, as it seems very possible that he was the same man who set up an impressive sculpted tombstone to his wife Regina at South Shields (Arbeia). The inscription on the latter reveals that she was also his freedwoman, and was of the Catuvellauni tribe encountered earlier in this chapter, whose territory was in southern England around Verulamium. These stones illustrate the mixed cultural background of many people who lived in places like Corbridge, Carlisle, and South Shields in the late second or early third century.

Fourth-century villas

The discussion in this final section centres on the last century of the Roman presence in Britain, and on the culture of rural villas. It shows how wealthy and prosperous the Romano-British elite had become (in comparison, say, to the equivalents in rural areas of Gaul), and how interested they still remained in claiming a 'Romanized' identity for themselves. For some—perhaps many—contact with the culture of other, more central parts of the empire was a real factor in this. Official postings (which were fundamental to a career in public life), commercial business, or the administration of properties abroad led to regular travel across the empire, and the elite in Britain must also have been affected by this, meeting their peers from other provinces or travelling themselves. Whereas early third-century Corbridge had reflected various different cultures from certain parts of the empire, the art of many of these villas is firmly grounded in classical Graeco-Roman subject matter and in the more homogenized culture of the empire's elite.

During the third century many regions in the Roman empire had suffered some decline, through external attack or internal unrest and economic crisis. Although less affected than elsewhere, Britain, too, experienced a period of disruption and insecurity after the growth and stability of the second century. This is reflected, for instance, in the decline in public building in towns: structures fell into disrepair, and there was little major public building other than town walls and

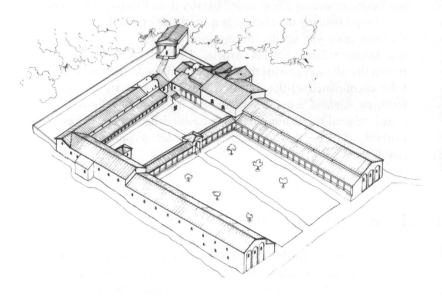

Figure 14 Reconstructed isometric view of Chedworth (Glos.), as it may have appeared in the fourth century. The wing in the foreground has not yet been fully excavated and its form is thus assumed. Facing east and situated high up in a commanding position in a combe in the Cotswolds on partially artificial terracing, the earliest visible part of the house lies across the head of the principal courtyard. A natural spring behind it was contained in a small *tempietto*, doubling as an ornamental water feature and shrine (*nymphaeum*). Wings—possibly of more than one storey—subsequently formed a second monumental courtyard, and (as particularly characteristic of the Late Roman period) provided further sets of rooms, probably for entertaining in different contexts and at different seasons in the year, with spectacular views across the landscape. Another terrace behind the north wing and at least one more complex downhill are likely to have contained service buildings and a home farm. The surrounding countryside contains numerous other Roman buildings including smaller villas, and much of it is likely to have been dependent on the main villa.

gates. But with the restoration of stability at the end of the century, one of the first signs of renewed vigour was in the building works and decoration to be found in the villas in the countryside.

'Villa' is a term that is used to include many types of establishment. Scholars have and continue to use it to mean different things, but basically it signifies a substantial rural house which may have been the centre of a working agricultural estate or the 'country house' owned by some dignitary from a nearby town (or both). Some estates may have been owned by institutions, or by wealthy landowners who lived elsewhere in the empire. In fourth-century Britain villas were concentrated in the South, particularly in good agricultural areas and in the orbit of small towns. They vary in plan (not least because some were developed over generations), but often incorporate aisled elements or courtyards (Figure 15). More significant perhaps for their 'Romanized' lifestyle is the often high quality of their decoration, with wall-painting and floor mosaics, and the sophistication of facilities (for instance, under-floor heating by hypocaust). These luxuries and comforts mark them out as places of high status. Although it is not always easy to tell from surviving evidence how particular rooms were used, many villas had imposing reception rooms as is clear from their layout and decoration. Rooms with a single or triple apse, for instance, were used for dining or the reception of visitors. In these houses owners were able to give public expression to their own cultural affiliations and powerful status in society. In so doing, they seem to have been speaking to a local audience (by showing off their wealth, for instance), but in the context of the much wider world of the empire. Their style of house and choice of decoration demonstrated their membership of an empire-wide elite and identification with the Graeco-Roman cultural tradition that it shared.

Mosaics

Mosaics are a good way of looking at this in greater detail. Owing to their considerable survival rate (especially compared to wall-paintings), they provide valuable evidence for reconstructing this aspect of villa life, and indeed for the art of fourth-century Britain as

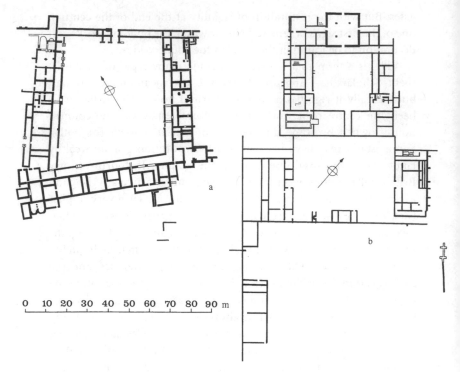

0 10 20 30 40 50 60 70 80 90 m

Figure 15 Partial ground-plans of two of the largest villas in Britain (North Leigh, Oxon., *left*; Woodchester, Glos., *right*). Neither site has yet been completely excavated, but even as seen here they stand comparison with some of the larger stately homes of Britain or Ireland in later ages. Like many of those, they seem to have evolved rather than been designed at a single time, though there is a clear trend in the Late Roman period towards pulling existing elements together to form a satisfactory whole. Woodchester displays most clearly the intention to employ architecture to impress and overawe visitors, by bringing them through the imposing central gatehouse in the right-hand court, from which, via a narrow gap in the opposing wall, they could glimpse across the inner court the great central reception room. When they eventually arrived at the latter, they would have been astounded at what is by far the largest mosaic yet found in Roman Britain (15 m. square), enclosed in a building that seems to have been of highly sophisticated design. Twelve other mosaics *in situ* (and evidence for more), the use of marble architectural veneers, and numerous fragments of sculpture, and there is no doubt that Woodchester's owners moved in the exalted social circles also represented by the Hoxne Treasure below (Figure 22 below).

a whole. Many floor mosaics were quite simple in design, but complex geometric and figured designs were also popular (if presumably more expensive to lay). In choosing to decorate their houses with mosaics, British villa-owners shared in fashions followed by their social counterparts across the Roman empire, and furthermore shared a choice of subjects and compositions. Part of this sharing was undoubtedly fostered by the fact that craftsmen seemed to have moved around to work when necessary: there is evidence to suggest that in the third century some moved from Continental Europe to the relative stability of Britain, while within Britain itself it has proved possible to trace the influence of particular local groups of mosaicists. These, moreover, are most likely to have used some kind of pattern-books to facilitate the reproduction of certain popular stock designs (although no such book has survived). But the prime motivation for this shared repertoire of mosaics must have been the desire to identify with the cultural values of the empire's elite.

Like their peers in North Africa and Cyprus (for instance), Romano-British villa-owners showed through the subjects of their floor mosaics the value they attached to a knowledge of Graeco-Roman mythology and literature; but as in these other regions, there were some distinctive local characteristics. In subject matter, British patrons seem to have had something of a penchant for rather obscure myths, but were less keen, it seems, on topics from popular culture (such as the scenes of the amphitheatre, or chariot-racing, or life on the estate, that were ousting mythological themes in North Africa). In terms of design, some common subjects were treated differently in Britain: the scene of Orpheus and the beasts is represented in a series of concentric figured friezes (as at Woodchester, for instance). Another aspect (which has parallels elsewhere, and other examples in the art of Roman Britain as was discussed in the last section) is the reproduction of scenes in styles that do not seem to match their classical content. The Rudston Venus mosaic (Figure 9) is probably the best-known example of this. It is hard to describe this style without using words such as 'provincial' or 'local' which have traditionally implied some negative, judgemental view based on the 'excellence' of classical art. A more fruitful approach is to set the piece in the particular context of its social production, as a provincial imitation of a classical culture aspired to but perhaps not fully understood. This particular mosaic adds some further questions about provincial art in the Roman empire, as the animals in the semi-circular panels along the sides include a lion and bull which seem to have come from the North African repertory of amphitheatre scenes, while another Rudston mosaic depicts a chariot seen head-on, also a North African type. Perhaps these were transmitted by craftsmen travelling across the empire, but what value did they have in their British context?

This question of value is an important and complex issue. Clearly, the subjects chosen for these Romano-British mosaics can throw a good deal of light on the culture of villas of this time. But there is an immediate difficulty about interpreting their meaning, especially at any symbolic level. This is true for much ancient art, but it is particularly acute here because so many of the subjects were long-established in Greek and Roman art. The question then must be what value they had in the context of fourth-century Britain: were there new ways of interpreting them, or had their original significance become trite and conventional? Another factor that needs to be taken into account is the polyvalence of many motifs in Roman art; images such as the hunt were open to more than one reading and so may have meant different things to different ancient viewers.

The Seasons (included in pavements at Lullingstone, Brading, Chedworth, and Bignor, for example) are another popular generic motif which can be read on various levels; they embody the fertility and abundance proper to a flourishing country estate and also symbolize the renewal of life in an eschatological sense. Other themes are hard to interpret in the immediate cultural context because they occur as isolated instances which are difficult to evaluate. Mosaics with particular literary references are a good example. They are actually few, but potentially important as evidence for familiarity with classical literature in Britain. The most extensive example is the pavement from Low Ham, Somerset, which shows episodes from Virgil's *Aeneid*, Books 1 and 4, but there are other pavements (Lullingstone and Frampton) with Virgilian themes (which are also found in wall-painting and some coinage in Britain). Some of these allusions are rather high-flown, but are they a sign of an individual's deep literary knowledge, or perhaps an instance of ostentatious tokenism? These are questions impossible to answer, but even so it is possible to take these mosaics as evidence for some appreciation, if not a specific understanding of Roman literature in fourth-century Britain. This can be reinforced by a number of other scenes which allude to a life of learning and philosophy (a popular theme in the art of the later Roman empire), including representations of the Muses at Branting-ham and Aldborough, the latter including an inscription in Greek.

Graeco-Roman mythology provided perhaps the richest repertory of scenes for these British pavements. There are images of individual gods and goddesses, such as Venus (as at Bignor and Rudston), Mars (Fullerton), and Bacchus (as at Stonesfield and Thruxton). Episodes from myths also occur, such as the rape of Ganymede (at Bignor) and Orpheus and the beasts (at Brading and Woodchester). Bellerophon killing the Chimaera is an instance of an episode found at several sites in Britain, including Lullingstone, Hinton St Mary, and Croughton, yet rare in mosaics elsewhere. Particularly interesting are pavements which contain several mythological scenes, which on the face of it at least, suggest some kind of deliberate grouping or cycle of episodes; it is not always clear, however, how far these are random collections of popular scenes, rather than significantly related. In some cases the subject of the mosaic may reflect the function of the room it decora-ted: just as the baths (as at Witcombe and Rudston) were often given aquatic motifs, so figures of lyre-players in reception rooms (as at Littlecote, whether Apollo or Orpheus) may represent the music played in that room. Connections like these can suggest something further about the cultural background of the mosaic scenes.

In some cases this background may involve religious practice or beliefs. For some pavements such a religious symbolism has been suggested: examples at Brading and Littlecote have been seen as representing 'Orphic' or gnostic (mystical knowledge) ideas. Clearly such scenes have the potential for this kind of interpretation, but whether it is historically relevant is practically impossible to decide. Indeed, as they were open to a range of significance, these scenes were perhaps read at different levels even in their original context. Bacchic symbols are a case in point. As in Roman art in general, Bacchic scenes and imagery are very common in these mosaics, raising a key question of evaluation: how much is conventional decorative work, and how much significant in terms of cult? This same question, inci-dentally, recurs for the silver plates of the Mildenhall Treasure. A similar issue, but with different ingredients, emerges in respect of representations of Orpheus and the beasts in British mosaics. As already noted this image, which had been such a popular topic in mosaics across the empire, seems to have been especially popular in Britain where it received a distinctive composition. This and their fourth-century date—well into the Christian empire—has led some scholars to propose for them a hidden Christian significance, calling in support other images of Orpheus in Christian catacombs in Rome. However, there is no other evidence to confirm this reading.

Even when explicitly Christian details have been incorporated into a mosaic's design, interpretation may still remain open to question. A pavement from Frampton (now lost) included the Christian Chi-Rho monogram as a feature in its otherwise conventional design, while a mosaic from nearby Hinton St Mary (possibly the work of the same craftsmen) has at the centre of the main room the bust of a young man set in front of a Chi-Rho (Figure 16). This is now usually accepted as an image of Christ (uniquely situated on a floor), and its presence raises important methodological questions about the interpretation of the other scenes in the design. These include as a parallel image, a scene of Bellerophon slaying the Chimaera (which may also have been depicted in the damaged central panel at Frampton), some genre hunting scenes in side panels, and four busts (perhaps of the Winds) at the corners. The point is whether the presence of the Christian element, powerful as it is, should as it were ' christen' the rest of the subject matter, or whether it is better seen as a self-contained feature which has no special value for the rest of the decoration. The overall assemblage of motifs in the Frampton mosaic suggests that the designer may have included the Chi-Rho as being one of a number of symbols invoking good fortune. Furthermore, there is no particular reason for automatically assuming that a Christian motif meant a villa-owner whose beliefs were exclusively Christian, nor even for expecting that Christian believers would see all mythological scenes as requiring 'conversion'. The situation at Lullingstone suggests that people were able to compartmentalize their attitudes to some extent. There a Christian chapel was set up in part of the villa close to the dining-room which retained its mythological mosaics of Bellerophon and Europa. Religious cult of various kinds had had a part in villa life (witness the water shrine at Chedworth Villa), so it is not surprising to see some degree of continuation after the advent of Christianity.

Figure 16 Decorative scheme of the fourth-century mosaic from Hinton St Mary (Dorset). The shape of the room—divided into two unequal parts— was a common one, often used for dining-rooms (*triclinia*) in which the smaller section contained the table and couches. For the mosaic designer this made two separate main panels more or less unavoidable. The smaller here depicts the myth of Bellerophon, mounted on Pegasus, slaying the Chimaera, a popular motif. The larger displays the bust of a beardless man in front of the Christian Chi-Rho monogram (the first letters of the name of Christ in Greek) and flanked by pomegranates (also encountered in Christian iconography). This might be an emperor (the monogram being adopted as an imperial symbol), but walking on an emperor's image would have rated as high treason. Gods, however, were a regular feature of mosaics, and it is almost certain that this is Christ.

Wall-painting and sculpture

This discussion has concentrated on the mosaics which decorated villas as these provide a usefully homogeneous body of material through which to look at issues of subject matter and iconography, but they would have been complemented in the houses by other forms of decoration and fine wares. Their walls would often have been decorated with paintings, sometimes on a similar theme: to judge from the fragments of painting which survive from Kingscote, the figure of Venus in the floor mosaic was possibly matched with a scene of Venus with the armour of Mars on the walls. Rather surprisingly perhaps, relatively few sculptures seem to have survived from villas, but these include pieces which have particular thematic relevance to villa culture. For instance, hunting is represented by figures of Diana from Chedworth and Woodchester, wining and dining by a marble group of Bacchus and his panther from Spoonley Wood in Gloucestershire (which was found in a grave), and ancestral values by two portrait busts found at Lullingstone, all of which could also have had religious significance. High-quality, often imported, tableware in fine pottery, silver, and glass would have formed part of the villa's household equipment, but was also exchanged between the wealthy and influential as gifts. Once again, a feature to note is the recurrence of similar motifs: hunting, for instance, was shown on a glass bowl from Wint Hill, Somerset and on the silver *lanx* (large rectangular dish) from Risley Park, Derbyshire.

To sum up this discussion, the wealth reflected by this lifestyle is one feature to emphasize, particularly in the context of this period. The private patronage of these Late Roman villa-owners contrasts with the relative lack of investment in public monuments in towns at this time. But the most striking feature in cultural terms is the continued vigorous life of traditional Graeco-Roman subjects and images. The terms in which these Romano-Britons chose to define themselves were, three hundred years or so after the Claudian Conquest, unequivocally Roman.

Conclusion

By concentrating on these three areas, this discussion has shown how interconnected were the culture and society of Roman Britain, and how this included, across time, a variety of social groups who used the arts as a means of articulating their own identities and agendas. The latter point is illustrated quite clearly near the beginning of the period by Tacitus' reference in the *Agricola* to the Roman introduction of cultural amenities and opportunities as a means of winning over the local population, and at the other end by the interests of the villa-owners.

A closer look at this use of the arts might suggest that it was particularly through themes and iconography that this identification is most easily recognizable. How different social groups made use of common themes, such as those taken from mythology, literature, or from the military or imperial repertory, can give some clues about their own standpoint. This is a particularly useful indication when the subjects have been appropriated, or adapted from the culture of another group as was shown, for instance, in the dedications made to local deities by Roman soldiers on Hadrian's Wall. The whole question of style in relation to subject matter is much more complex, and stylistic variations are therefore harder to interpret as signifiers of cultural background.

These aspects of the arts have an obvious bearing on the issue of Romanization, but it is important to reiterate that despite changes over time there is a heavy imbalance of evidence on the 'Roman' side. The 'local' ingredient (of particular interest perhaps in the earlier years of Roman presence) is practically impossible to track, especially at levels below the elite. Often we have to resort to inference about it, whether about the strength of cultural fear and resentment behind the Boudiccan revolt, or about the nature of the local cults which attracted Roman worshippers. But we may not always get this right: if the only route to British attitudes is through artistic media or historical evidence of Roman origin, then there is a very real possibility that we may misunderstand or fail to spot particular issues. It is for this reason that important questions about British resistance to Roman culture, for instance, often have to be left unanswered. There are also many 'grey areas' in our understanding: what, for instance, did the viewers of some of those fourth-century mosaics really make of their scenes? How far did they follow some of their more obscure allusions? And to what extent did they think of themselves as 'Roman', or 'British', or, for example, 'Icenian'? Or were even these categories redundant by this time? From 212 all free persons in the empire were Roman citizens, but even before that large numbers of people had a dual loyalty to Roman citizenship and their own places of origin.

Shining brilliantly (quite literally) through this grey mist, yet preserving many of these enigmas, are the 'Treasures' of Late Roman Britain—the Mildenhall, Thetford, Water Newton, and Hoxne hoards containing magnificent plate, some accompanied by jewellery and by cash in the form of gold and silver coins. They make a good place to end this chapter: not only do they show the continued use of images and artefacts imported from the wider Roman world, and the evident wealth enjoyed by some people in Britain in these last years of Roman rule, but they show the continued relevance of some important questions, as yet unanswered. To whom did they belong? Why were they hidden? And how should we evaluate them in their historical context of their contemporary society in Britain—or indeed in the context of its cultural history? Their dazzling richness and classicism makes it all too easy to forget the fact that for so many people in Britain across its Roman centuries such objects had little or no relevance to their culture. The experiences of this majority may scarcely have been touched by the various developments examined in this chapter, yet through the sources examined here there is little evidence by which we can tell.

Figure 17 The Romano-British expansion of agriculture and industry (salt production) in the Fens has been recorded from the air. At Spalding Common (Lincs.), contrasting with the natural watercourses a rectangular Roman farmstead in the foreground is reached by a drive from the Roman local road that runs up the right-hand edge of the photograph.

5

The human impact on the landscape: agriculture, settlement, industry, infrastructure

Richard Hingley and David Miles

The purpose of this chapter is to take an overview of the broad geographical patterns of human occupation in the British Isles within the imperial province and beyond in North Britain, the broad environmental background, and the regional patterns of change from the end of the first millennium BC to the fifth century AD. In particular this chapter will consider the impact of social change (sometimes called 'Romanization') on the British Isles as a whole, using the results of environmental analysis, aerial photography, and recent field surveys and excavations.

From his winter quarters in Gaul, Julius Caesar wrote a simplistic and misleading sketch of Britain's geography, but because he was the first and certainly one of the most influential foreigners to comment on the inhabitants (and to have his views inflicted on generations of schoolchildren) his ill-informed description has persisted. Even as recently as 1998, the broadcaster Jeremy Paxman in his national portrait *The English* could regurgitate the Roman propaganda: 'The original inhabitants of the country do not seem to have been a particularly advanced civilization . . . its priests encouraged human sacrifice and cannibalism. The most sophisticated tribe, the Belgae in Kent, grew wheat and flax, and while they could tend cattle, they were, apparently, incapable of making cheese and knew nothing about horticulture. That was the height of "English" sophistication before the arrival of the Romans, and the further you travelled from the south coast, the more "uncivilized" the tribes became!'

So history goes to the eventual victors. In fact Caesar—and about a century later the Emperor Claudius—launched his forces against an old country, populated by tribal people who had 6,000 years experience of exploiting their land, whether in Kent, the Pennines or the Orkney islands. These farming communities had a sophisticated appreciation of the potential of their landscape and their plants and animals. As the ancient geographer Strabo implied with his account of British exports—and archaeology makes clear—they were not primitive or subsistence farmers but agriculturalists who exploited their land, often in a sophisticated fashion, not merely to feed themselves but to generate a surplus so that they could support a warrior aristocracy and gain access to prestige goods—gold, foodstuffs, weaponry, clothing, and animals from the rest of Britain and the Continent.

The landscape

A general division of Roman Britain has often been made, dividing the province into two zones: the military district and the civilian district. These zones reflect and are defined by reference to relief, soil, communications, and, to some extent, climate. The lowland civilian district lies south and east of an imaginary line drawn from the mouth of the River Tees to the mouth of the Exe (Map A). This is an area of relatively young rocks, low hills, and large areas of flat ground—suitable for agriculture. The highland zone lies to the north and west of the line. Old rocks predominate and high hills and mountains are more common. Much of this area is less suited for arable agriculture, although some soils are highly fertile and considerable evidence for arable production exists throughout the highlands and

islands to the north and west of Britain. The highlands are also generally wetter and colder than the lowlands, providing less favourable
conditions for large-scale arable production.

Despite this division, human populations had inhabited the whole
of Britain for at least 6,000 years by the time of the Roman invasion.
Many areas of both the highlands and the lowlands supported very
dense populations prior to the Roman invasion. For instance, dense
Iron Age settlement occurred across much of the South and the
Midlands (particularly in 'Wessex' and in the Upper Thames Valley),
while roughly equal densities of sites occurred across much of the
north and west (for instance, in Cornwall, East Lothian, and parts of
the Western Isles). In terms of resources, both the highlands and the
lowlands were of importance to the Romans. The lowland zone
supported dense human communities which, given the peaceful
conditions imposed by Rome, could grow a surplus of arable crops
and animals. In some areas mineral resources also occurred which
were of value to the Roman state. The highland zones were also
important; the human population was probably less dense in some
areas, but taxes of crops and animals would have been raised. In
addition, much of the mineral wealth of Britain lay in those
regions—for instance gold at Dolaucothi in Wales and tin in
Derbyshire and the Mendips.

The highland/lowland divide is a general model that has been used
to characterize the evidence for Roman Britain, especially with regard
to the distribution of the Roman army across the province and also
with regard to the nature of civil society. It is often argued that the
highlands formed a 'military district', where the army remained into
Late Roman times and the civilian population continued to live in an
Iron Age manner. In contrast, it is usually suggested that across the
lowland zone the Roman army moved on swiftly after the Conquest,
leaving a population that became rapidly 'Romanised'. We shall see,
below, that these suggestions are rather oversimplified but they are
also generally useful.

These now conventional zones of landscape reflect the highland/
lowland model of regional contrasts first defined by Sir Harold
Mackinder in 1902 and promoted in the 1930s by Sir Cyril Fox
in his influential book *The Personality of Britain*. More recently other
analysts of the British landscape have challenged the twofold
division. Oliver Rackham divided England into three regions—a

central planned countryside framed by two zones, to east and west, of ancient countryside. This presages the classification in 2000 by Roberts and Wrathnell in *An Atlas of Rural Settlement in England*, which—on the basis of early modern and medieval settlement patterns and medieval woodland distribution—identifies a central zone of nucleated settlement running from the north-east coast and east Yorkshire to the central southern England. This central region, running north–south also roughly reflects the distribution of Romano-British villas from present day Dorset, Hampshire, and south and west Kent, through Gloucestershire and Oxfordshire to the East Midlands, the Lincolnshire Wolds, and East Yorkshire. Although there is no lack of native settlements, villas are rare or absent in the South-West Penninsula, Wales (except for close to the Severn Estuary), the Weald, the Fenland (except for the Fen Edge), and much of Norfolk, the West Midlands, Pennines, and the North-West.

At a regional and local level in Britain there was considerable variation in the character of the landscape that is not allowed for in the civilian/military district model. Hills, valleys, moors, and forests across the whole of the British Isles provided varying resources for local human communities. The variable geology of Britain provided a series of constraints and opportunities for the human communities. By the time of the Roman invasion, however, the landscape had been modified in major ways by generations of people. Large areas of forestry had been cleared from the Mesolithic onward and mixed farming formed an established agriculture system across the whole of Britain. The available environmental data and settlement evidence for the Roman period indicate variations in the ways that the landscape was used at this time. In general it would appear that much of the land had been cleared of trees, but forests and woods were a very important resource to Roman populations and they were managed for effective exploitation. In addition, extensive areas of marsh and bog covered parts of the lowlands in addition to extensive areas of the uplands. The lowlands of the Fens and the Wentlooge Edge (South Wales) were drained for agriculture during the Roman period, but other extensive areas of wetland survived (for instance, the Somerset Levels). Some rivers and streams may have been hard to cross, especially at times of flood, and efforts were made to manage and control these, while stone and timber bridges were also built across them. The pollen evidence (on which there is more below) indicates that in

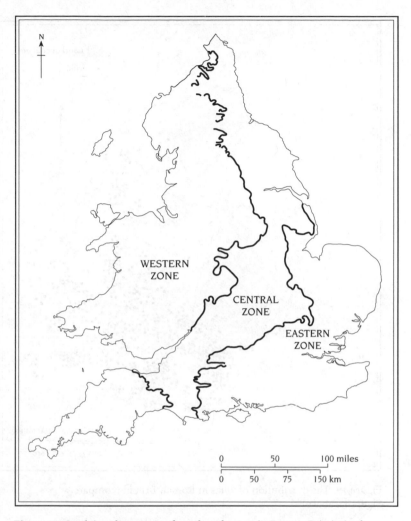

Figure 18 Studying the nature of rural settlement in Roman Britain in the conventional framework of the topographical division between highland and lowland zones (see Map A) will need now to be modified in the light of this mapping of rural settlement in England based on medieval and post-medieval data by Roberts and Wrathmell for English Heritage (see Further Reading). The central zone is one of nucleated settlements and mixed, relatively intense farming. Those to east and west are zones of more traditional dispersed settlements.

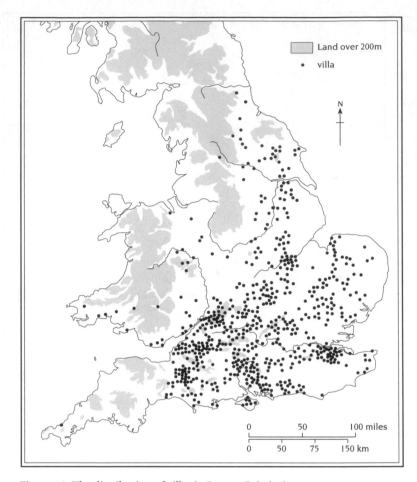

Figure 19 The distribution of villas in Roman Britain (compare Figure 18, above).

the course of the Roman period the long-term process of agricultural expansion originating in Prehistoric Britain contiued, for example, into the upland valleys of the eastern Pennines. Similarly in the Fenlands, pre-Roman reclamation continued and spread as ditched peasant farmstead and field expanded onto fertile land, taking advantage of the relatively dry condition in the earlier Roman period.

The nature of environmental evidence

Evidence for the climate comes from a number of sources, but none of these provide exact information. Classical literary texts provide some anecdotal evidence for major climatic events, and scientific methods of analysis include ice core analysis, study of glaciers, tree-ring studies, and analysis of peat growth. The combined evidence may suggest that the climate was slightly warmer than the present day following on from a relatively cool and wet Iron Age. It would also appear that colder and wetter weather set in during the late to sub-Roman period, when there is evidence of flooding in areas such as the Somerset Levels and the Fens.

Archaeologists can use the evidence of pollen, alluvium (flood-deposits), and colluvium (hill-wash) to study the past environment. The evidence can also help us to understand the interaction between people and the environment. Pollen analysis presents an understanding of the character of the landscape by presenting information about the relative amount of tree cover (indicated by tree and shrub pollen) and open land (indicated by the pollen of herbaceous plants). Petra Dark has studied forty-two pollen sequences that provide evidence for the environment of Roman Britain. These are spread across the country, but with a focus in the North and West (the evidence for the lowland zone is very incomplete, as peat bogs are less common in the South and East of the country). In spite of Caesar's description, much of Britain was already predominantly an agricultural landscape prior to the Roman Conquest.

Woodland

The climax woodland which covered most of Britain after the Ice Age was gradually cleared from the Mesolithic (about 6000 BC) onwards—first by hunter-gatherers who deforested areas to generate browsing for animals, and then by farming communities who needed pasture and, increasingly, arable land. From the Bronze Age onwards (about 2000 BC) fields were laid out in the landscape, and farming, both arable and pastoral, became more intensive.

Though much of the land was cleared of trees, nevertheless forests and woods remained a vital resource, particularly for fuel and building material. Studies of prehistoric waterlogged timbers from the Somerset Levels, Flag Fen near Peterborough, and sites in the Thames Valley reveal that prehistoric communities were skilled exploiters of woodland. Woodlands were not simply felled and cleared but managed, in order to grow standard trees for their long trunks, and coppice material for basketry, wickerwork, and fence-posts. Oak, hazel, willow, and lime were among the most useful trees to be cultivated. Some areas like the Weald remained extensively forested to supply the needs of the iron industry. Even in areas cleared for many centuries such as the Upper Thames, the poor sandy soils of the hills above Oxford were maintained as woodland to provide fuel for the large-scale local pottery industry. Rare fourth-century evidence for this ancient woodland came from a well at the Romano-British farmstead at Barton Court Farm near Abingdon. The nearby Roman wood, growing oak standards and hazel coppice, passed into the hands of the Abbots of Abingdon and St Johns College, Oxford, and still exists today.

Alluvium and colluvium

As land was cleared of forest and given over to arable fields, widespread erosion occurred. This process can be seen in Later Prehistory, when hill-wash built up in the valleys of the chalk downs and in the floodplains of rivers such as the Thames. Valley floors became wetter with increased run-off, and low-lying areas of earlier prehistoric settlement were abandoned. Alluvial deposits increased during the Roman period, reflecting the intensification of farming, the increased digging of drains, and the cultivation of winter-sown crops (encouraging the erosion of bare soils). Some of these low-lying areas, with waterlogged deposits blanketed by alluvium, have provided good evidence for Roman farming. At Claydon Pike in Gloucestershire, the Thames Valley floor was extensively grazed as open grassland in the Late Iron Age, particularly by cattle and lambs. Dung beetles were the most frequently preserved insects. Shortly after the Roman Conquest, the grassland was enclosed by hedges and given over to hay meadows, possibly an innovation of this period. Near Farmoor (Oxfordshire), where Roman hay meadow was also detected from plant and animal remains, a long iron scythe lay at the crossing of a stream onto the meadow. Romano-British innovations in land-use went hand-in-hand with new tools: shears also occur for the first time as new breeds of sheep are shorn rather than plucked.

Arable cultivation

Soil erosion was mainly the result of arable cultivation brought about by the demand for cereals and legumes. The principal prehistoric tool for cultivating the land was the ard or scratch plough, sometimes tipped with an iron sleeve or—in Scotland—with stone. With the ard it was necessary for the ox-team to plough in two directions to break up the soil. The resulting characteristic criss-cross pattern has been found on many sites from Wales and the South-West to Hadrian's Wall. The use of the ard continued into the Roman period: wooden ards were disposed of at Usk (Gwent) in the second century, and at Ashville, Abingdon (Oxfordshire) in the third. At the latter site criss-cross plough marks were also found in the Roman-period fields sealed by alluvium below the native settlement. By the Later Roman period ploughs had become more effective, heavier and equipped with a coulter which sliced through the soil ahead of the share. As a result the ground could be cultivated more deeply and broken up by ploughing in a single direction. Roman plough technology also improved with the development of the asymmetric share, which could both cut and turn the soil. Examples have been found at villa sites in southern England, at Brading (Isle of Wight) and Folkestone (Kent), and also in Wales at Dinorben.

Much of the evidence for Roman field systems has been destroyed in the past fifty years by modern agriculture. In the Fens, for example, the earthworks of Roman paddocks and fields have been almost entirely flattened. Now they can only be observed as soil marks or crop marks on aerial photographs. Similarly on the southern downs, the extensive field systems often called 'Celtic fields' (which were prehistoric in origin but cultivated into the Roman period) have notably disappeared. Field-walking indicates that these arable fields were manured; in the South-West, Wales, the Pennines, and the Cotswolds some of the fields and paddocks were surrounded by stone walls. Some of the best preserved are at Grassington in the Yorkshire Dales, covering about a hundred hectares. On the lowlands, water-logged field ditches at sites such as Farmoor have produced evidence for quick-set hedges of hawthorn and blackthorn set on or between earthen banks—apparently another innovation of the Roman period. Other intensively cultivated and well-drained areas reveal no physical evidence of fields. Perhaps, as is frequently observed in the Mediterranean today, field boundaries were indicated only by a plough-furrow or some other ephemeral marker—and persistent arguments between neighbours.

Crops

The evidence for Roman crops comes mainly from charred deposits scattered around settlements during processing, storage or consumption, from waterlogged remains—for example in ditches and wells—or pollen evidence from fens and bogs. It is only since the mid-1970s that excavators of Romano-British settlements have systematically searched for carbonized plant remains, so the national picture and regional differences are not yet very detailed. It is clear, however, that Iron Age crop production was very effective. Both in hill-forts such as Danebury (Hampshire) and lowland sites like Gravelly Guy (Oxfordshire), hundreds of underground pits or silos are found in which grain was stored. On hard-rock sites in the western and northern uplands or in wet locations such pits are rarely found, and evidence of crops is harder to come by. In the Iron Age the cereals most frequently grown were spelt wheat (*Triticum spelta*) and milled six-row barley (*Hordeum vulgare*). As the latter needs to be parched to remove the hull or husk its carbonized remains are frequently preserved. In spite of the inconvenience, the husk has the advantage of providing fodder for animals. Other Iron Age crops included the more ancient emmer wheat (*Triticum dicoccum*, which was grown on light soils), bread wheat, oats, rye, peas, Celtic beans, and flax. Systematic analysis of plant remains shows that arable weeds are also a useful source of information about crop cultivation. In the Thames Valley a series of sites between Abingdon and Lechlade have produced common spike-rush (*Eleocharis palustris*) in cereal deposits, indicating the advance of arable cultivation onto low-lying damp ground. In the North, heath-grass (*Danthonia decumbens*) from the Late Iron Age and Roman site at Thorpe Thewles may also indicate the cultivation of damp ground.

In the Roman period, below-ground silos are replaced by granaries, often with suspended floors supported on timber or stone posts. However so-called corn-drying ovens are a common feature of farming settlements in the South, and these are a rich source of evidence. Barley and spelt remain the most important crop plants, with the increasing cultivation of three species tolerant of a wide variety of soils: bread wheat, oats, and rye. Soil-nitrogen deficiency has been observed on some native sites in the Roman period such as Ashville, whereas the problem was not apparent at the neighbouring villa estate at Barton Court Farm.

Although the traditional crop-staples remained dominant, the arrival of a Continental population of soldiers, administrators, and traders from the Roman empire also stimulated the growing of exotic plants for foodstuffs and the garden. By the later first century AD, many farmsteads were cultivating coriander and opium poppies, and trees such as cherry, plum, and perhaps umbrella pine were grown. A formal garden has been found at the palace at Fishbourne, but, unfortunately, garden plants do not often leave remains. Some that do include rose and box, the staple of the Roman *topiarius*. Archaeologists have argued for many years about the presence of Roman vineyards. Grapes and raisins were certainly imported to cities such as York and London and have turned up in those places. There is no reason in principle why grapes should not have been grown in Roman Britain. At Wollaston in Northamptonshire, the discovery of grape pollen in Roman planting trenches seems to have clinched the argument.

Most Romano-British farmsteads were mixed, dependent on animals for manure, traction, dairy products, wool, hides, and meat. The study of Romano-British pastoralism is a rather neglected subject, not made easier by the fact that the soils suited to pastoralism are often acidic and bones are less well preserved. Specialist animal-rearers may also have often walked their produce off the site to market, to such towns as London, Exeter, or Cirencester, or to military garrisons. Cattle, sheep, and pig were the principal domestic animals in the Roman period, with cattle on the increase. Some sites may have specialized: on the Cotswolds the villa at Barnsley Park focused on sheep for wool, while a few miles away on the Thames gravel at Claydon Pike horse-ranching was important. In towns and high-status rural sites, cattle and pig were the main source of meat. Hens seem to be ubiquitous on Romano-British farmsteads, and occasionally egg-shells are found. The Cotswold villa at Shakenoak also had an important line in fish-farming.

The population: how many people lived in Roman Britain?

Judging from the number of settlements and the extent of agriculture, there was an increase in the British population from the Bronze Age onwards, through to the fourth century AD. Attempts have been made to estimate the population of Roman Britain on the basis of a number of factors, including the density of settlements produced by detailed field-walking. One estimate of 2.5 million people for Roman Britain has been made by Timothy Potter and Catherine Johns (see Table 1). Martin Millett used similar calculations to suggest a population of 3.6 million. The main difference between Millett's figures and those of Potter and Johns is that Millett argued for a population of 3.3 million in the countryside compared to the suggestion of 2 million by Potter and Johns. These figures do not

TABLE 1. *The population of Roman Britain according to Potter and Johns*

Site types	Total population
Major towns	120,000
Small towns/'local centres'	200,000
Army (in heyday)	60,000
People in *vici* (settlements) attached to forts	40,000
Countryside	2,000,000
TOTAL	2,500,000

include the Highlands of Scotland, which remained outside the Roman empire. Settlement is dense over much of this area, and another 250,000 people might well have lived here. All these figures are speculative as they are derived from a number of assumptions, but they do suggest a fairly great density of population. The Domesday Book, which was compiled in 1086, indicates a population of 1.75–2.25 million for England, and the Roman figures would suggest a comparable population density in Roman Britain. The population figures that have been derived from various sources have been used to create a population graph for Roman Britain.

The Roman empire as a whole could have had a population of around 80 million people, and estimates that exist for individual parts of the empire include 7.5 million for Italy and 11 to 12 million for Gaul and Germany. Roman Italy was very densely settled and had major towns and cities, while the provinces of Gaul and Germany covered far greater areas than Britain. The comparison of the potential population indicates a comparable density of population in Britain to that of other provinces of the Western Empire.

An analysis of the estimates quoted on Table 1 demonstrates that Britain was a fundamentally agrarian society at this time (Table 2). It appears likely that 10 per cent of the population lived in towns (including small towns), while soldiers and their dependants formed around 3 to 4 per cent of the population. Between around 83 per cent and 90 per cent of the population lived in the countryside and they were involved primarily in agriculture. Much of the population of the small towns may also have been involved in agriculture, while the army farmed as well (see below).

Most of the population, therefore, were actively involved in food

TABLE 2. *Percentages of the Romano-British population in various classes of sites* (% against total estimated population)

Classes of sites	Potter and Johns	Millett
Major towns	5%	No figure given
All towns	13%	6.5%
Soldiers	2%	No figure given
Soldiers and dependants	4%	3.5%
Country dwellers	83%	90%

production. Many of the most substantial towns lay in the lowlands, although the population of the largest of these is unlikely to have been more than a few thousand (see below). Most of the army was based in the highlands, with a particular concentration in the Hadrian's Wall corridor. The rural population was scattered throughout the province. Regional programmes of aerial photography and field survey in the lowlands suggests a density of at least one Roman-period site per square kilometre in many areas (Northamptonshire, Bedfordshire, and the Upper Thames Valley, for example). Further north, population density in what is today northern England and southern Scotland may have been rather lower, although some areas appear to have had concentrations of sites that are similar to the densely settled lowlands (the Solway Plain, and East Lothian, for instance). In upland Britain, river valleys and coastal plains were often densely settled.

The fullest evidence for Roman-period settlement comes from well-drained soils, where evidence is often derived through aerial photography. Field survey and excavation on heavier clay soils sometimes indicate a broadly comparable density of settlement. More evidence is required, however, to build a fuller picture of settlement densities across the province and this restricts the reliability of the estimate of the population of Roman Britain given above.

The vast majority of the population of Roman Britain would have been the descendants of the Iron Age British people. Large numbers of soldiers and traders certainly came into the island in the early period of Roman conquest and control, along with a limited number of administrators. Some of these people died in Britain, and examples of their tombstones have been found across the civilian and the military districts. Soldiers, administrators, and traders continued to come to

Britain from all parts of the empire throughout the period of Roman rule, and in the largest of the towns (notably London and York) a fairly mixed and cosmopolitan population existed. Many of the solders that served in the military district originated from other provinces and were moved to Britain. As time went on, however, soldiers came to be recruited locally and the individual army units often developed local loyalties. Despite the growth of a mixed population in some areas of the province, the rural areas of the civilian district are likely to have remained populated almost entirely by the native British.

The population included wealthy individuals, free poor, and slaves. The evidence is mainly derived from the inscriptions that have been found in the province. We know of some individuals who came to settle in the province who were citizens of Rome, and members of the British tribal elite will also have been made citizens by the emperor. Free provincials could join the army and would have become Roman citizens after twenty-five years of service. The British tribal elite would have had extensive lands and considerable wealth. Below them in the social hierarchy were other free landowners, and some of these people appear to have profited from the Roman control of Britain (see the discussion of the villa economy, below). There will also have been considerable numbers of tenant farmers, some perhaps fairly well off and some very poor. In addition, there were probably a considerable number of slaves who were dependent on members of the elite or owned by and employed in the local and central administrations. Slaves will also have been found in households lower in the social scale: there are, for instance, examples of slaves belonging to soldiers.

The agricultural landscape

The landscapes within which these people lived were highly variable. As we have seen, large areas of forest had been cleared over most areas of Britain. Much of the remaining woodland would have been managed to provide timber for building and for the charcoal industry. The landscape would generally have been fairly open, with a good mixture of arable and pasture. Some wetlands were drained, as noted above, and rivers and watercourses were canalized. Some wetland and moorland areas survived across the lowlands (for instance Dartmoor and the Somerset Levels), and these would have been exploited for wildlife and peat. It is estimated that some 4,500 tons of peat were dug from the central Cambridgeshire Fens before the onset of mid-third-century flooding. Extensive areas of moorland existed across the highlands, and wilderness survived on the mountains of the North and West. Much of the high ground over the whole of Britain would have been exploited for seasonal pasture.

Settlement patterns and settlement types

The population of Roman Britain lived scattered throughout this landscape in a wide variety of types of settlement, including towns, small towns, villages, villas, non-villa native settlements, forts and fortresses. The towns, small towns, villas, and forts are considered in other chapters and will not be discussed in detail here. They did, however, form part of the landscape and the military's relationship to urbanism will be addressed briefly.

Military infrastructure

The military and their followers may have formed around 4 per cent of the population of Roman Britain. The size of the armed forces in Britain was out of proportion to the total population and could only be supported because the soldiers were paid centrally by the Roman administration. The Roman army and administration swiftly created the infrastructure for Roman Britain. During the initial period of conquest, roads and forts were established to secure the country within the expanding province. In the lowlands the army swiftly moved on to conquer other areas further to the north and west. The roads that they built were a monumental element of the landscape. They can often still be seen today driving purposefully across the countryside as a series of straight lines. They also cut across the lands of people and communities and presumably severed the traditional lines of communication. For instance, in the Middle Waveney Valley (Norfolk) a Roman road slices through the grain of the existing field systems, ignoring local communities' pattern of fields, woods, and pasture. The Roman army had its own priorities: it was a powerful and aggressive organization that imposed the will of the Roman administration on the people of the lands that it conquered.

In friendly areas of Britain, forts were not necessarily required as the Roman administration would have dealt directly with the pro-Roman tribal leaders. In these cases the army may have negotiated over the land that they required. In unfriendly country, however, the forts would have been forced on the local population and supplies for the army acquired by compulsory purchase. Individual units of the army were followed around by a band of camp followers, including the families of soldiers and traders. These people often established a settlement (*vicus*) outside one or more of the gates of the fort, acting as a focal point for traders and others with services to offer the garrison. Often they remained to establish a new town once the army moved on, and many of the towns of the civilian district seem to have developed in this way (Cirencester and Exeter, for instance). By the end of the first century many of the soldiers were stationed in the highland zone and the army remained there throughout the period of Roman occupation. The forts became permanent settlements that survived into the fourth century and beyond, although military units themselves were sometimes moved around between them. Some forts also existed in the lowlands, for instance the large fort in the provincial capital of London and at Dover the second-century fort of the *classis Britannica* (the Channel fleet). In the third and fourth centuries a range of new forts (often called the forts of the Saxon Shore) were built around the south and east coasts of Britain.

Urban infrastructure

The larger town formed the administrative, social, and economic centres for the *civitas* as a whole, and also had an important role as a market centre for the surrounding population. Imported goods came into Britain from other parts of the empire, and it is likely that the major towns were the primary location for obtaining such goods. Various forms of industry and services were also attracted to the towns early in the period of Roman control. Some towns, notably Bath and Cirencester, seem to have villas clustered around them attracted by the services or the markets for foodstuff or the social and political life.

So-called 'small towns' also developed across Britain. These usually appear to have been unofficial developments, and often occur close to the boundary between the *civitates* and on the new network of roads. Small towns sometimes developed from Iron Age settlements, although others appear to have originated in the Early Roman period. Some small towns may have had administrative roles, but their economic role was probably more important in most cases. Many small towns were little more than nucleated villages, presumably with a market function and often a temple, as with the example of Heybridge in Essex. Usually, small towns have an irregular system of streets suggesting that they developed in an unplanned manner that contrasts with the official foundation (or re-foundation) of the *civitas* capitals. The market at small town sites sometimes encouraged the development of local industry: pottery production, glassworking, and ironworking. It is apparent, however, that Britain remained an agricultural society with only limited urbanism. The estimates above suggest that between 13 and 6 per cent of the population lived in towns (see Table 2). Towns and small towns were not uncommon in the civilian district, but in the North and West urbanism was very limited, with only two or three possible towns to the north of York, none beyond Exeter, the South-West, or in Wales other than the south coast. Urban centres in Roman Britain were small compared to the Mediterranean. The larger towns, such as London, Cirencester, and Verulamium, may have had a population of around 15,000 each, while the average small town might have been the home to a few thousand people.

The rural landscape

The rural population probably formed between 83 and 90 per cent of the people who lived in the Roman province. Beyond the Roman frontier in northern Britain, and most of Wales and the South-West Peninsula, there were no towns or forts and the entire population was rural. Settlements during the Iron Age across Britain were of a variety of forms, but people often lived in roundhouses set within different types of farmstead enclosure. Major changes occurred to the character of the civilian district during the Roman period. However, while the military district became home to thousands of soldiers living in forts, the changes to its native settlements appear rather more subtle than was the case in the lowlands.

Discussions about the rural landscape of the civilian districts of Roman Britain often focus on the definition of the term 'villa'. In written Roman sources a villa is usually the seaside or country estate of a wealthy member of the urban elite. Pliny the Younger, in his letters, describes proudly and affectionately his country house and its gardens. He seems more concerned with pleasure and aesthetics than with economics. We have no literary evidence about the villa's function or ownership in Britain. Only one name survives, *Villa Faustina*, possibly at the site of Scole on the Sussex/Norfolk border. Archaeologists define villas—Romanized farmsteads or country houses—by the evidence of their architectural traces: stone foundations, ceramic- or stone-tiled roofs, mortar floors, mosaic or plain tessellated pavements, under-floor heating, painted wall-plaster, window glass, and bathhouses. Some or all of these occur in any Romanized villa. In contrast to the British roundhouse—made essentially of local materials such as thatch, timber, and clay—the villa required specialist quarrymen, tile-makers, artists and craftsmen of various sorts, and a communications and financial system to support such a major investment and social statement. Villas come in a wide range of shapes and sizes, from a simple rectangular block to corridor houses with wings, and to the even more substantial courtyard houses reminiscent of the great country houses of Georgian England or Ireland. All of these represent the adoption of a Romanized lifestyle. Separate rooms and corridors differentiate the public and private. Guests, business associates, the family, servants, and tenants can be restricted to appropriate areas. Some parts of the building are for entertainment, pleasure, and relaxation; others for work and for meeting outsiders.

Some very early villas are among the most palatial. The Fishbourne complex on the South Coast near Chichester appeared fully-fledged at the height of Roman fashion and taste—an ostentatious showpiece, perhaps built at the Roman government's expense for their local ally and potentate, the leader of the tribe known to the Romans, flatteringly, as the *Regni* ('People of the Kingdom'). A rash of more modest Romanized villas spread across the South-East in the later first century and early second century. Particularly in the territories of the Trinovantes, Atrebates, Catuvellauni, and Dobunni, Romanized buildings were erected, probably by tribal leaders. By the fourth century villas had appeared widely across the countryside of southeastern, central, and north-eastern Britain. The most luxurious, such as Chedworth in the Cotswolds, compare with the wealthiest villas of Italy and Spain. Mosaics decorated with classical myths indicate that the owners were fully integrated into Roman culture. Many villas, however, were workmanlike farms forming an integral part of a market economy, providing the products of mixed agriculture to local towns and regional centres. They were linked into the network of roads, and were supported by the cash economy. The growth of the latter was stimulated not only by its convenience over barter in such a complex society but also by the collection of taxes in cash, requiring even the small farmers to acquire coins to satisfy the collectors of revenue. Some villas specialized: the Shakenoak villa in Oxfordshire in fish-farming, some in the Nene Valley were probably involved in pottery manufacture and metalworking, others along the East Coast in oyster-farming and salt production.

Villa buildings and the agricultural complexes of which they formed part were the centres of agricultural estates. Although we do not know the exact extent of any villa estates in Britain, several attempts have been made to reconstruct the sort of landholding that the villa economy depended upon. Each estate will have included a range of resources, including arable land, pasture, meadow, and woodland. It is likely that the villa-owner aimed to make his or her estate self-sufficient. Sometimes non-villa settlements are located close to villas, and it is likely that those who lived in the non-villa settlement were slaves or tenants of the villa-owning family, as perhaps is suggested at Stanwick in Northamptonshire.

Many of the villas of the civilian district were probably the homes of families that were descended from the Iron Age population. The limited evidence for landownership indicates, however, that some land was owned by landlords who originated overseas. A second-century writing tablet from the Walbrook in London mentions three men who owned a wood in Kent, and all three have names which indicate that their families originated overseas within the western empire (Spain, Gaul, and perhaps Italy). They may have obtained land in Britain and have been living in the province, but the land that they owned must have been taken (or purchased) from the native

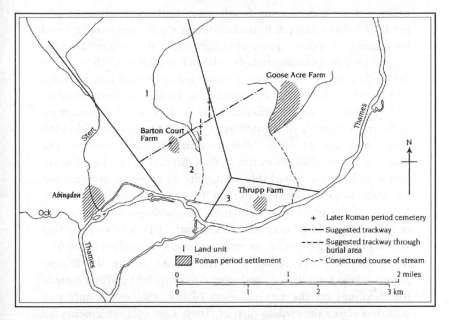

Figure 20 Theoretical approaches to land use have sometimes usefully been combined with physical evidence to suggest the possible layout of estates, as here around the excavated Roman villa at Barton Court Farm, adjacent to the Roman town of Abingdon (Oxon.).

owners. We also know that during the fourth century property in Britain was owned by Melania, a great Roman landowner. These two records of landownership indicate that some land in the civilian district was removed from the ownership of the native Iron Age families who had farmed it for generations. It is also certain that some land in the province will have been owned by the emperor. We have no idea, however, what percentage overall of the landscape of Roman Britain was removed from native ownership.

Turning to the countryside in more general terms, it is evident that no more than, at the very most, 15 per cent of the Roman settlements in the lowland zone were supplied with villa buildings, and the proportion is far lower across much of the highlands, where villas are very rare. Roundhouses, the dominant Iron Age form of dwelling, continued to be built throughout Roman times in many parts of the military district. Across the South many settlements changed as a result of Roman contact. Roundhouses on many sites were replaced by rectangular house types, although many of these rectangular houses are not elaborate enough to be called villas. On other sites in the civilian district roundhouses continued to be built into the third and fourth centuries (as, for instance, at Birdlip in Gloucestershire and Ashton Keynes in Wiltshire). At Birdlip, a small settlement including a number of roundhouses existed by the side of Ermine Street in an area in which villas are generally fairly common. The building of roundhouses in the civilian districts in the Late Roman period indicates a remarkable continuity in domestic architecture. The stress in past accounts of Roman Britain on the gradual 'Romanization' of the provincial population has, perhaps, led to the lack of a serious study of non-villa settlements. It is only recently that archaeologists have begun to realize that the roundhouse forms a major building type across southern Britain during the Roman period. These roundhouses and simple rectangular buildings formed the dwellings on the vast numbers of non-villa settlements that occurred across the civilian district. These non-villa settlements fall into a wide variety of types, from the extensive village-type sites of Cranborne Chase, the Fenlands, and the Upper Thames Valley to the grouped and isolated farms which are common all over the province. These sites are now being excavated in increasing numbers and this is leading to a more informed understanding of the Roman countryside. In some cases these non-villa settlements may have been the homes of tenants and farm workers who farmed land which belonged to the villa owners. In other cases, the residents of the non-villa settlements may have been independent landowners in their own rights. Many non-villa settlements have substantial buildings and enclosures that appear to demonstrate surplus wealth and the excavated remains from these sites sometimes suggests a fairly high standard of living. It is possible, therefore, that not all wealthy Romano-Britons lived in villas.

The locations of imperial estates (properties belonging to the emperor) are known for some parts of the Roman empire, but we are not certain where such estates were sited in Roman Britain. Some of them may have been fairly extensive and others may have been single small units of land. It has been argued that the Fenlands of East Anglia formed a vast imperial estate. The emperor would have owned the land but the local people—who lived in a dense series of non-villa settlements across the Fens—probably worked as tenants of the emperor. It has been argued that the settlement at Stonea Grange (Cambridgeshire), with its elaborate and substantial tower, may have been the administrative centre of this estate. The evidence for the substantial amount of investment in the drainage of the Fens at this time may well suggest a major input of public investment but, in the absence of conclusive evidence from inscriptions or literary sources, it is still not certain that the area actually formed an imperial estate. It has alternatively been argued that the people of the Fenlands were small-scale landowners who did have surplus wealth but invested it in different ways from the villa-owners.

In other areas of the civilian district, villas appear to be uncommon, for instance the gravel terraces of the Upper Thames Valley. Here a dense distribution of non-villa settlements occurs. It has been suggested for this area too that there was an imperial estate, but the same argument applies that the people who lived here may not have chosen to use the villa as a symbol of social status. They may have invested their surplus wealth in other ways, for instance the owner-ship of cattle. Within the Upper Thames Valley, a substantial non-villa settlement has been excavated at Claydon Pike (Gloucestershire). This was a substantial and elaborate settlement with considerable evidence of surplus wealth. The site also produced some Roman mili-tary finds, and it has been suggested that it formed part of an estate that was run by the Roman army to supply units with horses. If confirmed, this could support the identification of this part of south-ern Britain as imperial estate. Areas of the civilian district that do have a dense distribution of villas include the Gloucestershire and Oxfordshire Cotswolds, and the area of Hertfordshire around Veru-lamium. It is possible that the regional patterning that is evident in the distribution of villas across the civilian district is the result of people across Roman Britain choosing to live in distinct ways in the various regions.

In the North and West—and outside the province in the Free North—the nature of the landscape was very different. Ken and Petra Dark have suggested that a 'native landscape' survived in the high-land zone. We have seen that the military continued to have a pres-ence in the highlands, and it would appear that this presence may have inhibited the growth of towns and villas, although a few examples are known. The nature of the settlements varies from region to region but the typical native settlement across Wales, Cornwall, and the North (northern England and Scotland) was enclosed by an earth or stone bank and a ditch. The houses on these sites were often round and stone-built, so that they often survive in good condition. Particularly impressive examples occur in North Wales and Cornwall, while the brochs and duns of Scotland are monumental examples of roundhouses.

In some areas on the edge of the highlands, settlements developed in a way which was comparable to the situation in the lowlands. Villas are known in small numbers from the South West, northern Wales, and northern England (particularly in the North-East); they are not known outside the province in what is now Scotland. It is common during excavation on settlement sites in the highland zone to find 'Roman' objects (pottery and coins). This may suggest a good deal of trade between the native population of some areas of the highlands and Roman merchants. In Cornwall and North Wales in particular, many sites produce considerable quantities of Roman goods. In northern England and southern Scotland, however, Roman objects are far less common on native sites and it appears that trade may have been less significant. Indeed, the occasional coin and piece of pottery on sites in these areas may indicate collection of objects by locals from abandoned fort sites rather than trade.

Industry and the landscape

It is likely that one of the reasons that the Roman empire wished to conquer and control Britain was to gain more direct access to its mineral wealth, and it is significant that extractive industries developed swiftly. There is evidence for the exploitation of Mendip tin by 49. The army was initially heavily involved in exploiting metal deposits. Extensive industrial sites are know to have exploited tin and silver at Charterhouse-on-Mendip (Somerset) and gold in Wales at Dolaucothi (Dyfed), while the *classis Britannica* was involved in the extraction and processing of iron in the Weald of Kent in the first two centuries of Roman rule.

Some industries were fairly substantial in scale. The industrial workings at Charterhouse were associated with a Roman fort, as was the site at Dolaucothi. Both these mining sites had major complexes of mineral extraction remains and associated working; those at Dolaucothi including a major water-driven mill complex comparable to examples in the great state mines of Iberia. The Roman government required metals in large quantities—the army for their military equipment and for fort construction, the administration for buildings and other civil works and for the production of coinage. Considerable quantities of lead and other metals would also have been required during the development of the urban infrastructure in Britain, particularly in the later first and second centuries AD. Sites such as Charterhouse and Dolaucothi illustrate the scale of Roman mining in Britain; this exceeded anything that had been seen in the Iron Age. Stone was also extracted in large quantities in Britain to build roads, forts, military frontiers (Hadrian's Wall and the Antonine Wall), monumental public buildings, town walls, and villas. Some stone quarries have been located. A series are known along Hadrian's Wall, for instance. However, the Roman origin of many quarries will have been lost as a result of later extraction on the same sites.

Industrial manufacture was also important, and the scale of industry increased during the early period of the Roman conquest and control. The Roman army in Britain required access to a range of industrially produced goods, including pottery, glass, and metalwork. Although much of the material would have been imported into the country in the first few years of Roman conquest, other goods came to be made in Britain. The army produced some of its own goods, but a lucrative market also appears to have developed to supply the army, particularly in pottery. In addition to the demands of the Roman army and the administration, the local elite in Britain had grown accustomed prior to the Roman Conquest to a range of goods that were brought to Britain, including wine and fish sauce, high-quality glass, pottery, and metalwork. New methods of potting, including the potting wheel and harder fabrics, had been introduced to the South and East of Britain prior to the invasion. The demand for a range of goods increased after the Conquest as 'Roman'-style material culture became increasingly common on settlement sites throughout the lowland zone. Many of the items that occur on settlements were produced in the province. The pottery industry has been particularly thoroughly studied, but substantial manufacturing industries produced tile, metalwork, and glass throughout the Roman period. New types of kilns were introduced for potting and tile-manufacture, and new technologies developed around glass-making and metalworking. The scale of the industrial revolution that occurred at this time would appear to have been limited, however, from the restricted number of people that were not directly involved in agriculture (Table 2, above): Roman Britain remained a primarily agricultural society with only a limited proportion of the population involved in industry and trade.

The extent of the impact of industry on the environment and landscape of Roman Britain is uncertain. In some highland areas extensive areas of mineral extraction existed, although many of these have been damaged or removed by later extractive industries. It is likely that most of the Roman extractive industry was not on a comparable scale to modern industrial landscapes, although the remains at Charterhouse and Dolaucothi are impressive. In addition, major pottery production centres developed in many areas, for instance the Oxfordshire industry and around Water Newton in Cambridgeshire. Local people would have gained employment and money from an involvement in industry. On the local environment, however, these industries may have had a limited impact, as wood for fuel perhaps came into rather short supply. On the other hand, the fumes and other pollution produced by industrial processes may have proved to be a health problem for some who worked in industry and to their neighbours.

In the first two centuries of Roman control of Britain, many of the manufacturing industries appear to have been closely related to the towns. Early pottery production often appears to have occurred close to the *civitas* capital, presumably partly to exploit the market of the town. Through time, much of the pottery production moved away from the major towns and into the periphery of the tribal territory, perhaps in search of wood and other raw materials that were becoming scarce near the urban centres which were also using them in quantity for other purposes. We have seen that metal extraction was organized through the army in the early period. As time passed, leases on mine sites may have been let to private individuals. In the case of pottery, it is generally assumed that much of the production was carried out by local manufacturers, but certain major pottery industries developed which supplied the army, notably the makers of Black

Burnished Ware and Mancetter *mortaria*. It is not known how these industries were run, nor the extent to which the army itself was involved. Overall, much of the industrial production of Roman Britain may have been carried out at a local level, perhaps as a result of private initiative.

The sacred landscape

It has recently been suggested that the people who lived in the landscape of Roman Britain viewed it as sacred. The Roman author Pliny the Elder records that the people of the classical Mediterranean region considered the land and sea to represent divine spirits and it is possible that similar attitudes existed in prehistoric and Roman Britain. This may suggest that the local population viewed the act of conquest of the land by the Roman army as disrupting its sacred quality. The conquest and domination of Britain meant that traditional lines of communication and the meeting places of the community were disturbed by a range of alien monumental structures, including the roads, forts, and towns which were built by the Roman army and administration. In addition, we have seen that land may also have been removed from the ownership of the local population and given to people who had come into the island from overseas.

A tradition of the sacred character of the landscape is reflected in the evidence for the use of certain natural places and inherited ancient monuments during the Iron Age and in the period of Roman rule. Particular springs, wells, and caves may well have been treated as sacred by the local populations, regarding natural and semi-natural features as the dwelling-places of spirits. Artefacts were often deposited in these places, and the major temple complexes at Bath in Avon and Uley in Gloucestershire developed close to important springs. In addition, monuments constructed by earlier people sometimes continued to have significance at this time. Roman-period burials and other finds are fairly common on the sites of Neolithic and Bronze Age barrows. The most dramatic example, perhaps is a barrow at Bisley in Gloucestershire which produced six Roman altars. Roman temples sometimes came to be built in close proximity to monuments derived from earlier periods. At Haddenham in

Cambridgeshire a temple was built on top of a Bronze Age round barrow, while other temple buildings commonly occur within Iron Age hill-forts, as at Maiden Castle (Dorset). It is possible that the evidence for the Roman altars at barrows in Gloucestershire and the construction of temples on or within ancient monuments relates to the probability that these were significant locations within the landscape at which people met at special times. At Uffington Castle, close to the Uffington White Horse in Oxfordshire, a concentration of Roman finds within the hill-fort probably represents a significant meeting place for the people of the local community, though at this site there is no evidence to indicate that a permanent temple was constructed.

Temple structures started to be built in the Middle to Late Iron Age in Britain, and a range of temple sites are known across the highlands and lowlands during the Roman period. The temples that were built in the lowlands derived from at least two basic plans (rectangular and circular), and these possibly had native origins in the Iron Age. The temple-building tradition extended to the northern edge of the Roman province, as the Roman army and its associated civil population also built temple structures, but the idea does not appear to have been adopted by the native societies in northern Britain outside the province.

It is possible to attempt to distinguish a hierarchy of ritual sites. At a local level, rituals may have defined certain points in the landscape as significant, as in the case of the wells, caves, and barrows discussed above. Other significant finds are often made within settlement sites. For instance, at South Shields Roman fort at the mouth of the Tyne a deposit in a ditch outside the west gate produced a number of animal skulls, part of the head of a statue, and two fragments of pottery lion-heads which had formed spouts on *mortaria*. Some temple buildings appear to have related to single communities, as in the case of Claydon Pike in Gloucestershire, while others probably had rather wider local followings, for example the temple associated with the small town at Heybridge in Essex. Certain cults associated with local places developed into important sanctuaries, as at Coventina's Well at Carrawburgh on Hadrian's Wall and at Uley in Gloucestershire.

At Uley the temple developed close to a healing spring, while the origins of the temple-complex at Bath were presumably similar. Bath became a highly important sanctuary, and had one of the few major classical-style temple buildings that are know to have been built in Britain. The temple site at Gosbecks (Essex) is associated with a theatre, and a similar relationship has recently been claimed at Verulamium (St Albans) between the temple at Folly Lane and the theatre. Bath and Gosbecks were presumably tribal sanctuaries, and drew worshippers from far afield. The temple at Frilford (Oxfordshire) was located close to a boundary between the *civitates* of the Atrebates and the Dobunni. It was surrounded by an extensive settlement, including a substantial amphitheatre. Again, it is likely that this represented a tribal or pan-tribal sanctuary, and there may be similar sites which are yet to be located. At the top of the hierarchy of religious sites was the temple to the Emperor Claudius at Colchester in Essex, a massive building of regular classical form constructed prior to AD 60. It was the focus for the provincial cult, and perhaps for meetings of all the *civitates* of Britain. It is of interest that this cult centre was created only a few kilometres from the native sanctuary at Gosbecks noted above. Perhaps a visit to the centre of Roman worship within the *colonia* required a prior call at the traditional tribal site.

The end of the Roman interlude

The ending of Roman control caused major changes to the landscape of Roman Britain. Accounts of the end of Roman Britain, however, often make these changes appear very sudden, while the process of change may have appeared very gradual to the people who lived in Britain at the time. One major factor was that the collapse of Roman rule caused the ending of the money supply to Britain. Coinage, as we have seen, was vital to the urban system and the villa economy—it was also vital to the maintenance of the army. With the withdrawal of the Roman administration, the money supply to Britain dried up.

Major changes had occurred to the larger towns and to some of the small towns in the third and fourth centuries as they were provided with circuits of town walls. These are often considered to have been defensive—a sign of troubled times. However, they were also a symbol of civic pride, and were substantial and well-built features of the urban landscape. Other public buildings in many of the towns ceased to be repaired during this period, and it has been suggested that many towns only survived into the fourth century as 'administrative villages' as their marketing and social roles fell away. There is some evidence for trade and industry in Roman towns in the late fourth century, but this falls away as the monetary economy collapsed at the start of the fifth. Nevertheless, despite the changes in the towns of the province, urban centres survived into the fifth century and in some cases beyond, as in the case of Wroxeter in Shropshire.

The collapse of the money economy caused the ending of the major pottery and tile industries as these depended on cash to operate. Pottery and tile ceased to be readily available in the towns and the countryside. The economic basis of the villa economy was similarly destroyed as the demand for surplus agricultural goods was reduced. As a result, villa-owners did not have the surplus wealth to maintain their luxury houses. In addition, wealthy rural settlements may have become subject to raiding by bandits as the maintenance of law and order within the province collapsed. Some rural sites appear, on the other hand, to have continued to be occupied into the Anglo-Saxon period. The pollen evidence is unclear, but does not seem to indicate much change in the intensity of agriculture or a major regeneration of woodland. There may thus have been a good degree of continuity in the nature of the agricultural use of the countryside at the same time as the distinctively Roman elements of the villa system ended. In the military districts some forts appear to have been abandoned during Later Roman times. Elsewhere, however, during the collapse of Roman rule soldiers appear to have continued to live where they had formerly been stationed. It has been suggested that, when the Roman administration ceased to be able to pay the troops, soldiers at some forts supplemented their incomes by increased taxation of the local populations. This may indicate that army units had developed local loyalties, and that quasi-military units survived into sub-Roman Britain at sites such as Birdoswald on Hadrian's Wall (Cumbria) and elsewhere in the North and West.

Change in Late and post-Roman Britain may have been gradual, but the outcome was that by the end of the fifth century AD the landscape of Britain no longer contained the distinctive features that had made it Roman. A few towns and small towns lived on as small villages sheltering inside their Late Roman defences. The major urban public buildings and urban infrastructure had collapsed. In the countryside the villas and temples were falling down, although the estates continued to be cultivated by local communities. In the military zone, some forts were used by local groups who recalled their military origin, and perhaps also still felt some loyalty to Rome. The forts themselves were by this time looking more like native settlements, although elements of their original Roman form may still have showed through. Into this environment new peoples were coming from regions to the north and north-east over the seas. The landscape of Britain was swiftly changing, and by the end of the fifth century can no longer be considered Roman.

Figure 21 This mass of Late Roman plate from the hill-fort at Traprain Law in south-eastern Scotland outside the frontier may have been loot from Britain or Gaul, but as some individual items are cut up, folded, or crushed it might represent payment in precious metal by weight to tribesmen outside the frontier for political or military purposes.

6

The edge of the world: the imperial frontier and beyond

David J. Breeze

Caesar in 55 BC received a longer triumph for his foray into Britain
than for his conquest of Gaul. Standing on the Channel coast in AD
43, the army of the Emperor Claudius mutinied at the order to cross
the ocean. In the fourth century, after the accumulation of over three
centuries of detailed knowledge, Roman writers still treated the land
beyond Hadrian's Wall as if it were a mystical country inhabited by
strange and exotic peoples. This is particularly disturbing, for all our
written sources are Roman (or Greek) in origin and are not balanced
by any observations from the indigenous inhabitants of Britain. Even
the only reference to the locals ('Brittunculi') in the most important
new material discovered in the last thirty years, the Vindolanda
writing tablets, is open to interpretation. Mainly concerned with
internal army matters, Vindolanda has not yet provided a document
that provides a strategic overview of the northern frontier, but we
should not be surprised at that. By far the greatest amount of paperwork undertaken by any bureaucracy relates to the minutiae of
administration—orders and receipts, casework and consents—not
strategic planning, and in this the Vindolanda archive is
representative.

Roman Britain, however, is not devoid of statements of purpose.
Suetonius wrote baldly that Claudius invaded Britain because he
required a triumph. Agricola, stated Tacitus, invaded Caledonia

because the northern tribes were acting in a threatening manner. Hadrian, according to his much later biographer, built his wall to divide the Romans from the barbarians. Antoninus Pius, we are informed in an otherwise enigmatic statement, conquered the Brigantes because 'they had attacked the Genounian district which is subject to Rome'. Severus invaded Caledonia because he wanted to take his sons away from the fleshpots of Rome, the army needed stiffening, he himself liked fighting—and because the locals were troublesome: his aim according to Cassius Dio was to conquer the rest [of the island]. In the course of the fourth century it would appear that the Romans lost the initiative and became essentially reactive to external invasions and pressures, be it from Picts, Scots, Saxons, Franks, or the unlocated Attacotti. Rome's aim became to hold what it already possessed or, as we are informed by Ammianus Marcellinus in the case of Count Theodosius, recover what it had temporarily lost.

Archaeology has an essential role in helping us understand the contacts between Rome and the peoples on both sides of the frontier. This survey will encompass not only Rome's relations with the Caledonians but also Ireland, and compare the areas immediately within the northern frontier with the other parts of Britain on the periphery of the empire. Where appropriate 'evidence by analogy' will be used. Here, too, is one of the most significant aspects of the Vindolanda writing tablets: the basic similarities between them and documents from the eastern frontier of the empire validate the use of the eastern material to help illuminate the British frontier.

Ancient geography

Britain may have been known to the Greeks from at least the sixth century BC through voyaging from Marseilles. The voyage of Pytheas (another Massiliot), probably sometime between 322 and 285 BC, is better recorded, though it excited incredulity. It would appear that from Cornwall he sailed completely round Britain, which he described as a triangle. Pytheas was informed that six day's sail to the north of Britain lay the island of *Thule*, probably either western Norway or Iceland.

Caesar knew that Britain was an island, while a contemporary of Claudius, Pomponius Mela, recorded that there were thirty Orkney islands and seven *Haemodae* (probably Shetland). Pliny the Elder, who died in 79 before the Agricolan campaigns into Caledonia, added the Inner and Outer Hebrides to the list of islands, and he was the first to mention the Caledonian Forest, his contemporary Lucan recording the Caledonii.

Agricola's campaigns, including the voyage of his fleet in the final season, will have added further information relating to geographical features, tribes, and place names, conveniently recorded in Ptolemy's *Geography* produced sixty years later. At the same time the historian Plutarch recorded another official expedition led by Demetrius of Tarsus, who had been commissioned by the emperor to sail to the nearest of the islands around Britain and make enquiries and observations. Demetrius recorded that there were many deserted islands scattered around Britain, some inhabited by holy men: he probably explored the Hebrides.

In 81 or 82 Agricola drew up his army facing Ireland, and Tacitus was later to record that Roman information on its approaches and harbours was tolerably well known from the merchants who traded there. This is supported by Ptolemy's *Geography*, in which the amount of material on the interior of Ireland is in sharp contrast to that available on Scotland beyond the Great Glen.

The amount of geographical information available to the Romans about the periphery of the empire in Britain was not inconsiderable. It is all the more ironic therefore, that some of these places, including the Caledonian Forest and *Thule*, which the Romans usually but erroneously equated with Shetland, became bywords for far-off mystical places.

The location of the frontier

The frontier history of the province is covered elsewhere in this volume. Here, it may be noted that for most of the life of Roman Britain the frontier lay on the Tyne–Solway line. This was effectively the northern boundary of the province from 43, throughout the years that the Brigantes formed a client kingdom. In the 70s the tribes of the Welsh peninsula were conquered, and subsequently Agricola pushed north, presumably aiming to eliminate the frontier by completing the conquest of the island, but his northernmost gains lasted less than ten years. The Antonine advance was of rather longer duration but still only twenty years (*c.*142–*c.*160). The Severan foray, again with the intention of completing the conquest of the island, was over in three or four years (208–*c.*211). Other Roman expeditions beyond the frontier appear to have been of a reactive or punitive nature only. In the main, all these expeditions appear to have been confined to eastern Scotland. Agricola, for example, probably did not venture beyond the Great Glen except by sea—though he may have reconnoitred up Strathspey into the Highlands. Agricola, according to Tacitus, and Severus, according to Dio, reached the end of the island, though where exactly is not specified. So far as we know, no Roman soldier set foot in Ireland.

The causes of war

Relations between Rome and its neighbours were not on the same basis as those between modern sovereign states. Rome saw itself as free to intervene beyond the frontier as it wished to ensure that its best interests were maintained. Certainly during the early years a good case can be made for Rome following a general policy of expansion in Britain, though at a rather staccato pace, with the aim of conquering the whole island. Even in the early third century, the Emperor Septimius Severus saw himself as 'expander of Roman dominion' (*propagator imperii*).

The known examples of Roman official activity beyond the frontier in Britain are all in relationship to warfare, with the sole exception of the voyage of Demetrius of Tarsus. As the Romans liked a *casus belli* to justify their aggressive activities, it is not always possible to be certain about the real circumstances behind their intervention. Thus, in 82 'Agricola fearing the threatening movement of the Caledonian tribes, invaded their territory'. Yet the Caledonians only prepared for war because a strong Roman force arrived on their borders having conquered their neighbours. It is impossible to believe other than that this was offered as a justification for the action which Rome intended to take in order to pursue its expansionist policy.

Sixty years later, it is possible that the 'Genounian incident' quoted by Pausanias masks a similar justification for the actions of Antoninus Pius, which can most plausibly be explained as resulting from his own need for a triumph exactly as Claudius had a century before. Certainly Fronto recorded that the emperor controlled the actions of his army from his palace as the helmsman controls the ship, while this was the only time that Antoninus Pius accepted the acclamation *Imperator* ('Conqueror') after his accession.

In the early third century again a local reason—that there was a rebellion among the northern barbarians which was so serious that either more troops were required or the presence of the emperor— was offered by Herodian for the invasion of the territory of the Caledonians and Maeatae. However, it is interesting to note that Herodian used a similar phrase a few years later to justify the presence of the emperor on another frontier suggesting that this was a *topos* (conventional element in such accounts, not necessarily true in any particular instance), while Cassius Dio offers several other reasons for the intervention which have nothing to do with the local situation, as we have seen.

Yet, in spite of its power, Rome failed to complete the conquest of the island. In the 80s, the Flavian expansion came to an abrupt end in the face of disasters on the Lower Danube, as a result of which reinforcements were demanded from Britain. In the second century, during Gibbon's 'Golden Age', Antoninus Pius chose a more limited advance in Britain than seeking to further unfinished business and complete the conquest of the island. Severus, according to Cassius Dio, came to complete the conquest of the island but his untimely demise at York prevented consolidation of his conquests and led to their abandonment by his sons. Thus ended the last attempt to eradicate the frontier in Britain. As a result, Rome was faced with having to live with a land frontier and the necessity of using other methods of controlling events beyond it.

The nature of the frontier

The nature of the frontier altered over the centuries. Indeed, in earlier centuries in the Roman empire there was no boundary which could be recognized on the ground, it was simply the outer border of the city states or tribes who formed the empire. These cities and tribes did not require garrisons to enforce loyalty.

After the loss of three legions in the Varian disaster of AD 9 in Germany—which followed closely on the Illyrian Revolt in the Balkans—the Augustan advance halted. Tiberius was content to follow the advice of his predecessor Augustus not to expand the empire. It was under Claudius that, ironically, we see the first results of a generation of lassitude. First, it would appear, individual units came to be spread along the empire's boundary: we can first recognize this on the Lower Rhine. Then in the 80s we can recognize the addition to the outermost line of forts of other features designed to aid frontier control, towers and fortlets. These remained, however, 'open' frontiers, and it was Hadrian who took the next step of adding a physical barrier in the form of a fence, turf rampart, or stone wall. In the first plan for Hadrian's Wall, there were no forts on the wall line itself. These physical arrangements allow us to recognize the different functions of the troops in the forts behind the Wall— frontier defence—and those on the Wall in the milecastles and turrets—frontier control. The move of forts onto Hadrian's Wall blurred that distinction, and the two aspects were further blurred on the Antonine Wall where forts and rampart, defence and control were closely integrated, at least physically. This was underlined by the increasing density of forts on the line. The first move, some decades earlier, had been to shorten the normal distance between forts—20 km (14 miles)—by placing a unit in between the forts on the outermost line. This 10-km (7-mile) pattern can still be seen on Hadrian's Wall. This spacing also seems to have governed the pattern on the Antonine Wall which, in the first scheme, entailed forts at 8-mile intervals with fortlets at each mile between. In the second plan for the Antonine Wall the distance between forts was further reduced to 3.5 km along most of its length. The reoccupation of Hadrian's Wall did not see a move to repeat that close density; rather there was a return to the concentration of troops in individual forts and the abandonment or reduction in importance of many of the minor structures. The 'frontier' was not a single line but a multi-layered arrangement. To the north of Hadrian's Wall lay four outpost forts. Behind the barrier lay many hinterland forts, focused on the main roads through the wall at Newcastle, at the Port Gate, and at Stanwix. These were supported by the legions well to the south at York and Chester.

Frontier regulations

Hadrian, we are informed by his fourth-century biographer, built his wall to divide the Romans from the barbarians. Divide, it certainly did. Hadrian's Wall, and the briefly held Antonine Wall, formed distinct barriers from sea to sea. Yet neither was impermeable. Both appear to have been erected with considerable provision for movement across the frontier, for each seems to have been provided with gates at mile intervals, though the lack of evidence for causeways across ditches outside milecastles and fortlets on both frontiers raises a question as to how such movement might have taken place. The history of Hadrian's Wall suggests that there was an over-provision of crossing points. While few milecastles are known to have had their gates blocked completely, many were narrowed later in the second century so that they were only usable by pedestrians and not wheeled traffic as in the original plan. Nor is it clear for whom the gates were provided. Little evidence survives for trade across the frontier. Perhaps they were provided for the use of local farmers moving their beasts between different pastures. Possibly, however, their main purpose was not civilian but military, to facilitate the movement of the army in the frontier area.

We know that on other frontiers regulations governed the movement of people into the empire. They could only enter unarmed, under guard, by day, and upon payment of a fee; on one frontier at least they could only trade in specified market places. In 70 the Tencteri of Germany requested restoration of their traditional rights of free movement and settlement on each side of the Rhine, presumably abrogated during the recent civil war, and forced the Roman *colonia* at Cologne to repeal all local taxes and restrictions on trade.

It seems probable that similar regulations operated in Britain, and that customs duties were payable on crossing the frontier. There is, of course, considerable evidence for trade between Rome and its neighbours elsewhere, especially on the eastern frontier. Perhaps of more immediate relevance are the references to soldiers obtaining corn from beyond the Danube in 105, and to Marcus Aurelius restricting trade on the Middle Danube. Also under Marcus, laws forbade the export of iron, wheat, and salt to the enemy. Yet not only is trade into Britain from the north and west rarely possible to recognize archaeologically, but the only Caledonian known by name within the province—Lossio Veda, who erected an altar at Colchester—was probably a soldier, as he dedicated it to Mars Medocius and the Victory of the Emperor.

Treaties

Treaties existed on the British frontier. In 197, we are informed that the Caledonians broke their promises—presumably their treaty with the Romans. In 209, Severus concluded peace with the Caledonians and Maeatae, although they subsequently revolted; and after his father's death in 211, Caracalla signed a new treaty. In 367, the Scots and Picts ignored agreements made with Rome and attacked the frontier. It seems likely that throughout most of the Roman period treaties governed relations between Rome and its northern neighbours.

Cassius Dio provides some details of the contents of the treaties concluded with the German tribes north of the Danube in the 170s and 180s. The tribes could only assemble at certain designated places, where they could only meet under the supervision of a Roman officer. Settlements were forbidden within a certain distance from the Danube, and tribute was payable to Rome. Only one of these conditions might be recognizable archaeologically—the absence of settlements in a zone immediately to the north of the frontier—but there seems to be no such negative evidence from Britain, though the nature of archaeological evidence does not allow certainty about the continuity or otherwise of settlements throughout the Roman period. It has, however, been argued that meeting places similar to those on the Danube existed north of Hadrian's Wall in the third century. Unfortunately, the evidence is open to different interpretations. The seventh-century *Ravenna Cosmography*, a list of places in the known world, includes a heading 'various *loca*' in Britain. The problem is whether *loca* is being used to mean just 'places', or in a specific sense to mean 'meeting places' as mentioned by Cassius Dio in referring to locations beyond the Danube agreed by treaty. The north British places include the *locus Maponi*, *locus Manavi*, *locus Dannoni*, the *Segloes*, and *Tava*. The last is presumably the River Tay, but the *Dannoni* would appear to be the Dumnonii of Ptolemy and the *Segloes* his Selgovae, two tribes of southern Scotland. The *locus Maponi* is the 'place of Maponus', a local god, whose name survives today in Lochmaben and the Clochmabenstane which stands on the north shore of the Solway near Gretna. A stone also acts as a reminder of the *Manavi*, the Clackmannanstane, and that name also survives in Slamannan, both at the head of the Forth Estuary. But are these meeting places operating under treaty arrangements and under the watchful eye of Roman soldiers, or simply a mixed bag of locations? The former interpretation is attractive but we cannot be certain.

On the Continent, literary sources demonstrate that the Romans intervened to support particular kings or tribal factions, but support for any states, kings, or chiefs can only be inferred—not proven—north of Hadrian's Wall. Traprain Law offers a particular example. This major hill-fort in East Lothian lay in the territory of the Votadini. The relative lack of Roman forts in their territory (they did exist at High Rochester and Inveresk, for example) and the continuing occupation of the hill-fort throughout most of the Roman period, coupled with the high quality of the Roman objects found at the site, has led to the suggestion that this state was pro-Roman, that it may have had a 'favoured nation' treaty with Rome, or was perhaps a client state. The late fourth- or early fifth-century treasure found on the site, however, poses a peculiar problem. All of the 120 or more silver bowls, dishes, cups, flagons and spoons were cut up, crushed, or broken. Is this material better interpreted as part of a subsidy paid to the tribal leaders or as their loot from a raid or raids into the empire? Unfortunately, we know little about the history of the objects while the context of their final deposition does not necessarily have much to tell us about the mechanics that caused them to come to northern Britain.

Rome might support its treaties and relationships through subsidies (or bribes, depending on one's point of view). High-class Roman artefacts and coin hoards north of the frontier have been interpreted as such diplomatic gifts or subsidies, but they are few in number. Only three glass vessels (one from Aberdeenshire and two from Orkney) might be interpreted in this way, though it is also possible that such items were purchased from Roman traders. Coin hoards may be a better pointer towards the existence of subsidies, bribes, or straightforward payment: in 197 the Roman governor had to purchase peace and the return of prisoners of war from the Maeatae. Several coin hoards in Scotland date to the late second and early third centuries and may relate to this action or to the Caracallan settlement. Yet, in addition, hoards dating to the late third and the first half of the fourth century have been found well beyond Hadrian's Wall.

Rome clearly did not rely upon treaties or subsidies alone to maintain control over the lands beyond Hadrian's Wall. It might retain a physical presence through the basing of troops in forts north of the wall. In the first plan for Hadrian's Wall, three outpost forts were established in the west, at Bewcastle, Netherby, and Birrens. Intended from the first, it seems possible that the purpose of the regiments based there was to protect those members of the Brigantes who had been isolated from their fellow countrymen in the province by the construction of the Wall. It was probably in the 180s that a major change took place to these dispositions. Birrens, the most westerly fort was abandoned, and two new bases were established to the north of the eastern sector of the wall along Dere Street. These were at Risingham and High Rochester, which had the distinction of being the most northerly known fort in the Roman empire for over 100 years (though for a time there was almost certainly at least one outpost further north near Jedburgh). Each of these two eastern forts was the base of a thousand-strong mixed infantry and cavalry unit, one of the largest regiments in the provincial army and also one of the rarest, as there are only five of this type known in Britain. It has been suggested that two more such units were based in the western outpost forts, but the evidence is not clear. Additional troops at the eastern forts were scouts (at both) and an irregular unit at Risingham. Netherby was called 'Fort of the Scouts' (*Castra Exploratorum*) which may be an indication of its garrison. We can only presume that the function of these soldiers was to patrol southern Scotland and maintain surveillance over the tribes perhaps as far north as the Tay. These scouts were presumably the ancestors of those abolished in the aftermath of the 'Barbarian Conspiracy' of 367, when the 'areani' betrayed the Roman positions to the enemy, the Picts.

An argument has been advanced that after 367 the Romans replaced the scouting arrangements with a series of buffer states north of the Wall. This hypothesis was primarily based on the Roman names of the rulers of these kingdoms supported by the interpretation of the name of one, Patern Pesrut, as Patern of the Red Cloak which, it was argued, indicated the gift of Roman insignia. This thesis, however, has not found favour beyond students of Roman Britain. Doubt has been cast on the value of the relevant literary sources, while it has been suggested that the names could equally indicate adoption of Christianity, not imperial establishment. It has also been pointed out that Patern is more likely to be 'of the red shirt', not red cloak. Red is a common dye at Vindolanda, while purple was the colour of imperial investiture, as we know, for example, through the inauguration of Clovis as king of the Franks. The lack of Roman artefacts north of the Wall in the late fourth century might also argue against continuing friendly contact across the frontier.

There were occasions when the treaties failed to keep the peace other than in 197 and 367. The commander of the Sixth Legion erected an altar at Kirksteads 5 km west of Carlisle, probably in the late second century, to record his thanks for successful actions beyond the Wall. To the east, at Corbridge, a prefect recorded slaughtering a band of 'Corionotatae', but whether these were members of an unattested tribe or a band of brigands, is uncertain. An undated tombstone at Ambleside, 50 km south of the Wall, perhaps erected in the fourth century, commemorates one or two soldiers killed in the fort by the enemy.

The army

A substantial Roman army was maintained in Britain. In the early second century, this included three legions, each about 4,800 strong and formed of Roman citizens, and over 50 auxiliary units (originally 'support' drawn from the allies of Rome), a total paper strength of over 40,000, though documents suggest that units might be up to 25 per cent below strength. In the second half of the third century, this army was much reduced in size. Many of the forts in northern England appear to have been abandoned. In the fourth century, the army was reinforced by new units, based in northern England and on the Saxon Shore, while at the very end of the century a field army was stationed in the island.

It may be that the army was maintained at such a strength in the second century because it had to protect the province from a powerful enemy. Certainly, there are many references to trouble on the northern frontier and the best generals of the day were sent to govern the province. The decline in army strength during the years which we believe were peaceful—and its reinforcement at a time when the Picts and Scots were growing in power and menace—might be taken to support such a conclusion. However, the fact that the Caledonians and their allies were unconquered (rather than that they were unconquerable) might in itself have led to the continuation of a significant army in Britain, especially since the province was relatively isolated as it was an island. In contrast, the South-West Peninsula of England was conquered, and it was then possible to remove all troops from the area. Most units based in Wales were similarly withdrawn after the tribes were subjugated. With the construction of Hadrian's Wall and the Antonine Wall further units were withdrawn. It is possible that the light garrison left in Wales was primarily concerned with control of mining.

It is useful, also, to compare Britain to another peripheral part of Europe, namely Spain. The conquest of the Iberian Peninsula had taken two hundred years. A similar stretch of time from 43 would take Britain into the middle of the third century, a time of civil war and chaos when the tide of history had turned against the empire and expansion. In short, the invasion of Roman Britain occurred too late in the life of the empire for the task to be completed, and this time lag was compounded by the even greater distance of northern Scotland from Rome.

Supplies

The Roman army had a voracious appetite for food, medicines, arms and armour, pottery, leather, and many other items, including stone, lime, timber, and turf for building. Wherever possible, goods were obtained locally, but the provision of supplies in Britain was exacerbated by the location of the army in the less fertile and, from the perspective of Rome, peripheral parts of the island. It may be noted that most forts were placed in relation to the better farm land and only located elsewhere for strategic reasons, to control routes, for example, as at Hardknott and Low Borrow Bridge, or in Wales, perhaps, in order to supervise the mines. In the centuries before the Conquest, farming seems to have expanded in northern Britain—at least the pollen evidence showing intensive destruction of the tree-cover suggests as much. This may have aided local supply of the army—and the provision of turf for fort ramparts—but it also forced the use of substandard timber for construction: alder, for example, instead of oak and roundwood instead of squared timbers in the second century. When it came to other goods Britain itself could not meet all the requirements of the army, and a wide variety of items, including wine, spices, and pottery were imported from the Continent.

While some goods were purchased, others might be obtained through requisition or taxation. The normal method of supply was through requisition at set prices, which might be more advantageous to the seller than the purchaser: this method is described by Tacitus in the *Agricola*. Taxation was normally paid in cash, being collected by the local cities. In two cases, in frontier areas, we know that taxes could be paid in kind: the Frisii paid in ox-hides and the Batavi through recruits. It is possible that taxes were paid in similar fashion in areas of Britain where there was no monetary economy. The only documentary hint at taxation in the frontier zone of Britain appears in an inscription recording T. Haterius Nepos, *censito[r] Brittonum Anavion[ens(ium)]*, in the reign of Trajan, and who is now presumably to be equated with the man of the same name mentioned on a Vindolanda writing tablet of about 100. Nepos would appear to have been taking a census, presumably preparatory to taxation, in an area usually interpreted as Annandale, on the north-west frontier, presumably territory of the Brigantes. The last phase at the late first-century fort and annexe of Elginhaugh by the Firth of Forth has been interpreted as a collection centre for cattle, possibly in connection with the payment of tax or tribute. It has been suggested that some of the units with British names stationed on the Continent were originally raised from the northern tribes conquered during the Agricolan advance, but this is impossible to substantiate.

While the relationship between the army and the local rural community is opaque, we can be certain that it existed, that local farms were expected to contribute in some form to the supply of the army, and that soldiers behaved in precisely the same high-handed and grasping manner as is recorded elsewhere in the empire and is now attested for the first time on the northern British frontier at Vindolanda. From here a 'transmarine person' wrote to 'his majesty' (the governor at least, possibly the emperor) to complain that he had been beaten—though an innocent man *not from Britain*—and that his complaint had been ignored by the centurion. It is possible that this man was but one of the many people attracted to the military zone by the possibility of making money. Others included Barathes of Palmyra, himself buried at Corbridge and his wife at South Shields, and various people who erected inscriptions in Greek presumably betraying an origin in the eastern provinces, as well as merchants, traders, and craftsmen, such as the potters who established workshops at Corbridge, Inveresk, Bearsden, and many other sites.

Britain is recorded twice as exporting corn, under Augustus and again in the fourth century. It is possible that these two instances reflected a normal pattern and that the farms of southern Britain were normally able to supply most of the grain for the North. Certainly, evidence from Bearsden on the Antonine Wall and South Shields by Hadrian's Wall indicates the transport of grain to those two sites. That there was interest in local production, too, is suggested by the close physical relationship between the fort at Old Carlisle in Cumbria, its civil settlement, and the surrounding farmland, as revealed by aerial photographs. Recent evidence from Scotland indicates the growing of wheat at farms on the Lothian plain, while the unprocessed state of both wheat and barley found at the nearby Roman fort of Elginhaugh also points to local production and supply.

In matters of supply, it is possible that the frontier was no barrier and that goods were purchased from beyond. A report of 105 from Stobi in modern Bulgaria records soldiers collecting food beyond the Danube, while a purchase of cattle from beyond the Rhine was witnessed by two centurions, suggesting that it was a military order.

The native people and their settlements

The discussion so far has been mainly based upon literary and documentary evidence. In moving to consider the evidence about native people, the sources are more restricted. They consist of the evidence of archaeology, and Roman accounts of their opponents: the latter hardly offer objective views. There have also been fewer surveys and excavations of civilian and native sites in comparison to military installations. This is compounded by the general paucity of finds on rural sites which renders them more difficult to date. Within the border zone on the nearer side of the frontier, the haul of finds during an excavation might consist of two or three sherds of Roman pottery, a glass bead or fragment of a glass bangle, some iron fragments, and quernstones. There is only one coin known from a non-military site in Northumberland. There are in the frontier zone of northern Britain no conspicuous grave groups such as are found in Germany.

The people of the peripheral parts of Britain were organized into states, just as those elsewhere in the island. These states were capable of combining their forces to fight their common foe as the struggle against Agricola's army demonstrated. This indicates a certain level of political sophistication. The main evidence for warfare before the Roman invasion consists of the existence of defended sites and of weapons. Roman accounts describe the fighting tactics of their enemies, and this suggests that warfare between the various states of Britain was a regular occurrence. Tacitus recorded that the Caledonians' main strength lay in their infantry. Their chiefs employed the chariot, a war machine abandoned in Continental Europe by this time. The battle of Mons Graupius commenced with the leading warriors driving up and down between the rival armies in chariots and goading the Romans before dismounting to fight on foot. Beside the kings or chiefs and the warrior caste, there may also have been a priestly class as there was elsewhere in the Celtic world. Certainly

Druids lived on Anglesey, while Demetrius of Tarsus mentioned holy men on British islands, probably in the Inner Hebrides. The people of the North and West in the main followed a mixed farming regime. The major clearance of woodland in Scotland had been during the Neolithic period: the earliest dated cultivation of cereal crops in Scotland is about 3,500 BC. There was accelerated woodland clearance in the second half of the first millennium BC, with the result that the Romans will have entered a relatively open, farmed landscape, still with many trees but perhaps no more than today in many parts of Scotland. Cattle and sheep were reared and cereals (mainly barley) grown, with the diet supplemented by wild animals such as deer, fish, and wild fruit. Evidence for cultivation has been found high up the valleys of Northumberland and on bleak moorland. This was not a mere subsistence economy. Sufficient was produced to allow time for the construction of defended settlements, major forts, and, in Scotland, large stone-built houses such as duns and brochs.

The normal type of domestic dwelling in the North, Wales, and the South-West is the round house. These buildings could be substantial, consisting normally of a low wall of stone with a roof of thatch, skins, or other organic material supported by timbers. Roundhouses might be found singly or in farmsteads of two or more houses, where one might serve a purpose other than living, perhaps a byre. Sometimes the clustering is such that the group of houses might be termed a village, but in such cases it has not so far proved possible to identify the house of a village chief. These villages might be open or enclosed. In some areas sites defended by one or more ramparts and ditches might be located on hilltops. It has generally been assumed that such hill-forts were the equivalent of towns, but it has also been suggested that some might have only been occupied occasionally, served as markets, or had a mainly religious function. Only in the Late Empire do rectangular houses appear in settlements and these remain scarce, though, of course, the farm enclosure might be rectilinear in any period, often depending on the topography. Such distinctions as there are between different areas have been tentatively attributed to the differing traditions of the various states.

The impact of Rome

It is to be expected that the invasion and conquest of these tribes will have caused severe disruption to the upper echelons of society. Not only might many warrior leaders have been killed but others would be disaffected and not prepared to cooperate with Rome. On the other hand, there were always some that would. It might be expected that the post-Conquest leaders received or acquired symbols of their new masters in the form of Roman artefacts. In Scotland during the first-century occupation, Roman objects, admittedly few in number, are mainly found on higher-status sites: in south-west England, it has been suggested that those sites with Roman artefacts were the homes of the new leaders.

The longer term impact of Rome on the indigenous inhabitants of the peripheral zones is not easy to determine, for rural settlements in these areas are not rich in artefacts, as has already been noted. In northern Britain several changes in rural settlements have also been considered to reflect the impact of the Roman presence. These include the abandonment of hill-forts as a result of the imposition of the *pax Romana*, the growth in the size of settlements, the extension of settlements into the uplands, and the introduction of stone as a building material for houses. Unfortunately, few sites produce sufficient diagnostic finds, nor have enough finds been radiocarbon tested in order to allow close dating. Nevertheless, it does seem that some of these changes may have occurred before the arrival of the Romans. Recent work on two of the largest hill-forts of southern Scotland, Burnswark and Eildon Hill North, suggests that the defences of both were abandoned *before* the Roman advance, though pottery indicates some continuing occupation of the sites. Settlements certainly grew in size and in some cases spread over abandoned hill-fort defences, which could as much be the outcome of a shift in population patterns as a result of the abandonment of hill-forts as the result of a growth in population due to the outlawing of warfare by Rome. The use of stone in the construction of houses may be the result of the major clearance of woodland, which we can now see had taken place in the second half of the first millennium BC.

The impact of Rome may not have been the same in each area

under consideration. For example, it has been argued that there is a lack of a hierarchy of settlements in northern England. Villas occur in Yorkshire as far north as the Tees, but—with one or two exceptions—not in the military zone in the North of England as defined by the distribution of forts. Beyond the frontier, in today's southern Scotland, a settlement hierarchy appears to reassert itself, with undefended roundhouses, protected farms and settlements, brochs (stone-built towers), duns (round or oval stone houses), and souterrains (underground passages attached to stone or timber houses) all present. A distinction has also been drawn between settlement patterns north and south of the frontier itself. North of the Solway, the settlements are fewer in number, more highly defended and more rarely have associated field systems. An inference drawn is that this reflects the socio-economic effect of Hadrian's Wall, agriculture being encouraged in the shelter of the barrier. While this has long been considered a possibility, the proposition is based upon the distribution of undated sites located through aerial photography. Yet the hypothesis gains some support from the analysis of botanical remains to the east which suggests that there were less advanced agricultural practices in the farms beyond Hadrian's Wall than those in its hinterland.

The situation in south-west England is broadly comparable to southern Scotland, with rounds (small enclosed homesteads), courtyard houses, and souterrains present, though only one villa has been recognized west of Exeter. In Wales, villas occur along the southern coastal plain, but not in central or northern Wales where a military presence was maintained into the fourth century. Yet Roman artefacts tend to be more numerous than in northern Britain, and a greater degree of Romanization is also indicated by activities such as ironworking and the construction of rectangular buildings in some farms. There is also more evidence for a settlement hierarchy, with some hill-forts continuing in occupation at one end of the spectrum and unenclosed hut-groups existing at the other, beside the enclosed farms which form the bulk of the known rural settlements.

It has been suggested that the army in the North of England acted in effect as the top strata of society, creaming off agricultural surpluses and preventing the growth of a settlement hierarchy. Yet, the settlement hierarchy in the South-West is relatively flat even though there was no military presence. Villas, which are dependent on a strong agricultural base, while absent from much of Wales, the South-West, and the North are also absent from most of Norfolk and Suffolk, certainly the seaward part that the discovery of metalwork hoards suggests was a relatively rich area. Perhaps in different areas people had alternative ways of demonstrating their wealth. Could the people of upland northern Britain, central and northern Wales, and Devon and Cornwall have preferred to keep their wealth in some other form than villas, such as cattle?

While major sites, such as Traprain Law, certainly existed in the periphery before the arrival of the Romans, it is fair to state that the latter introduced urbanism. However, the urban settlements in the frontier region related entirely to the army. Outside each fort normally lay a civil settlement. The Roman army on campaign attracted camp followers, and the later physical expression of this is the civil settlement. For all we know, the inhabitants of the civil settlements were the descendants of the earlier mobile camp followers: there is certainly no evidence to indicate that they were immigrants from the adjacent rural settlements, though that is not to say that such movement did not occur. Indeed, the paucity of Roman objects on rural settlements is not only a major hindrance to clarifying the relationship between Rome and the indigenous population, but also emphasizes that the main distinction on the frontier is not between military and civilian but between town—as represented by fort and civil settlement—and country. Within this framework, Carlisle and Corbridge, both of which we now know maintained a military presence within their urban framework through much of the period, can be seen simply as larger towns which were as parasitical on the army as the civil settlements outside forts. Aldborough and possibly Carlisle, and perhaps even Corbridge which acquired walls, each became a *civitas*. In Wales, Caerwent and Carmarthen performed a similar role, but there were no towns in North Wales and none west of Exeter. This inability to develop an independent urban market in turn may have had an effect on the development of villas, which, in the southern part of the island, generally occur within close proximity to towns.

The evidence from these three areas is broadly similar, but interpretation is another matter. Geographical determinism might be considered to play a part. Many parts of the peripheral zones were upland areas with a relatively poor agricultural base. Yet there are significant areas of good agricultural land in these areas, such as the Lothians and Buchan in Scotland or the South Wales plain, and such areas, and beyond, were capable of providing the agricultural surplus which enabled the construction of significant structures from Neolithic chambered cairns to brochs and hill-forts. Remoteness might play a part in the lack of artefacts on rural settlements, but not all of the people of the countryside of northern and western Britain were remote from the urban centres represented by forts and their attendant civil settlements. Nor is there much to distinguish the proximity or otherwise of a rural site to an urban centre based on the number of artefacts found.

The paucity of Roman artefacts on rural sites in the military zone remains a significant problem. The army normally paid for supplies in cash, though the payment did not always arrive, while individual soldiers might be corrupt and grasping. But if supplies were obtained locally, how were they paid for in a non-monetary economy? If this was a barter society, it is not reflected in the appearance of Roman artefacts on native settlements as they are very scarce. If supplies were paid for in cash, where are the coins? Did they disappear in taxation, normally paid in cash, though areas without a monetary economy might be allowed to pay in kind?

A more radical view has been offered, that some inhabitants of Roman Britain rejected the symbols and appurtenances of Roman rule, Roman-style houses, and Roman artefacts. It may be difficult to distinguish that explanation from an interpretation of the continuing use and construction of roundhouses in the countryside throughout the province as an indication of the traditional innate conservatism of the farming community. Nor is the phenomenon ubiquitous. While Roman artefacts are found in hoards on rural sites in Wales, for example, and reached more settlements in Antonine Scotland—and in greater quantities—than in the first century, it has been suggested that the lack of Roman artefacts in hoards beyond the frontier in north-east Scotland, an area rich in indigenous metalwork, may be the result of a desire to stress local identity. Even where Roman culture was adopted, it may not have been embraced wholesale. The brooches worn by native people in north Britain, for example, hark back to local decorative traditions.

In contrast to the pattern pertaining in first- and second-century Scotland, in the South-West Peninsula in the second century there was both a decline in the quantity of Roman artefacts reaching the rural settlements (there was a similar decline in Cumbria in the third century) and a change in the style of the settlements themselves to forms which continued into the fifth and sixth centuries. It has been suggested that these changes reflect society's delayed acceptance of the consequences of being conquered, and possibly also the withdrawal of the army, which, as we can see from the distribution of Roman artefacts in Scotland, had a major impact on the presence and distribution of objects. It has also been suggested, however, that the lack of Roman artefacts and the creation of their own architectural style—which survived the demise of Roman rule—may be deliberate actions on the part of the inhabitants to reinforce their own identity, only adopting those Roman features which best fitted local conceptions of the acceptable and rejecting the rest. It is possible, therefore, that a range of differing factors, social, economic, and political, led to the paucity of Roman material on the farmsteads and villages of the peripheral zone of Britain, with the motivation varying across the country and changing through time.

Religion

A relationship between Roman and native religions may certainly be detected on the frontier (see Chapter 4). While Rome brought its own gods, and, through its far-flung empire, allowed exotic sects such as the eastern mystery religious to penetrate to the northern frontier, it also readily adopted and adapted local cults. Thus local gods suddenly appear in epigraphic or sculptural form and sometimes are equated with Roman counterparts, Mars, for example, in the case of Belatucadrus and Cocidius. Dedications to each of these local gods is relatively restricted geographically. This may indicate ancient religious loyalties but perhaps also former political groupings. Inscriptions to the Veteres—perhaps the 'old' gods—tend to lie in the eastern and central sectors of Hadrian's Wall; Belatucadrus and Cocidius were mainly favoured in the western half of the wall. It is possible that Bewcastle was the shrine of Cocidius, *Fanum Cocidii*. Another god whose shrine may have been in the same area is Maponus, whose name survives today in both Lochmaben and Clockmabenstone on the north shore of the Solway Firth.

Occasionally, the god's temple survives, for example, that to Antenociticus at Benwell or to Coventina at Carrawburgh. At Carrawburgh a particular pre-Roman tradition is represented, the deposition of gifts to the gods in a watery context. The pull of Coventina was so great that worshippers continued to throw objects into her well even after Christianity had become the official religion of the empire. Between the Walls, three large ironwork hoards have been interpreted as votive deposits because they were found in lakes or bogs, while beyond the frontier, two caves in Fife and a third at Covesea on the Moray coast contained several Roman artefacts and it is possible that they were gifts to the local god(s). Religious sites can also be a sign of specifically Roman activity in the countryside. Two rural shrines are known in Northumberland, while the discovery of dressed and numbered stones at Easter–Langlee has led to the suggestion that a Roman temple stood on a hilltop near Newstead. Religion, thus, not only emphasizes that it was possible for Roman and native traditions to meet, but it also opens up altogether different windows on the local people and their ways.

Artefacts beyond the frontier

The number of Roman artefacts found beyond the northern frontier is relatively small. They are in general confined to the coast, though some coin hoards have been found inland, including one at Fort Augustus deep in the Highlands. The paucity of such material may be the result of closing the frontier to trade or at least restricting it: note the law of Marcus Aurelius cited above forbidding the export of certain items to the enemy. Such artefacts as are found beyond the frontier are not always easy to interpret. While diplomatic gifts might account for some of them, there are other possible reasons. Objects may have been brought by local people returning from raiding expeditions or from service in the Roman forces; by traders, missionaries, travellers by sea blown off course, adventurers, Roman invaders, or refugees. Some objects may not even have been used for their primary purpose but acquired simply for status. Nor does the presence of Roman objects beyond the frontier necessarily indicate any deep desire to adopt Roman culture; conversely we should be wary of reading too much into the lack of Roman objects.

It is worth reminding ourselves that trade was not a Roman invention. Stone axes, for example, had been traded across hundreds of miles centuries before the arrival of the Romans in northern Britain. Political or family links may also have accounted for the movement of some objects. It has been suggested that the appearance of a fragment of a Roman amphora dating from the late first century BC or the early first century AD at the broch of Gurness in Orkney may hint at alliances between the British tribes.

As we have seen, there is little direct evidence for trade across the northern frontier. The many references to Roman traders operating beyond the empire's other frontiers might lead to an assumption that such activity also occurred in Britain. In earlier centuries Strabo recorded that trade had existed between the southern British states and Rome. The Britons exported cattle, gold, silver, slaves, and hunting dogs and received in exchange ivory bracelets and necklaces, amber glassware, and 'similar petty trifles'. There is evidence to suggest that some 'petty trifles' travelled in a north–south direction in northern Britain, for moulds for making dress fasteners have been found at Traprain Law. Trade certainly existed with Ireland. Tacitus records that 'the interior parts are little known, but through commercial intercourse and merchants there is better knowledge of the harbours and approaches'.

Roman finds from Ireland are not numerous, but they are interesting. Roman objects date mainly to the first to second centuries and the fourth to fifth. The earlier material is mainly restricted to the east and north coasts, but the later material penetrates further inland to the south of the island. Some Roman objects, coins and artefacts, appear to have been used as gifts to the gods. At Newgrange, for example, 19 Roman coins, some of high denomination, were deposited, together with jewellery, around the entrance to the tomb. Long cist graves at Brayhead, with a coin to each skeleton, suggest familiarity with Roman custom, perhaps even the presence of a Roman trading post (burials containing Roman objects have also been found in Scotland). The trend from cremation to inhumation in burial practice may also be consciously copying the changing Roman fashion. The recent recognition of a gate constructed in a 'Roman' manner also indicates cultural links. While Roman influence on certain artefacts has been suggested, these objects are very scarce. A different activity—raiding—is recorded in the fourth century, but items which might have been brought to Ireland (or Scotland) as a result of this activity are few in number. We cannot even be certain how objects such as the Coleraine Hoard or the Traprain Treasure reached their destinations. Are they the product of barbarian raiding or imperial subsidy?

Missionaries beyond the Roman frontier are not attested during the period of Roman rule, but if the names of the late fourth- and fifth-century kings of southern Scotland can be interpreted as evidence for their Christianity, then the results of such activity can be recognized. St Patrick, a Christian and the son of a Christian, possibly born in north-west England, wrote in the second half of the fifth century to the Christian Coroticus, king of Strathclyde. At about the same time St Ninian established his church at Whithorn in south-west Scotland, whence, we are informed by Bede, he undertook missions to the Picts.

Rome as a neighbour

The Roman army must always have been a threatening presence, a threat to the individual (through punitive action, corruption, or venality) and to society in general (again through punitive action, interference in internal affairs, and by offering an alternative model of society or action). Its power could be awesome, not just in military matters but in its ability to organize. Rome's willingness to interfere in the affairs of its neighbours, we might expect, would have been annoying to those neighbours to say the least, but also potentially destabilizing. It was also unpredictable. In the military dictatorship which was the Roman empire, so much depended upon the whim of one man. An emperor might order invasion, as did Claudius in 43 and Antoninus Pius in 138/9, or retreat, as Claudius dictated to Corbulo when he instructed him to withdraw from across the Rhine in 41 and as Domitian from Scotland in or about 87.

The disposition of Roman forces may offer a hint of one aspect of the relationship between Rome and its neighbours. Interestingly, on both Hadrian's Wall and the Antonine Wall the weight of troops was not towards the well-populated areas but to those largely devoid of people. The reason for this may be that the leaders in the populated areas understood the importance of maintaining peace and therefore avoiding Rome's interference, while the lack of people in other areas north of the frontier resulted in the army having to resort to greater effort to maintain watch and ward.

The third century is believed to have been a time of peace, and certainly no wars are recorded after the campaigns of Severus between 208 and 211. The disposition of military forces in the North lends force to this assumption, for many forts in northern England seem to have been abandoned at this time. The situation was to be changed radically in the face of the threats of the fourth century. New regiments were stationed in northern England on the roads leading north to the frontier, while both east and west coasts were fortified. A chain of towers was built along the Yorkshire coast. The measures on the western coasts are not so coherent, but they included building several new forts in the most up-to-date military architecture and refortification of other sites, for example along the Cumberland coast.

The northern tribes placed the frontier under great pressure during the second century and again in the fourth. We do not, however, know the reason for their attacks on the province: destruction, booty, or settlement within the empire are all possible aims. From the first through to the fourth century, tribes beyond the Roman frontier had sought to move within the empire. There is no evidence to suggest that such actions occurred in Britain. But if sought it was unsuccessful, for it appears that no 'barbarians' settled within the shadow of Hadrian's Wall.

If the disposition of Roman forces might help us understand the pressures on the frontier, the Roman presence might help explain events beyond it. Towards the end of the Roman period we can recognize again the existence of states beyond the frontier. Some of these states may be the successors of first-century tribes. The 'Goddodin' were, philologically, the fourth-century descendants of the first-century Votadini, while the kingdom of Strathclyde occupied roughly the same area as the earlier Dumnonii. Beyond the Forth a different pattern emerges. The twelve tribes of Ptolemy gradually coalesce into the unitary kingdom of the Picts. Here, perhaps, is Rome's greatest gift to its neighbours, for it has been argued that its powerful presence in the southern part of the island caused the northern part to unify, consciously or unconsciously, as the only way to survive.

The reason for the location of the frontier

As we have seen, for most of the life of Roman Britain the frontier lay on or around the Tyne–Solway line. Why did the frontier settle at this point? Various reasons have been offered. Arguments that the Caledonians were too fierce for the Roman army to subdue or the mountains too high are subjective, ignoring the known ability of the army to overcome stronger enemies or higher and more extensive mountain ranges elsewhere. It might be argued that there was no economic value in conquering northern Scotland, but it is far from clear that the Romans would have been swayed by such considerations. The reason offered by the second-century writer Aelius Aristides for not subduing northern Britain, namely that it was not worth conquering, may be an excuse rather than a reason: Strabo had earlier stated that Britain was not worth conquering because the Romans gained enough from customs dues, yet a few years later Claudius ordered the invasion of the island.

Twenty years ago, a different view was offered, that the Romans required the existence of the right socio-economic infrastructure in order to achieve a successful permanent occupation. A developed infrastructure was necessary for the imposition of the self-governing administrative system which the Romans preferred and which, together with a market economy and trading network, created an efficient system of food supply. Thus, the Roman province of Britain should only have consisted of the southern and central parts of England, but here, as in certain geographically favoured areas of Continental Europe, the Romans were able to extend their rule some distance beyond the areas that had the necessary infrastructure. In North Britain, Central and North Wales, and the peninsula of the South-West, it was argued, urbanization never materialized beyond the shadow of the army. Nor had the tribes of these areas developed a monetary economy—or at least coinage—in the years before the invasion of 43. The Welsh tribes were capable of inflicting an embarrassing defeat on the Roman army and the northern states had indicated a political sophistication in the face of the Roman threat, yet they still appear to have been insufficiently far advanced to offer the necessary socio-economic infrastructure to enable the Romans to undertake a successful occupation.

There is, however, also a political and military dimension to this discussion. The Romans saw client kingdoms as parts of their empire, and thus can be seen to be doing little more than restoring the status quo when they conquered *Brigantia* in the 70s after the overthrow of their client queen Cartimandua. Perhaps the disruption to the western frontier by the Welsh tribes—as well as appreciation that the geographical area to be conquered was not great—led to advance here: certainly the geographically restricted nature of the South-West Peninsula will have been an inducement to conquest. Yet, still at this time, the underlying thrust of Roman actions led them to seek expansion. Thus, Agricola did not stop at the northern edge of *Brigantia*, nor at the next isthmus, but pushed onward, apparently in an attempt to complete the conquest of the island, an achievement which Tacitus believed had been attained. Severus also aimed at completing the conquest of the island. It was political considerations which led to the failure of such actions. Agricola's conquests were abandoned in the face of more serious problems on frontiers closer to Rome, while Antoninus Pius had more limited ambitions, and Severus' sons other priorities. It may thus have been political reasons which brought the frontier deep into northern Britain rather than follow the fringes of the Midlands, just as geographical reasons dictated that the sea was the boundary to the west, with the result that the 'marginal' lands of the North, West, and South-West, which shared so many characteristics in common, lay on both sides of the frontier. This does not invalidate the hypothesis that the appropriate socio-economic infrastructure was necessary for successful Roman rule. The Roman advance ground to a halt in the peripheral zones beyond the 'natural' boundary, and the fact that Roman civilization failed to make any significant impact here points to the validity of the hypothesis.

Conclusion

There is value in comparing the peripheral parts of the Roman province with each other, and also those areas immediately beyond with each other. In the peripheral zone within the province the same general conditions prevailed, little recognizable settlement hierarchy coupled with a relative paucity of Roman material culture. Undeniably, all areas were geographically and agriculturally disadvantaged. It *may* have been possible to grow cereals in many of these areas and at relatively high altitudes, but in quantitative terms, Cornwall, Wales, and northern Britain could not compete with the breadbasket of southern England. Furthermore, while these three areas were relatively remote in that they lay on the fringes of the richer part of the island, the mountainous nature of the terrain led to considerable remoteness *within* these three areas.

It might be argued that the lack of settlement hierarchy and general poorness in artefactual terms of the settlements in northern Britain was because the army siphoned off excess production and wealth, but this proposition is difficult to sustain in Wales and Cornwall. It has been argued that the lack of Roman artefacts on native sites and the continuing construction of roundhouses represented a conscious rejection of Roman culture. Yet, it is difficult to know whether a more significant reason might not lie in the traditional conservatism of farmers, reinforced by general paucity of the agricultural base.

Interestingly, there are differences of pattern between northern Scotland and Ireland. In spite of long-standing geographical knowledge of northern Scotland, it does not appear to have become as well known to the Romans as Ireland, nor is the number of Roman artefacts found there great. Geography may not be the only reason for this: perhaps Ireland had more goods to offer Roman traders. The existence of major political 'central places' such as Navan may indicate that Ireland was more socially and economically advanced than northern Scotland and was therefore more attractive to entrepreneurs from the empire—and would have been more susceptible to Roman rule if invasion had ever taken place. What is clear is that in all these peripheral areas fewer roots of Roman origin took hold—apart, that is, from Christianity.

Figure 22 This silver-gilt pepperpot in the form of a Late Roman empress is one item in a great treasure carefully packed and buried at Hoxne in Suffolk not earlier than 407, certainly after the seizure of power from Britain by Constantine III and possibly after the end of Roman rule, events in which the owners may have been caught up.

Conclusion

Peter Salway

Britain and Rome

This concluding chapter provides an opportunity to recall some of the principal themes introduced by the contributors to this book and to look at one or two of the most significant in a little more detail. It will be noted that in some instances there can be more than one interpretation and, moreover, that on occasion individual contributors have differing opinions. There are, indeed, many cases in which the surviving information is insufficient for absolute certainty, and scholars can come to different but valid conclusions, provided that they do not run contrary to the evidence.

In the course of the preceding chapters we have seen the British Isles go through a series of transformations. Lying at the periphery of the Roman world, the Isles were first affected by long-distance trade from the south, and then gradually drawn more and more into the orbit of the culture that had its centre in the Mediterranean. The effects, of course, diminished within the British Isles the further away from Continental Europe the location of any particular indigenous peoples happened to be (or, to be more accurate, the further in terms of ease of travel). The process accelerated from the middle of the first century BC when Roman armies arrived at the Channel: the political, economic, and cultural consequences of being near neighbours of the dominant power in the Western world profoundly affected the Isles. From Caesar onwards, little could happen (at least in the nearer parts of Britain itself and arguably more or less everywhere) without Rome's influence being in some way felt, even if only as a huge background presence that could not be ignored. It is not entirely surprising that actual conquest did not come for a century after Julius

Caesar's brief expeditions, since Rome clearly regarded Britain as lying within its sphere of influence like other regions just outside its frontiers, and expected that British rulers should recognize its authority like client kings elsewhere. The imperial poet Virgil encapsulated Roman belief when he described Rome's god-given destiny to rule as being without limit. In the particular case of Britain there was, after all, the fact that Caesar had imposed tribute and dynastic arrangements on the Britons of the South-East. It was immaterial whether or not they had complied once Caesar was safely out of the way. The legalistic Roman mind must have regarded the obligations as in place, and under the empire Britain was considered—in the language of imperial eulogy if not elsewhere—as 'more or less Roman' long before the Claudian Conquest. The presence of noble British exiles at Rome as suppliants to the emperor will have reinforced Roman attitudes. Not only could it be seen as implying a recognition by Britons of Rome's function as international arbitrator, but also gave an excuse to intervene—provided, of course, that it was in the interest of whoever was in power at Rome. It is, indeed, very significant that it was not till internal factors at the highest level within the empire precipitated invasion that Rome actually moved to incorporate Britain as a directly ruled province. As the geographer Strabo had said in the Augustan period, from the perspective of the balance of advantages, in his day Rome got more profit from Britain as it was than if it had conquered the country, taking into account the costs of imperial rule.

Emerging archaeological evidence hinting at the presence in Britain of Romans—metropolitan, provincial, possibly even military—in the period between Caesar and Claudius, is not yet enough for certainty but entirely believable. Epigraphic evidence from outside other frontiers records the presence of Romans as communities of resident aliens, and historical sources record military intervention in neighbouring states in support of or against local rulers where it suited Rome's interests. Conversely, it is likely that the exiles were not the only prominent Britons to have travelled within the empire, whatever their politics (in reverse, one recalls Commius Caesar's Gallic former friend and subsequent enemy, who fled to Britain and apparently founded a British royal dynasty). At the top level, residence at the imperial court in Rome by foreign princes from client kingdoms within and outside the imperial frontiers—willingly or as hostages—

was not uncommon. Julius Agrippa, grandson of Herod the Great, had a decidedly uneven relationship with successive emperors both at Rome and subsequently in his kingdom, but had been brought up from childhood in Rome within the imperial family. The role he (and his son) adopted as advocate with Rome for Jews and Judaism reflected ethnic origin, but was not out of line with common practice among Roman aristocrats who assumed or inherited an obligation of honour as 'patron' to represent at Rome the interests of distant communities with whom they had a personal connection. Indeed, the overall involvement in Roman politics and culture would not have seemed out of place in a prominent native-born Roman of the period, most of all in an actual member of the imperial family. It is therefore not surprising to find archaeologically in pre-Conquest southern Britain material signs of aristocratic wealth of Roman origin, such as the contents of the great Lexden tumulus near Colchester or the superb Augustan silver cups from Hockwold, in Norfolk. These may, indeed, have been diplomatic gifts, but should not conjure up visions of trinkets for 'natives'. It is probably truer to see the culture of Britain—at least in the South and East, and at the top layers of society, and to varying extents in different places—as converging with the Roman way of life.

The Conquest and 'Romanization'

It may seem to be stating the blindingly obvious to remark that the Conquest hugely accelerated this process of 'Romanization', were it not for the fact that that view has been under attack from two different directions. On the one hand, some now argue that the 'Conquest' was hardly a conquest at all, that Roman rule was largely welcomed— or at least accepted—by British aristocracies who were already extensively Romanized, and that that welcome lasted till disillusion in certain parts of the new province exploded in the Boudiccan rebellion. This theory is chiefly based on archaeological and art-historical analysis of the material evidence for the penetration of Roman culture. It does, however, run the risk of equating preferences of taste and style—and readiness to adopt superior standards of comfort—with political alignment. It is much more likely that the picture was very variable, with different British tribes and their rulers welcoming or resisting the Roman invasion, depending on a mix of local circumstance between and within British tribes and of perceived advantage to Rome, and often irrespective of degree of local cultural Romanization.

It is easy to pursue the argument of cultural convergence—as the contributors to this book have not—to the point where the Claudian invasion becomes only a minor landmark in a long process. Ironically, alleged unimportance of the Conquest can also form part of the opposite cultural argument (that Britain was only superficially touched by the Roman way of life) promoted by those who see the period of Roman rule as a passing phase in the history of Britain that is relatively unimportant compared with the founding of the Anglo-Saxon kingdoms, from which (in terms of political organisms) there is a direct line of descent to the present day. Others mete out the same treatment to the Saxons, and regard the Battle of Hastings as marking the real beginning of history in mainland Britain. Yet it is also possible to maintain that AD 43 was quite as momentous as 1066. It is, of course, true that closer study of the backgrounds to both the Claudian Conquest and the Norman reveal that the changes were not quite as clear-cut as popular history would have them. Normans in influential positions in Edward the Confessor's England, family connections between English, Danish, and Norman ruling families, and Saxon nobility supporting William against Harold have interesting echoes. But when it came, the Norman Conquest was a brutal shock that ruthlessly imposed a new political system and in a relatively short time had dispossessed a large proportion of the native upper classes. Despite the continuities that scholarship has traced, the popular belief that Norman England was radically different from Saxon England is unshaken (and not too far from the mark). Why, then, is the arrival of the Romans not considered as momentous in the history of Britain as the Norman invasion? One answer must be that Roman Britain is seen as a failure because it came to an 'end' and Norman England a success because it gradually evolved into English-speaking state or states that were the direct ancestors of the United Kingdom. This, however, is history by hindsight, and one of the purposes of this book is to look at the Roman era as four extraordinary centuries in the story of the British Isles.

Some consequences of absorption into the empire

Perhaps what marks out the imposition of Roman rule as a real turning point is that it introduced fundamental changes that affected everyone, either directly or indirectly, whereas before the Conquest the Roman way of life had, as we have noted, only seriously influenced members of the British elite, and that much more in the South-East than elsewhere. While it is probably true that the *everyday* life of the Iron Age rural population—and therefore the bulk of the population—went on much as before under Rome, the underlying changes in the parameters within which society worked were profound. Moreover, some of the most important features were not static throughout the Roman era, but themselves changed in highly significant ways, as the preceding chapters have shown.

In recent years it has been unfashionable among commentators to attribute historic change to particular 'great men'. A more balanced view accepts that individuals operate within the circumstances of their times and often within major historic changes of direction, but that their contributions can be critical. It is difficult, for example, to argue away Alexander the Great or Luther or Lenin. Earlier in this book we noted the role played by Claudius' personal political circumstances, notably his need to establish a military reputation to cement the shaky hold on the throne to which he had been propelled by *coup d'état*. Moreover, the urgency was not just the fact that retaining the support of the troops is vital to a ruler in any age—particularly one whose power originates in a coup—nor in Claudius' case the immediate circumstance that a failed revolt by a provincial commander had just revealed that the loyalty of the frontier legions could not be taken for granted. It was also the peculiarly Roman importance placed on military reputation. As Cicero had succinctly put it a century earlier, more glory was to be gained by expanding the empire than by administering it. This is critical in understanding the Roman ruling classes. The eternal pleasures of power, status, and fame were given an extra edge in the upper echelons of Roman society by the extreme importance attached to bringing fresh honour on the family and showing respect to the ancestors by equalling their successes. At the level of emperor, it would be difficult to trump adding a new province by war. And in the case of Britain, Claudius, intensely interested in the study of history as he was, will have been acutely aware that he had an opportunity not only to add glory to the name of the Julio-Claudian family but to do it in a fashion that would outdo all the previous efforts towards Britain represented by the inconclusive expeditions of Caesar, the much anticipated but unfulfilled Augustan intervention, and the recent aborted attempt of the late unlamented Caligula. Furthermore, Britain as a theatre for victory also carried the added kudos that it lay across the dreaded Ocean and that the Britons were reputedly savages. Caesar's troops had hesitated at the point of landing, and—despite another century of cross-Channel contact—the common soldiers of Claudius' own army were to need a direct appeal that accidentally touched their sense of the ludicrous before they would trust themselves to the sea or venture outside what they regarded as the known world.

Roman views of Britain and the Britons

Virgil, searching for a poetic expression of the despair of Italian farmers dispossessed to reward military veterans, ranks Britain alongside Africa, Scythia, and Persia as remote parts of the earth to which the refugees might flee. In the case of Britain he adds the vivid phrase, 'the whole wide world away'. This is, of course, more than half a century before the Claudian Conquest. It may therefore at first seem strange that the view of Britain as an unbelievably far-off island inhabited by barbarians can still be found in literature at the end of the fourth century, when Britain had been part of the empire for so long and so many Romans from other parts of the empire had served in the imperial service in it or visited it on business. This is, however, a phenomenon with plenty of parallels today. We still immediately recognize in cartoons—or (very significantly) in advertising—the stereotype of a Frenchman, with beret and striped vest or blue dungarees. Yet those who visit France regularly nowadays hardly ever see those items—and some of us have never heard the accordion played! It is significant that stereotype Britons appear chiefly in literature, where they are effectively a literary device, or in imperial propaganda.

Figure 23 The Spirit of Place. The seen and the unseen were closely
connected in the ancient perception of place, each having its guardian deity
(*genius*). A legionary centurion of the Second *Augusta* dedicated an altar
(*left*) at Auchendavy on the Antonine Wall to the *genius* of the Land of
Britain. On behalf of the Emperor Domitian a Greek academic, Demetrius of
Tyre, explored the islands off Britain, and (*right*) was almost certainly the
dedicator of two silvered bronze plaques in Greek from York. The upper—to
'the gods of the governor's residence'—shows the same consciousness of
place. Without it, one would suspect that the lower plaque—to the marine
deities Oceanus and Tethys—was no more than a learned reference (meant to
flatter those who recognized it) to Alexander the Great on the River Indus at
the other end of the world. It is, however, interesting to find the same
comparison between the geographic extremes re-emerging in a Christian
context when Constantine portrays himself in letters to the East as having
himself brought conversion all the way from the remote Ocean around
Britain.

Just as it had suited Caesar and Claudius to play up their daring in carrying Roman arms across the ocean, so it was still flattering two and a half centuries later in a laudatory address to the emperor to characterize the visit of Constantius I to the furthest parts of Scotland as almost mystical. Constantine the Great, similarly, made great play of mind-dazzling distance when he wrote to correspondents in the East of having been elevated to the throne in York at one end of the empire and carried power and the Christian faith to the other. There is, however, a further aspect of the Roman view of Britons to explore. At the very end of the fourth century and the beginning of the fifth, we find the court poet Claudian lauding the emperor for victories in Britain won in his name. Significantly, among the enemies defeated on land are 'tattooed Picts' and by sea the Scots (who have roused 'all Ireland', whence they have not yet at this period migrated to Scotland). This reminds us that direct Roman rule only ever extended over about half the land area of the British Isles. However much like north-western Gaul the South of Britain may have appeared, there were unconquered 'barbarian' peoples as near neighbours, with whom there must at best have been an uneasy relationship. One begins to see that the stereotype was not completely without substance—and, indeed, that it could be reinforced by the direct experience of influential Romans serving in the army and administration in Britain.

In the uppermost levels of Roman society—the senatorial families of whom Cicero is thinking when he talks of the greater glory of extending the area of Roman rule over administering it—the conventional career of those ambitious to emulate the successes of their ancestors was marked by occupying in succession a defined series of public posts, some military, some civil, with age limits and prerequisites. The pecking-order of these posts was acutely understood by those eligible, and the messages sent out by who was appointed to what, and when, were of great interest in an age when reputation was all. There were very few posts towards the top of the pyramid, and there competition was intense. In formal terms, the culmination was the consulship, the supreme constitutional magistracy. But beyond the consulship were the great provincial commands. Those without substantial military garrisons were—in theory—in the gift of the senate (the most prestigious being Africa and Asia), and those that included major forces fell within the remit of the emperor, who appointed their governors direct, notionally as deputies to himself. Of the latter, under the Early Empire, it is said that the governorship of Britain ranked alongside Syria in conferring the highest prestige. Just why that should be so is worth considering. With a garrison of three full legions (sometimes four) plus a large number of regular auxiliary units its military establishment was remarkably large: it has been calculated that at times it represented 10 per cent of the entire imperial army. It also had unconquered tribes with whom there was always the possibility of war. This was not necessarily seen as a disadvantage by those who wanted the appointment: it is unhistorical to project back into the past modern attitudes to war and peace. There was space, too, for actual territorial expansion of the empire. In the particular context of the period from Boudicca to Diocletian, there is some disagreement here between the authors of Chapter 2 and Chapter 6 above on whether the emperors were more or less permanently committed to expansion in Britain. The author of the latter has pointed out in discussion that there were more years without war than with, and that the army in Britain spent far longer periods in establishing, maintaining, and sometimes retracting frontiers than in offensive action. Yet it can be argued that acceptance of a limit to Roman claims of universal right to rule seems rarely to have been on the cards, whatever practical circumstances actually dictated. It is certainly true that Britain seems to have been a theatre of choice for emperors like Claudius and Antoninus Pius needing a military reputation, and that it retained an attraction beyond the Early Empire for emperors campaigning in person (Septimius Severus and Constantius I with major campaigns beyond the northern frontier, possibly also Constantine, Constans, and Magnus Maximus). It is probable that the potential propaganda advantages taken into account by these emperors were not just Britain's stereotypical reputation: any success could be more easily magnified and failure minimized than in provinces closer to the metropolitan centres of power. Cynically, it could also be pointed out that Britain was cut off from the Continent by the Ocean, and that military disaster there would not seriously affect the empire at large.

The army

It is well-recognized that the army played an extremely important part in the everyday working of the Roman empire, particularly under the Early Empire before the elaborate structure of the imperial civil service had fully evolved. In the provinces governors, for example, would have been left without staff if deprived either of the troops directly attached to them or the many soldiers on detachment stationed in ones and twos around the province for specific purposes. Without this, the infrastructure such as the Imperial Post would have not functioned; the systems of justice would have broken down without soldiers acting as gendarmerie and as clerks, gaolers, and executioners; and direct interventions to assist local communities would have been impossible without specialists such as architects, surveyors, and water engineers. Intelligence agents fed the administration with information; and behind it all the main formations of the army were the means to enforce internal security if it ever became necessary. Although modern conceptions of the Roman army concentrate mostly on the army at war, this highly disciplined and multi-skilled army certainly spent most of its life in peacetime activity, and there must have been many soldiers who never saw action in the whole of their careers. It is thus not surprising that a striking feature of the Late Roman civil administration is that it took on more and more of the trappings of the military: this was essentially the style in which the general population had always experienced the impact of central government.

There is another side to the Roman army that is much less often appreciated. There is plenty of evidence that it was not universally popular, particularly in the frontier provinces and near the highways by which troops were moved about the empire. But the problems were greater than a tendency of troops to behave badly or—at a more official level—to demand unwelcome requisitions from local communities of supplies and subsidies. A combination of the high value put on reputation—particularly military reputation—and a very long-established tendency for troops to become more attached to their own commanders than to the state meant that the possibility of civil war was never totally absent, even under the firmest of emperors.

Huge resources must have been wasted over the centuries as Roman armies fought one another, yet the empire did not collapse. That fact makes it much easier to understand why in the early fifth century no one seems to have realized that the continuance of that tradition was about to bring the whole edifice in the West finally crashing down.

The emperor in person

Examples of military intervention by emperors in person in Britain have been noted at many points in this book, whether it was a matter of conquest (Claudius or Septimius Severus) or reconquest (Constantius I) or major military reorganization (Hadrian's Wall), but it is possible to trace examples of their direct influence in other ways as well. It is highly likely, for example, that the dedication inscription of the city forum at Wroxeter—erected by the *civitas* of the Cornovii in honour of Hadrian—reflects personal intervention by the emperor during his visit to Britain to revive a failing Flavian urban initiative. The intention, it would seem, had been to create a city on the site of a former legionary base, intended to act as a pacifying influence by drawing the locals into participation in normal provincial life. In this case we can reasonably infer the likely purpose. However, the serious-minded modern historian can easily be led astray by assuming that all imperial decisions were conditioned by considerations of state or taken under the imperatives of politics. An emperor's personal taste or whim might just as easily be involved, and this could influence the actions not only of those few unfortunate emperors generally accepted as unbalanced such as Caligula, Commodus, or Elagabalus but also some of the greatest such as Hadrian, whose personal aesthetic passions not only had a huge effect on the culture of the empire but were matched by a notable level of intellectual arrogance. The execution of his predecessor Trajan's supreme master of large-scale design Apollodorus for criticizing Hadrian's personal forays into large-scale architecture is well known, but one is tempted to speculate, for example, that the original scheme for Hadrian's Wall that proved to need so much modification owed more to intellectual neatness and visual effect than practical military appreciation of the terrain. Personal sentiment towards particular regions on the part of the emperor could also profoundly affect their fortunes. It has been suggested that the remarkable flowering of the Romano-British villas in the first half of the fourth century—implying high prosperity and confidence among the provincial elite—owed much to personal favour from Constantine the Great towards the place that had seen his successful usurpation of power and its leading citizens. The reverse of the coin is the ultimately failed usurpation of Magnentius, and the subsequent decimation of the elite by the victor: the villa-culture was never so brilliant again. One is tempted to suspect that recollection half-a-century later of those good times lies behind the curious statement in the ancient source that the British usurper Constantine III was chosen in 406/7 'because of his name': he certainly strove to make capital out any association in people's minds with the imperial family of the glorious past by adopting the style 'Flavius Claudius Constantinus' on his coinage and renaming his sons as Constans and Julian.

An imperial visit or intended visit could have considerable effects, even without any particular intention on the part of a visiting emperor. It is generally thought that the residence of the imperial family and major officers of state at York at the end of the reign of Septimius Severus—in effect the temporary transfer of the central government of the empire—had substantial effects on that city. The ceremonial arrivals and departures of emperors were great events, sometimes permanently recorded in coinage or the visual arts, and it is known, too, that palatial accommodation was provided in anticipation of a possible visit even where no actual arrival is known to have taken place. The curious history of the enormous basilica of Roman London—the largest north of the Alps—may well reflect one or even two such events. It replaced an earlier Flavian forum of normal size for a provincial city, and has been shown archaeologically to have had two phases, with the probability that construction had been begun around the end of the first century, abandoned, and restarted early in the second. We do not yet have certainty about the exact relative dating to the basilica of the fort at London—in itself not only large but also an extreme rarity in a city under the Early Empire—or of the rebuilding in stone of the existing Flavian timber amphitheatre or the reconstruction of the Huggin Hill baths. But it is not unreasonable to suspect that some of these activities related to the visit of Hadrian. Might the earlier phase of the large basilica also be material evidence of an expected imperial visit? Tacitus, eager to pin any available blame on the Emperor Domitian and to show Agricola in the best possible light, described Britain as completely conquered and then almost immediately let slip. The emperor is likely to have seen it in an entirely different light—even after the closure of the legionary fortress at Inchtuthil, which could be regarded as a sign of total pacification in Scotland rather than retreat. It is tempting to see the great monumental arch constructed at the port of Richborough in the late first century as intended to mark the completion of conquest, and its location on the site of the principal—or only—beachhead of the Claudian invasion as highly symbolic. To take this hypothesis a little further, one can begin to suspect that a visit by the Emperor Domitian in person to Britain in the late 80s or 90s was anticipated (he was indeed in Germany in 89, and might have intended to come on to Britain). It is possible to imagine great building projects being put in hand but halted if the visit was postponed due to the military emergencies that are attested elsewhere in the period, or abandoned with the murder of the emperor in 96 and the subsequent solemn *damnatio memoriae*, the official erasure of his memory.

Imperial assistance in local projects is well attested right across the empire, sometimes on the initiative of the emperor himself, but very often in response to appeals from the provinces. It is certain that the presence of emperors will have caused a flood of petitions from communities in Britain for assistance in public projects or the settlement of disputes. A huge amount of the time of any emperor was taken up with responding to such approaches. Britain's distance from the centres of imperial power will have made it more difficult for communities to mount such petitions than in the case of most other provinces, and the importance of making the very best use of the very rare imperial visits must have seemed great. But there were other channels. Right from the days of the Roman Republic senators had regarded it as a duty that reflected well on themselves to represent at Rome the interests of provincial communities with which they had some personal or family connection. A fascinating insight into the way in which the Roman empire actually worked is provided by a remarkable inscription from the modest Roman county town of Caerwent, the *civitas* capital of the Silures of South Wales. This stone seems to fit into this context, with an interesting twist. It is dated to just before 220. The *ordo* (the membership of the council of the

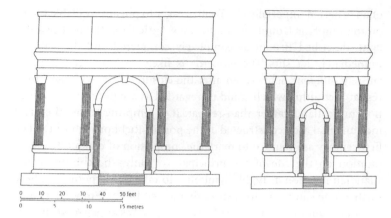

Figure 24 Reconstruction of the four-way commemorative arch built at Richborough under the Emperor Domitian, very significantly on the site of the Claudian invasion bridgehead. This was probably after the Battle of Mons Graupius, marking what seemed to be at the time the completion of the conquest of Britain. It was encased in Carrara marble and bore gilded bronze statuary. It is possible that after the murder of this much-hated emperor the monument was defaced: it was certainly stripped and converted into a watchtower in the third century and demolished in the fourth.

civitas) erects a monument in honour of Tiberius Claudius Paulinus, formerly commander of the Second Legion stationed nearby at Caerleon, subsequently governor of the senatorial province of Narbonensis (Mediterranean Gaul) and then of the imperial province of Lugdunensis (Northern and Central Gaul). The career ought to indicate that he was a man on the way up. The Silures must have made his acquaintance when he was legionary commander, and one presumes from the inscription that they were impressed by him (and he with them). The top of the inscription is missing, but it has been suggested that the councillors were hoping that he would act as 'patron' when they needed some favour from the imperial authorities. As they do not mention any particular act for which they are grateful, it was probably a matter of hope of future benefit rather than thanks for past actions. They may or may not have known that he was about to return to Britain as a governor, but the fact that he actually became governor of Lower Britain (rather than the province of Upper Britain in which the Silures were situated) suggests that it was influence with

Figure 25 Statue base from Caerwent (*Venta Silurum*): an example of local government (a *civitas*) in action at arguably the peak of the system before the worst of the upheavals of the third century. Just before 220 the council (*ordo*) of the *res publica* of the Silures of South Wales has by decree (*ex decreto*) set up this monument in honour of Tiberius Claudius Paulinus, formerly commander (*legatus legionis*) of the Second Legion *Augusta* stationed nearby at Caerleon (*Isca*), then governor (*proconsul*) of Gallia Narbonensis (Provence), and currently governor (*legatus Augusti*) of *Gallia Lugdunensis* (Central Gaul). The status of such a *civitas* had recently changed: since the *Constitutio Antoniniana* of 212 (the empire-wide declaration of universal citizenship) *all* its citizens had Roman citizenship, with the remedies access to Roman law bestowed. A monument such as this, however, makes it clear that friendly relations between the local worthies of a distant province and a member of the senatorial aristocracy near the top of the imperial administration whom they happened to know personally were still as important as when their *civitas* was merely *peregrina*, or 'native'. From his names, Paulinus' own family were probably provincial in origin and enfranchised two centuries earlier: this inscription underlines the continuous capacity of the empire to absorb and integrate.

the emperor that they had in mind, not favours from the provincial administration. By a strange coincidence, we do have an inscription from Gaul recording exchanges between this Paulinus and a provincial worthy, Titus Sennius Sollemnis. The latter describes himself as 'friend' (*amicus*) and *cliens*. This relationship of mutual obligation between greater and lesser that lay at the centre of Roman society and in which membership of a great man's *clientela* could go far beyond individuals to whole communities, even whole provinces. The content of that Gallic inscription reveals just how mutual the services could be, and how intertwined the interests of governors and provinces could become. It records how an attempt had been made to accuse Paulinus of misconduct before the central council of the Gallic provinces (a committee of leading provincials, whose resolutions were one of the few formal ways by which provincials could aid or damage the careers of governors). Sollemnis had used a procedural device to halt the motion, and spoken to such good effect that the accusation was dismissed. It is not impossible that behind the Caerwent monument—apparently erected while Paulinus was still in his second post in Gaul—lay some move by the Silures to show support while he was in political danger at the Council of the Gauls, in hope of favours to come. Sollemnis certainly did well subsequently at the hands of Paulinus when the latter had taken up his appointment in Lower Britain, receiving the offer of a post on the governor's staff and a number of expensive gifts. Nowadays this might carry a whiff of political corruption: the very different attitude of Romans is neatly underlined by the fact that these gifts are meticulously listed on the inscription in exactly the same manner as honours would be recorded then and now.

Rules, documents, and literacy

In the first century the Silures had been a fierce tribe that took over three decades to subdue. In the early third century—and now all Roman citizens—they have become deeply embedded in the Roman way of life, their *respublica* now a fully-functioning element in the system of empire, with all its network of rules, conventions, dues, and ties of mutual advantage built up over centuries. Indeed, for provincials to survive and prosper once absorbed into the empire there was little alternative, since the change was so great. Much weight has been placed on the writing tablets from Vindolanda, as indicating not only a society dominated by documentation, but also a high level of literacy profoundly affecting everyday life. It has, indeed, been pointed out that huge quantities of documents must once have existed, since few transactions of an official or semi-official nature took place that were not confirmed in writing. We know, for example, that permits to travel via the network maintained for the Imperial Post were signed by the emperor and bore an expiry date. That implies perhaps hundreds of examples a year across the empire from that class of documents alone, and every one consigned to the rubbish bin once used or out of date. On an altogether greater scale, we have to imagine thousands and thousands of tax receipts issued, all essentially ephemeral. The discovery at Vindolanda of the bonfire that represented the clearing out of an office underlines not only the sheer amount of paperwork on which Roman society ran but also the extent to which the written document had become a throw-away item too much part of everyday life to be treasured.

It may be objected that Vindolanda is not representative of Roman Britain as a whole, since the documents are entirely from a military milieu, some official, others from individual soldiers or dependants—and we know that the Roman army was literate. Moreover, local British do not appear, except as subjects of scorn. That argument has to be regarded with caution, as the Vindolanda collection dates almost entirely to around 100, with a great deal more Romanization of the province to come. It collapses when the equally fascinating collections of votive tablets from sacred sites such as Bath and Uley are considered, or the small but significant number of graffiti on pots, tiles, domestic instruments, and walls, for they reveal that the everyday concerns of ordinary civilians with no discernible military connections and from parts of the country without significant garrisons still found their outlet in writing, however informal. Moreover, the Vindolanda tablets are not alone, single examples having turned up elsewhere. Only a little later than the Vindolanda tablets, the writing tablet from Roman London dated to 118 referred to in Chapter 5 above records in careful legal language an adjudication following a site visit in a property dispute relating to a wood in Kent. This is the same world as is familiar to us in literature from the classical Mediterranean, as in Cicero's discussion of whether the seller of a house is obliged to inform the prospective vendor of defects known to him that are not visible. It is of course true that one might find written documents in a legal context even in societies generally illiterate. One would not, however, expect in an illiterate world to find containers, such as the ubiquitous amphoras in which olive oil, fish sauce, wine, and similar products were imported, labelled—as they sometimes are—with shipper and contents. That implies reliance upon written information at a much more everyday level of activity. And in the final analysis, even today it is not necessary for everyone in the community to be literate or even semi-literate for societies based on written material to work.

All these transactions are, it should be noted, being conducted in Latin. A small number of Greek inscriptions have been found in Britain, and a few words of other languages are recorded, but almost

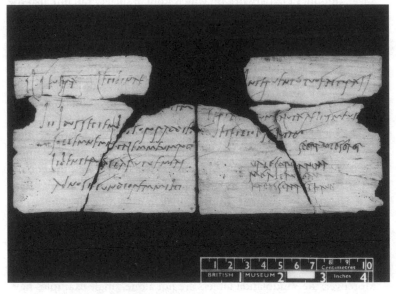

Figure 26 Claudia Severa dictated this letter to a secretary when she invited her friend Sulpicia Lepidina, wife of the fort commandant at Vindolanda on the northern frontier around AD 100, to visit her on the occasion of her birthday. However, in adding an affectionately pressing postscript to the formal invitation, she has given us an extended example of her own handwriting.

nothing in native Celtic. This is also largely true in Gaul—and even there, when Gallic does occur, either Roman or Greek script is employed. In Britain, at any rate, if you needed or wanted something written, you expected it to be in Latin, and you required Latin (or a good interpreter) to navigate yourself round this complicated world in which the written word was king. Nor was that necessarily a disadvantage: the fact that the parties to that Kentish property document seem to have had Gallic, Spanish, and possibly Italian ethnic origins vividly illuminates the obvious but not always remembered point that Latin—whether originally imposed as on recruits to the Roman army or acquired as the unavoidable currency of life beyond the isolated rural settlement—was the *lingua franca* that made the workings of this sophisticated society possible. Nor was this only at the level of officialdom or business. In cosmopolitan places such as London or the ports or some of the civil settlements outside military establishments a remarkable kaleidoscope could be observed. It would be difficult to find anywhere a better instance of ethnic mix and social mobility than is represented by the handsome monument to his late wife erected in the cemetery outside the stores base and port of South Shields on the Tyne by a Syrian civilian from the great city of Palmyra in the deserts of the eastern frontier of the empire. The inscription itself is bilingual, being in Latin with a lament in Palmyrene, but the rather shaky Latin itself has suggested an author more at home in Greek. Furthermore, we learn from the text that the dignified Roman matron portrayed in the accompanying relief sculpture was not only British—from the *civitas* of the Catuvellauni centred on Verulamium—but had been a slave before he freed and married her. One can only speculate what the family spoke at home: if her native tongue was Celtic, the household could have commanded four languages. The one certainly common tongue was Latin, the medium that made Roman Britain work.

Slave and free

Slavery is an emotive subject but has to be addressed head on. It certainly existed in Roman Britain, just as it also existed in Iron Age Britain: manacles and chain-gang collars have been found, and

Strabo records the slave trade between Britain and the Roman empire, clearly involving Britons selling other Britons to Romans. We also know that slaves were part of society in Anglo-Saxon England. There is relatively little archaeological evidence for slavery in Roman Britain, though research on the subject is active and may produce new light. On the other hand, the substantial epigraphic evidence for freedmen and freedwomen (slaves freed by their masters) implies the prior presence of slaves. And this practice of emancipation (sometimes purchased out of savings, often in the master's will, and sometimes—as in the case of Regina cited above—clearly out of affection) reminds us of a cardinal element in Roman slavery. Our modern perception is heavily coloured both by cinema representations of Spartacus and the like and by black slavery in the New World. There were certainly terrible instances of barracked slavery and forced labour in quarries and mines (including by convicts). This is particularly well-attested on the great estates of Italy under the Roman Republic, and will have been fed by the huge supplies of new captives during the wars of conquest. However, with major expansion of the empire ceasing after the early second century AD, the supply of slaves, will mostly have declined to those home-born from slave parents. Moreover landowners under the empire are recorded as doubting the productivity of unwilling slaves on the land as against that of free estate workers and tenants. Outside the labourer level in agriculture and industry, many slaves (especially educated slaves with professional skills) had a very different life, with substantial numbers in responsible positions. Those at the very top—such as the imperial slaves (*servi Augusti*) who were influential and feared officers of the emperor—could be important people. Freedmen certainly often were—for example Narcissus, the enormously rich secretary to the Emperor Claudius, whose speech to the hesitating troops of the force assembled opposite Britain in AD 43 tipped the balance and prevented the invasion from being aborted. Large numbers of freedmen also founded prosperous free families. Though the status of a freedman imposed some restrictions, these did not apply to their children, who were full citizens. It is very important not to paint too rosy a picture: as slaves they had had none of what we would now call human rights and were subject to the whim of their masters, but it is conversely true that being a slave was not in Roman times an absolute and irreversible condition. Emancipation was a substantial element in social mobility: it certainly fed the professional middle classes, and there are even examples of slave origins of senatorial families.

Decision-making and its location

Mention of matters of property earlier in this chapter leads also back to another theme touched upon at the beginning of this book, that decisions affecting Britain—even at the local level—were now often taken elsewhere. As mentioned in Chapter 5, it is known that in the empire at large very substantial amounts of property fell into the hands of the emperors in one way or another. Some of it was subsequently given away again, as supporters and favourites were rewarded, but since the personal property of the last emperor was absorbed into the general imperial estate at the beginning of the next reign the cumulative effect was probably a greater and greater holding. Decisions on these lands cannot have avoided being coloured by factors outside the particular localities. This factor, however, went beyond imperial properties. While it is very likely indeed that the majority of villa, farm, or temple estates in Britain were in the hands of Romano-Britons, we cannot ignore the phenomenon of the multi-millionaire with what would now be called 'global' interests, particularly in the western part of the empire in the Late Roman period. The Italian lady Melania, mentioned in Chapter 5, decided in 404 to give her huge wealth to the Church. This included estates not only in Italy itself but also in Spain, the North African provinces, Sicily, and Britain, which she sold off one by one. Similarly, the fourth-century senator Symmachus had at least fifteen different houses, in Rome, Italy, and Mauretania. Such magnates had the power to affect large numbers of people: one of Melania's estates, for example, is said to have included sixty-two settlements. When considering individual parts of the empire such as Britain, therefore, it is never wise to assume that even at the private level decisions were taken for local reasons alone—or at all.

At a political level, many examples have occurred earlier in this book of decisions taken outside Britain—often primarily for non-British reasons—that affected Britain, such as Caesar's or Claudius' invasions or the dreadful purge of alleged disloyal elements in Britain following the defeat of the usurper Magnentius. But there were also political moves originating in Britain itself whose driving forces were external to the Isles. It is very noticeable, for example, that almost all the serious uprisings in Britain that were part of Roman politics—as opposed to that of Boudicca which was a native rebellion against Roman rule as such—were aimed not at possession of Britain alone but at the imperial throne. Clodius Albinus, Constantine the Great, Magnus Maximus, and Constantine III all sought to become emperor in the fullest sense. Even in the case of Carausius and Allectus, their realm not only extended onto the Continent but they portrayed themselves as equal participants in the governmental system of multiple emperors that was established by Diocletian. Indeed, that system itself aided this conception, because, although in practice different members took responsibility for different geographical parts of the empire, in theory they governed it all collectively and the area in which each emperor was based was irrelevant.

Later Roman Britain

The changes that occurred in Roman Britain in the third and fourth centuries that have been traced in this book did not mirror exactly those in other parts of the empire, but the overall shifts can be paralleled elsewhere. Britain certainly suffered less from barbarian incursions and civil war in the third century than many other provinces, particularly those on the near Continent. This led to its Late Roman reputation as a place of notable prosperity, reflected in recorded incidents such as the summoning of skilled craftsmen by Constantius I from Britain to Gaul after his recovery of the island from Allectus to help rebuild the great city of Autun, which had been seriously damaged in an earlier civil war. These *artifices* were available because Britain had a surplus of them (some had, no doubt, been working on Allectus' would-be imperial palace in London and maybe other *grands projets*, now not required). Half a century later, the Emperor Julian was constructing a fleet of transports and great warehouses to bring grain from Britain to feed his armies on the Rhine, short of supplies from Continental sources devastated by hostile action.

Other major changes that we have seen in Britain reflect those elsewhere in the empire, though often with a British twist. The nature of the empire had evolved from a system in which a relatively small number of Romans governed provinces whose largely non-citizen populations ran their own day-to-day affairs through the *civitates* and other local bodies to one in which the central government operated a very large measure of direct rule over the now all-citizen population through a vastly increased military and civil imperial bureaucracy. It is not surprising that such changes are mirrored in the archaeological record. In the *civitas* capitals of Britain, for example, expenditure on public buildings and other civic amenities tails off in much the same way as in many other parts of the empire. The private donors on whom civic authorities had largely relied were always to a substantial extent local worthies who served on their councils and were expected to reciprocate local honour with generosity. It is not therefore surprising that signs of munificence in the municipalities decline as simultaneously local office became a burden rather than a pleasure and the paths of ambition for provincials shifted from the civic arena to the imperial service. Perhaps the most striking example is the manner in which many of the town-hall basilicas ('forum-basilicas') show clear evidence for change of use or disuse. The shift of power, ambition, and private expenditure away from the *civitates* is the context, but it does not justify an automatic assumption that the towns were no longer of any importance. The modern example of London's County Hall, sold and converted to private uses on the abolition of the civic authority for whom it had been built, must cause us to pause when assuming that the loss of its basilica implies that a Roman city was in terminal decline. The demolition of London's huge basilica—now two centuries old and shown archaeo-logically to have become decrepit and possibly unsafe—need cause no surprise when local power was shifting away from civic elites to the agents of central government. In the particular and spectacular case of London that may well have been accelerated by the actual presence in the city of a would-be imperial central government in the persons of Carausius and Allectus and their retinues, with different needs in the way of official buildings. The mood across the empire of change—not collapse—is nicely caught by an inscription from a North Italian town that records the relocation of statues by order of the provincial governor from the forum, because few people now saw them there. Certainly the argument that the disuse of forum-basilicas indicates a failure of towns in Britain and is a symptom of weak Romanization leading to an eventual peculiarly British end collapses when one observes other Roman provinces. Valeria, a town on a comparable scale in central Spain, displays the same phenomenon: a town basilica converted to other uses by the end of the third century. In the same region, a similar town—Segobriga—presents other evidence that if encountered in Britain would probably be interpreted as a sign of terminal decline: both the theatre and the amphitheatre went out of use, and their sites were occupied by low-class fourth- and fifth-century housing. Yet we also know that Segobriga survived long after the end of Roman rule, indeed right through the Visigothic period as well. If the towns of Late Roman Britain were really no longer vital, the provision of ever-more powerful and spectacular defences to many would be very difficult to explain, let alone the fact that in Britain (unlike some other provinces) these defences enclosed most of the built-up area of the Early Empire conurbation. We must be seeing the rising importance of centralized government: the modernized defences, the fewer but larger houses, and the apparently much greater extent of open ground (perhaps now private gardens and parks) are exactly what one would expect of the burgeoning official class of the Late Empire, clustering where important officers were located. The fourth-century multiplication of imperial officials of high rank based in London that was noted in Chapter 3 above provides an excellent example. Such a 'kremlin' situation is, admittedly, much easier on the imagination in those many Continental towns that have small Late Roman defensive circuits within the much larger extent to which the urban areas had spread during the Early Empire. The contrast, however, is more likely to derive from the historical accident that far more British towns had relatively recent walls that could be updated than from any fundamental difference of function. Late Roman towns were *different* from those of the Early Empire, not dead.

The Church

It was noted in Chapter 3 above that there is plenty of archaeological evidence for the persistence of paganism in nominally Christian Britain. Indeed, for the whole of the fourth century there was a long drawn-out rearguard action in the empire at large against the Church, much of it coming from people in the top levels of society. However, the conversion of Constantine and the transformation of Christianity—effectively from persecuted sect to state religion—did inject a fundamental new element into the empire. Indeed, it is not difficult to argue that for its long-term consequences the unconstitutional elevation of Constantine to the throne at York was the most important single event that occurred in Roman Britain, possibly—on the stage of world history—the most important in the history of the British Isles. It is not necessary to be a Christian to think on these lines. Indeed, without a belief in divine providence, it is even more remarkable as a historic event. Certainly within the history of the Roman empire alone, it is unlikely that the Church would have had anything like its effect had Constantine and his successors not decided that it was an imperial duty to support correct doctrine and little by little increasingly to use the power of the state to enforce it. It was, of course, not just a matter of a perceived religious duty on the part of believers to encourage the worship of a true god. The persecutions of Christians—at least the most recent and most terrifying ones—had been launched chiefly because it had been thought that the travails of the empire were due to the anger of the pagan gods. The restoration of their worship had therefore seemed an essential part of imperial recovery. The spectacular victory of Constantine under the Christian banner over his traditionalist rival Maxentius at the Battle of the Milvian Bridge reversed this situation. It is ironic that Maxentius was no persecutor—indeed, notably tolerant towards the Church—but the full support of the exclusive Christian god was clearly now what the state needed for its well-being and therefore had to secure. In the second half of the fourth century the removal of the altar of Victory from the Senate House in Rome became a major matter of contention, and by the end Theodosius I had legislated to forbid pagan observances even in the home. Equally striking at the time—and with much longer consequences extending through history to the present day—was the use of political and military power to support particular versions of Christianity. This was often political, but also reflected the immemorial Roman belief that in religion exact adherence to prescribed ritual was vital for it to be effective. Britain has the melancholy distinction—in the person of Magnus Maximus—of having seen the elevation of the first emperor to employ the death penalty for heresy.

The fourth-century emperors also profoundly shifted the balance of influence in society not only by giving special privileges to the Church and clergy—as has been touched upon—but also endowed churches with vast amounts of wealth confiscated from temples. In many cases pagan temples had accumulated great wealth over the centuries, and were often in practice the depositories of the reserves of civic communities. Churches were also much enriched financially by the gifts of the pious rich, as we have seen above in the case of Melania and her husband. Such a shift not only represented a shift of comparative wealth but also tied the Church into the Late Antique system of society based on large-scale property-owning among whose great landowners it was beginning to be numbered.

It is not perhaps surprising that the collapse of this society in Britain after the end of Roman rule also seems to have brought down the Romano-British Church. It is very significant that St Germanus' famous encounter at Verulamium in 429 with doctrinally heretical British Christians (whose magnificent apparel—so characteristic of the Late Roman rich—is stressed in the source) should have taken place at one of the relatively few sites where there is archaeological evidence for the continuance of elements of a Roman lifestyle. Overall, however, the Church that survived in the fifth century in western Britain and spread outside the former Roman borders in the North and spectacularly to Ireland reflected the alternative austere and monastic tradition that had been emerging on the Continent alongside the more worldly manifestations of the creed. The Romano-British Church thus became the parent of the decidedly different Celtic Church which had such a huge effect on the succeeding history of the British Isles but which, one can argue, would not have been born without it.

Economic change

The changes in the towns in the Later Roman period also seem to reflect important changes in the general economy. Studies of ceramics and other commodities show a substantial drop in imports and dominance of markets by such British centres of production as the Oxfordshire potteries. Much of the commercial quayside of Roman London went out of use from the third century, reflecting this substantial drop in imports. Britain was becoming increasingly self-sufficient. The effects of inflation during the imperial political chaos of the third century have probably been overestimated: decline in long-distance trade in the empire was not necessarily to the detriment of the more outlying provinces. It will have been positively advantageous to local producers as these areas caught up in technology and in the development of a fully-operating money economy. It must be true that the presence of far fewer troops in Late Roman Britain (particularly of the most highly paid units) sharply reduced the amount of money coming in to pay and sustain the military establishment—and from that to circulate in the economy. However, the vast increase under the Late Empire of officials receiving salaries and other financial benefits may well have begun to balance this out, not to mention the huge accumulation of private wealth by the land-owning classes. At least equally important may have been the consequences of the Late Roman innovation of large-scale detailed management by the agents of the central government of the supply system for the official military and civil establishment. This included the direct production of arms, uniforms, and the like in state-run factories, at least one of which is known in Britain from documentary sources, though its exact location is uncertain. It also included the setting-up of storage depots, which we may imagine receiving not only supplies directly produced, but also the results of the large-scale taxation in kind that the reformed fiscal system introduced by the Emperor Diocletian. Fourth-century Britain may, indeed, be seen as a sort of life-form in which the circulation of money—or equivalents in kind with a defined monetary value—was central to existence. Taxpayers had to work to earn in order to pay up, and expenditure by the government and by those who benefited by the operation of the system (not least by the elaborate structure of exemptions of various kinds) kept the mechanism turning. The rich certainly became richer: whether the poor became poorer is usually assumed, but difficult to prove. Social mobility had been a notable feature of the Early Empire: under the Late Empire an individual's prospects of betterment cannot have been helped by imperial attempts by regulation to keep people in the occupation to which they had been born, attempts not limited to the labouring classes though perhaps especially hard on the peasant farmer. The municipal middle classes were undoubtedly impoverished—at least those who did not manage to escape into the new bureaucracy, the army, or the Church. It is certain that across the Roman world high status continued to be reflected through ownership of land (the vast holdings mentioned earlier are only extreme examples), but there is a real shift from wealth and power displayed through public munificence towards personal display through possessions, including a developing delight in fashion, especially elaborate and colourful clothing. It is not entirely surprising that we see archaeologically a flowering of the luxury trades: on the one hand a startling growth of grand villas (including examples of highly sophisticated and, by previous standards, exotic architecture) and the decorative arts they stimulated, on the other the portable chattels of extraordinary richness known to us from the almost exclusively Late Roman treasures that have been found in Britain. The latter, too, reflects the growing tendency towards marking official occasions by elaborate gifts in kind: presentations in gold and in plate became meticulously graduated according to rank. This must to some extent have become a circular process, in which reception of such gifts and their display demonstrated the favour in which the recipient was held in imperial circles and consequent status and influence. It is not difficult to imagine these possessions on show at dinner parties in the entertainment suites that are a feature of the late villas: literary and archaeological evidence supports the popularity of elaborate dining among the upper classes of the Late Roman world, a trend towards which Tacitus had satirically noted already in late first-century Britain.

The 'end' of Roman Britain

Readers will have realized in the course of this book that there are major differences of opinion about what happened in Late Roman Britain and how it came to an end. The tendency is to look for a single cause, while the probability is that there were many causes that contributed to the outcome. We can perhaps pick out one or two that are underplayed. At one time it was generally held that the Late Roman army was a shadow of its former self. This is a view that was in part driven by the same notion of a 'classic' period and subsequent decline (rather than change) that we saw earlier in relation to literature, the arts, and government. The Late Roman regular army—at least for the first three-quarters of the fourth century—is nowadays more often seen as having changed to meet new circumstances, but still efficient, well-equipped, and highly trained. That training had always been fundamentally rooted in the possession of immensely experienced middle-ranking and lower officers and a high proportion of long-service individuals in the ranks, whose knowledge was passed on to succeeding generations. This must have been powerfully reinforced as the higher commands passed increasingly from the third century onwards to full-time professionals. And it was not, of course, only military affairs that depended on the efficiency and extraordinary adaptability of the army. The very wide use of contingents of troops and individual soldiers—particularly specialists—in the practical and administrative business of government throughout the empire that we have noted earlier was central to its effective functioning and survival.

The presence of 'barbarians' in the Late Roman army—perhaps a quarter of the officers in the fourth century—has often been cited as evidence of decline. This is very misleading, because it conflates the existence of many men in the fourth-century *regular* army who were first- or second-generation immigrants (chiefly—in the West—Germanic) with the temporary presence of very large contingents of 'barbarians' in the armies of the late fourth century and fifth *under their own leaders*. The former became thoroughly Romanized (a process that the army had been carrying out for centuries), the latter were essentially free agents who could change sides without warning, depending on who would pay them or offer the best prospects of plunder or (increasingly) land. It is only necessary to recall that the Alaric who so sensationally sacked Rome in 410 and became a byword for barbarian assault on civilization was the same Alaric who was one of the commanders of the powerful contingents of Goths in the army with which the Emperor Theodosius the Great at the Battle of the River Frigidus in 394 regained the western half of the empire for the second time from usurpers. It is significant that it was Roman actions that turned Alaric into such a powerful enemy. Disappointed of an expectation that his services to Theodosius would be rewarded with an appointment at the top of the Roman military hierarchy he became an independent *condottiere*, backed by the Gothic warriors who had followed him to the Frigidus. It is in this context—the paid employment of non-Roman allies in the course of internal imperial politics—that the Sack of Rome occurred. Alaric and his Goths had not been paid off after being contracted to take part in an attack by western Roman forces on the eastern part of the empire that was aborted for internal reasons.

It is now widely accepted that the real change in the quality of the Roman army had been marked by the death of the Emperor Valens and the destruction of perhaps two-thirds of the eastern part of the regular army by the Goths at the Battle of Adrianople in 378, leading to the loss of that vital core of experience. In 382 Theodosius, the new emperor, made an agreement giving large groups of barbarians land within the Danube frontier under their own chieftains in exchange for military service—from which they could withdraw at will. Making up the loss of experience in the eastern army might have been possible by drawing on the units stationed in the West, but in 383 the usurpation of Magnus Maximus that started in Britain progressively cut Theodosius off from the western provinces. Five years later, in 388, he decisively defeated Maximus' forces, using substantial contingents of Germans and Huns, just as he was subsequently to employ Alaric at the Frigidus in 394. Thus the western army suffered major defeats twice in the same fashion in a relatively short space of time, and one suspects that its regular components were henceforth in no better shape than those in the East.

It is against this background that what happened in Britain in the early fifth century has to be investigated. There is still no agreement among modern writers on the period: one or two of the theories have been aired earlier in this book, and the titles listed in the Further Reading section for Chapter 3 have deliberately been chosen to include the full gamut of opinion. What is fairly common ground is that very much less of Roman Britain survived than of Roman Gaul. Yet among specialists on the Early Anglo-Saxon period it is becoming widely accepted that the major invasions of Britain that were once thought to have brought substantial movements of Germanic peoples into the country at this time did not take place. There does, therefore, seem to be a gap lasting for most of the first half of the fifth century in which the withering of the Roman way of life in Britain has to take place unaided by large movements of new peoples inward from outside. This does not, of course, rule out the involvement of Germanic chieftains on a much smaller scale but in a similar fashion to Alaric. Quite small bands of fighting men could have a disproportionate effect once the regular army—and the structure of command to coordinate it—was no longer on hand. What marks out the end of the first decade in Britain from the neighbouring provinces—indeed from the other dioceses in the Praetorian Prefecture of the Gauls—is that the final end of Roman rule was an actual expulsion of imperial officials and positive rejection of the vast network of rules and regulations on which the system operated, from top to bottom. It does not matter that the emperor to whom the officials answered was the usurper Constantine III: the system will have been unaltered. Even if those who seem to have appealed to Honorius in 410 accepted that their action would involve the return of that structure, it clearly did not happen. Many suggestions have been put forward for the motives of those who so decisively rejected the system, and indeed they were probably many, complex, and through lack of evidence, effectively unknowable. One very striking apparent difference from Late Roman Gaul and Spain is that we have no evidence for the provincial elite of Britain—in the sense of permanent residents rather than imperial office-holders posted to Britain or absentee landlords—occupying high office in the empire at large, or, indeed, of this elite containing anyone of senatorial rank. If this was really so, then there may have been at least three major consequences. It is easy to imagine that the disadvantages of the imperial system—with its huge demands for money and manpower—seemed to the British elite not to be counterbalanced by the personal advantages enjoyed by their counterparts across the Channel. Support for local usurpers may have been augmented by hope of high office, rank, and wealth. If this was followed by disillusion with the would-be emperors' relative lack of success—accompanied by no lifting of the burden of supporting the system—then rejection becomes understandable. Among other grievances, Late Roman landowners particularly resented the conscription of farm workers into the army in a period of severe labour shortage. If that army no longer even provided peace and security in Britain, being drained to support Continental adventures, then confidence is likely to have collapsed. And once the administration had been dismantled—and, right at the centre of the system, there was no longer an imperial authority to issue warrants of appointment and make rulings on matters that could not be settled locally—then lack of experience amongst the leading locals of government at the higher levels and of the dense network of personal contacts that made Roman systems work may well have made it extremely difficult to organize anything on a larger scale than the landed estate or group of estates or—in a few places—possibly the *civitas*.

This rejection is the critical difference between Britain and Spain and most of Gaul (the principal exception being Armorica, where the British example set off something similar). In those provinces there had been no general revolt against the structure of Roman administration, and the incoming Germanic peoples found a functioning system to take over. Indeed, in many areas Roman administrators continued to operate, but answering to new rulers who took over the imperial role. Many of the latter will have had long experience of the empire, and some will actually have served it. In this they were probably substantially different from the Saxons who eventually arrived in Britain. On its side, the Roman civil service encountered by the incomers in the Continental provinces had by this time had many years of involvement with individuals and groups with a Germanic ethnic background—as we have noted earlier—both within the imperial borders and as neighbours without. Even the incumbent Roman landowning class which had been at the centre of Late Roman society in those provinces—and been heavily involved in wider imperial politics—was not entirely dislodged. In many regions formal or informal arrangements emerged by which a proportion of the landed estates were surrendered to the newcomers in exchange for military protection. Indeed, the way of life on some of the great villa estates seems to have continued surprisingly little altered for a remarkably long time. The foundations of the kingdoms of Merovingian France and Visigothic Spain were being laid down.

In Britain, we have not just to imagine the consequences of the sudden disappearance of the people who ran and enforced the system and the rendering inoperative overnight of the legal and practical authority behind it. We have also to envisage the effects on the structure of Romano-British society of halting the mechanism of economic life in its tracks. Most of the troops have almost certainly gone, to prop up Constantine's regime on the Continent, not to mention serving his rebellious generals. The civil officials have now been expelled. The inflow of money to pay army and administration (the spending of which in the provinces was a major prop of the monetary economy) had already become extremely unreliable, but the collection of taxes will have continued till the enforcers were expelled. Once they were expelled and their paperwork empire was dismantled, however, it is inconceivable that it continued. Some local attempts may have been made to raise money for local purposes, but what was at the very centre of the circulation of money had suddenly evaporated—the unremitting need to make surpluses in order to be able to pay taxes, the demands for which everyone knew would come. It is not surprising that the economic system fell apart. Even if physical security and freedom of movement had survived, it is very difficult to envisage how the complex network of trading, production, and craft industry could have continued without the vigorous circulation of money. And even if cash or its equivalents had still been available, the evaporation of an enforceable and universal legal framework in which agreements could be relied upon or debts collected irrespective of the respective locations of producer and client must have crippled all but local economic activity. The closing of the large centres of pottery manufacture is the clearest indicator in the archaeological record—indeed it was not just the factories: the country seems rapidly to have gone from a state in which pottery was a throw-away commodity to one where ceramics were almost unknown.

The growth of the money economy mirrors the overall development of Roman Britain. It is probable that even the Roman Britain of the Early Empire would have disintegrated if there had been an imperial withdrawal—the very large garrison of that period, for example, must have contributed hugely in expenditure and practical involvement. Nevertheless, the highly devolved early system of government in which so much was left to locals *might* have bequeathed a workable structure, particularly while there were still client kingdoms. The vast growth and centralization of the Late Roman state will have made it very much more improbable. If the theory that Roman Britain was only superficially Romanized and was more or less defunct is correct, then one ought to be able to observe a general continuation of everyday life after the end of Roman rule *outside* the specifically Roman centres of activity such as villas and cities, with a gradual return to the quite high prosperity of the Iron Age. It does not seem to happen, except in some isolated places. We can, indeed, be certain that there were now vast variations from place to place and very significant differences in the degree and speed of change, but overall the condition of the British Isles inside the former Roman boundaries must have been much worse after the termination of Roman rule than before its start. The problem was, in short, not too little integration but too much. We do not know how long the process of disintegration took once the core of the system had been removed, but—perhaps in slow motion—Roman Britain without Rome had imploded.

Further Reading

Introduction

Background and reference: general

Boardman, J. (ed.), *The Oxford History of the Classical World*, 1986.

Cunliffe, B. W. (ed.), *History of Prehistoric Europe*, 2000.

Elton, H., *Frontiers of the Roman Empire*, 1996.

Greene, K. T., *Archaeology, an Introduction: The History, Principles, and Methods of Modern Archaeology*, 1983.

Greene, K. T., *The Archaeology of the Roman Economy*, 1986.

Hornblower, S., and Spawforth, A. (eds.), *The Oxford Classical Dictionary*, 3rd edn, 1996.

Howatson, M. C. (ed.), *The Oxford Companion to Classical Literature*, 2nd edn, 1989.

Kent, J. P. C., and Painter, K. S., *The Wealth of the Roman World: Gold and Silver, AD 300–700*, 1977.

Lane Fox, R., *Pagans and Christians*, 1986.

Talbert, R. J. A., *Barrington Atlas of the Greek and Roman World*, 2000.

Background and reference: British Isles

Collingwood, R. G., and Wright, R. P., *The Roman Inscriptions of Britain* (generally referred to as *RIB*). Vol. I, 1965; revised, 1995. This has been followed by an index, and a second volume in eight parts, variously compiled by R. Goodburn, S. S. Frere, R. S. O. Tomlin, and H. Waugh, 1983–95. Vol. III is in preparation. Finds subsequent to a particular section are recorded in the annual epigraphic reports in *Journal of Roman Studies* (to 1969), and *Britannia* (from 1970).

Cunliffe, B. W., *Iron Age Britain*, 1995.

Darvill, T. C., *Prehistoric Britain*, 1987.

Frere, S. S., *Britannia: A History of Roman Britain*, 3rd edn, 1987.

Frere, S. S., and St Joseph, J. K. S., *Roman Britain from the Air*, 1983.

Ireland, S., *Roman Britain: A Sourcebook*, 1986: most of the literary sources in translation, other than the longest (principally Caesar, *Gallic Wars*, and Tacitus, *Agricola*).

Jones, G. D. B., and Mattingly, D., *An Atlas of Roman Britain*, 1990.

Mattingly, H., and Handford, S. A. (trans.), *Tacitus: The Agricola and the Germania*, 1970.

Ordnance Survey, *Map of Roman Britain*, 4th edn, 1978: two sheets (scale 1:625,000) and gazetteer.

Rivet, A. L. F., and Smith, C., *The Place-Names of Roman Britain*, 1979.

Salway, P., *Roman Britain* (Oxford History of England, Vol. Ia), 1981.

Salway, P., *The Oxford Illustrated History of Roman Britain*, 1993.

Salway, P., *A History of Roman Britain*, 1997: revised version of the text of *The Oxford Illustrated History*.

Todd, M., *Roman Britain*, 3rd edn, 1999.

Wilson, R. J. A., *A Guide to the Roman Remains in Britain*, 3rd edn, 1988.

The transformation of Britain: from 55 BC to AD 61

Bradley, R. J., *The Social Foundations of Prehistoric Britain*, 1984.

Cunliffe, B. W., *Greeks, Romans and Barbarians: Spheres of Interaction*, 1988.

Holder, P. A., *The Roman Army in Britain*, 1982.

James, S., *The Atlantic Celts: Ancient People or Modern Invention?*, 1999.

Macready, S., and Thompson, F. H. (eds.), *Cross-Channel Trade between Gaul and Britain in the Pre-Roman Iron Age*, 1984.

Wiseman, A., and Wiseman, T. P., *Julius Caesar: The Battle for Gaul*, 1980: Caesar's *Gallic Wars* in translation.

A second start: from the defeat of Boudicca to the third century

Breeze, D. J., *The Northern Frontiers of Norman Britain*, 1982.

Burnham, B. C., and Wacher, J., *The 'Small Towns' of Roman Britain*, 1990.

Casey, P. J., *Carausius and Allectus: The British Usurpers*, 1994.

Johnson, S., *Hadrian's Wall*, 1989.

Wacher, J., *The Towns of Roman Britain*, 2nd edn, 1995.

The fourth century and beyond

Bland, R., and Johns, C., *The Hoxne Treasure*, 1993.

Dark, K., *Britain and the End of the Roman Empire*, 2000.

de la Bédoyère, G., *Golden Age of Roman Britain*, 1999.

Esmonde Cleary, A. S., *The Ending of Roman Britain*, 1989.

Faulkner, N., *The Decline and Fall of Roman Britain*, 2000.

Jones, M. E., *The End of Roman Britain*, 1996.

Kulikowski, M., 'Barbarians in Gaul, Usurpers in Britain', *Britannia*, 31 (2000), 325–45.

Maxfield, V. A. (ed.), *The Saxon Shore: A Handbook*, 1989.

Painter, K. S., *The Mildenhall Treasure: Roman Silver from East Anglia*, 1977.

Culture and social relations in the Roman province

General

Birley, A. R., *The People of Roman Britain*, 1979.

Huskinson, J., *Experiencing Rome: Culture, Identity and Power in the Roman Empire*, 1999.

Aspects of Romano-British art

CSIR (*Corpus Signorum Imperii Romani*), Vol. 1, fasc. 1–8: catalogues of stone sculpture from Roman Britain.

Davey, N., and Ling, R. J., *Wall-Painting in Roman Britain*, 1982.

Henig, M., *The Art of Roman Britain*, 1995.

Ling, R., 'Mosaics in Roman Britain: Discoveries and Research since 1945', *Britannia*, 28 (1997), 259–95.

Neal, D. S., *Roman Mosaics in Britain*, 1981.

Scott, S., *Art and Society in Fourth-Century Britain—Villa Mosaics in Context*, 2000.

Toynbee, J. M. C., *Art in Roman Britain*, 1962.

Toynbee, J. M. C., *Art in Britain under the Romans*, 1964.

Religion

Green, M., *The Gods of the Celts*, 1986.

Henig, M. E., *Religion in Roman Britain*, 1984.

Johns, C., and Potter, T. W., *The Thetford Treasure*, 1983.

Painter, K. S., *The Water Newton Early Christian Silver*, 1977.

Thomas, C., *Christianity in Roman Britain to AD 500*, 1981.

Watts, D., *Christians and Pagans in Roman Britain*, 1991.

Social groups and sites

Allason-Jones, L., *Women in Roman Britain*, 1989.

Bowman, A. K., *Life and Letters on the Roman Frontier: Vindolanda and its People*, 1994.

Crummy, P., *City of Victory: The Story of Colchester—Britain's First Roman Town*, 1997.

Keppie, L., *Roman Inscribed and Sculptured Stones in the Hunterian Museum, University of Glasgow*, Britannia Monograph Series 13, 1998: includes the distance slabs from the Antonine Wall.

The human impact on the landscape: agriculture, settlement, industry, infrastructure

Dark, K., and Dark, P., *The Landscape of Roman Britain*, 1997.

Hingley, R., *Rural Settlement in Roman Britain*, 1989.

Millett, M., *The Romanization of Roman Britain: An Essay in Archaeological Interpretation*, 1990.

Potter, T. W., and Johns, C., *Roman Britain*, 1992.

Roberts, B. K., and Wrathmell, S., *An Atlas of Rural Settlement in England*, 2000.

The edge of the world: the imperial frontier and beyond

Bateson, J. D., 'Roman Material from Ireland: A Re-consideration', *Proceedings of the Royal Irish Academy*, 73, C, 2 (1973), 21–97. See also the report of the Colloquium on Hiberno-Roman Relations and Material Remains, *Proceedings of the Royal Irish Academy*, 76, C, 6–15 (1976), 176–292.

Bowman, A. K., and Thomas, J. D., *The Vindolanda Writing Tablets*, 1994 (= *Tabulae Vindolandenses* II).

Breeze, D. J., *Roman Scotland*, 1996.

Breeze, D. J., and Dobson, B., *Hadrian's Wall*, 4th edn, 2000.

Hanson, W. S., *Agricola and the Conquest of the North*, 1987.

Hanson, W. S., and Maxwell, G. S., *Rome's North-West Frontier: The Antonine Wall*, 1983.

Maxwell, G. S., *The Romans in Scotland*, 1989.

Chronology

Entries in italics give the names and dates of Roman governors of the British provinces, where they are known or can reasonably be conjectured.

125–123 BC	Permanent Roman presence established in southern Gaul, increased penetration of Roman culture northwards, changes appearing in Britain
c.100	Development of Portland and Hengistbury Head as trading ports
58–51	Caesar's conquest of Gaul
56	Defeat of Veneti, Gallic domination of communication with Britain broken
55	First expedition of Caesar to Britain
54	Second expedition of Caesar
54–51	Gallic revolts (52 Vercingetorix)
52	Commius flees to Britain
49–44	Caesar as *dictator* (49–45 Civil War, 48 death of Pompey)
44–30	Further civil wars across Roman world
31	Battle of Actium, victory of Octavian over Antony and Cleopatra
30	Suicides of Antony and Cleopatra; Octavian (Augustus) sole ruler; effective end of Roman Republic
34, 27, 26	Projected expeditions of Augustus to Britain?
16	Roman diplomatic activity towards Britain?
c.16	Romanizing coinage of Tincomarus begins
c.15	Coinage of Tasciovanus appears, Catuvellaunian expansion begins?
by 12	Permanent Roman bases on the Rhine
AD 9	Destruction of three legions in Germany (*Clades Variana*), imperial expansion under Augustus ends
before 14	Tincomarus and Dubnovellaunus suppliants at court of Augustus; coins of Cunobelinus, issued first at Colchester, then Verulamium; British rulers dedicate offerings on Capitol in Rome
39/40	Adminius exiled from Britain by Cunobelinus
40	British expedition of Gaius (Caligula) aborted
40/3	Death of Cunobelinus

41/2	Verica flees from Britain to court of Claudius
43	Claudian invasion, Claudius accepts British surrender in person; invasion force includes legions Second *Augusta* and Fourteenth, almost certainly Ninth and Twentieth (recorded in Britain soon after)
43–7	*Aulus Plautius*
*c.*43–6	Vespasian campaigns westward
by 47	Conquest of South and East of England completed
47	Aulus Plautius becomes last Roman outside imperial family to receive a formal 'ovation' in Rome
47–52	*Publius Ostorius Scapula*
47	First Icenian revolt suppressed
47–52	Campaigns of Ostorius Scapula on Welsh border
48	First Roman intervention in Brigantia
49	Foundation of Colchester as *colonia*
*c.*50	Foundation of London
51	Caratacus finally defeated in battle, surrendered by Cartimandua, ceremonially displayed at Rome, and pardoned by Claudius
52–8	Conquest of Wales continued; second Roman intervention in Brigantia, supporting Cartimandua against Venutius
52–7	*Aulus Didius Gallus*
57/8	*Quintus Veranius*
?58–61	*Gaius Suetonius Paullinus*
60	Paullinus attacks Anglesey
60/1	Revolt of Boudicca, destruction of Colchester, London, and Verulamium
61/2–3	*Publius Petronius Turpilianus*
63–9	*Marcus Trebellius Maximus*
*c.*66/7	Fourteenth Legion withdrawn by Nero for Caucasus campaign
68–9	'Year of the Four Emperors'
69/71	*Marcus Vettius Bolanus*
69/70	Fourteenth Legion back in Britain after first battle of Bedriacum
69	Venutius makes war on Cartimandua
70	Fourteenth Legion transferred to Germany
71–3/4	*Quintus Petillius Cerialis*
71	Second Legion *Adiutrix* posted to Britain
71	Final defeat of Venutius by Cerialis

71–84	Conquest of northern Britain and Wales completed
73/4–77/8	*Sextus Julius Frontinus;* Silures defeated in Wales; major public works begun in Romano-British cities
77–83	*Gnaeus Julius Agricola*
83/4	Battle of Mons Graupius
83/96	*Sallustius Lucullus*
85/92	Second Legion *Adiutrix* transferred to Danube
?87	Inchtuthil evacuated
90/100	Foundation of Lincoln and Gloucester *coloniae*; at London stone fort constructed, second basilica started; Richborough victory monument built
by 98	*Publius Metilius Nepos?*
?97/8– *?100/1*	*Titus Avidius Quietus*
*c.*100	Frontier on Tyne–Solway line, Scotland largely abandoned
?100/1–3 *(or later)*	*Lucius Neratius Marcellus*
108/130s	Final withdrawal of Ninth Legion from Britain
c.115/18?	*Marcus Appius (or Atilius) Bradua*
117/38	Hadrianic fire of London
118–22	*Quintus Pompeius Falco*
122	Hadrian visits Britain, the Wall begun, revival of public building in cities; Sixth Legion posted to Britain
122–4 *(or later)*	*Aulus Platorius Nepos*
124/131	*Trebius Germanus*
130/1–2/3	*Sextus Julius Severus*
132/3–5 *(or later)*	*Publius Mummius Sisenna*
138/9–?42/3	*Quintus Lollius Urbicus*
140–2/3	Antonine conquests in Scotland, by 143 Antonine Wall begun
?142/3–?5	*Cornelius Priscianus?*
by 146	*Gnaeus Papirius Aelianus*
150s	Serious trouble in the north, Antonine Wall evacuated, Hadrian's Wall recommissioned
*c.*155	Verulamium extensively damaged by fire
by 158	*Gnaeus Julius Verus*
158/9–61	*. . . . anus*
*c.*160/3	Final abandonment of Antonine Wall

161/2	*Marcus Statius Priscus*
161–80	Reign of Marcus Aurelius, major wars on Danube and in East, serious pressure on empire from outside begins
162/3–?6	*Sextus Calpurnius Agricola*
c.163	Hadrian's Wall restored
169/80	*Quintus Antistius Adventus; Caerellius Priscus?*
175	Surrendered Sarmatian cavalry sent to Britain
180/230	Land walls of London built
177/8–184/5	*Ulpius Marcellus*
c.182/3	Major warfare breaks out on northern frontier of Britain
184	Victory in Britain
mid-180s	Earthwork defences begin to be provided for previously unwalled British towns
185	Army in Britain sends delegation to demand dismissal of Perennis, Praetorian Prefect
185/?7	*Publius Helvius Pertinax*
191/2–?3	*Decimus Clodius Albinus* (193 proclaimed in Britain as emperor)
193–7	Britain under rule of Clodius Albinus as emperor
197	Victory of Septimius Severus at Lyon, Britain falls to Severans
197	Restoration of forts in northern frontier region begins
197–?200/2	*Virius Lupus*
?202/3–5	*Gaius Valerius Pudens*
205/7	*Lucius Alfenus Senecio*
205	Restoration of Hadrian's Wall begun
?208/13	*Gaius Junius Faustinus Postumianus*
by 213	*Gaius Julius Marcus*
197/213	Britain divided into two provinces
197/c.250	*Pollienus Auspex (Britannia Superior); Rufinus (Brit. Sup.); Marcus Martiannius Pulcher (Brit. Sup., acting)*
208–11	Campaigns of Septimius Severus and Caracalla in Scotland, imperial court in Britain, Geta effectively regent
?208/11 (or later)	Martyrdom of St Alban
211	Death of Septimius Severus at York
211–13	Caracalla makes frontier dispositions in Britain, possibly finalizes division into two provinces
212	Murder of Geta by Caracalla in Rome
212	*Constitutio Antoniniana* (Roman citizenship extended to almost all free inhabitants of empire)

by 216	*Marcus Antonius Gordianus (Britannia Inferior)*
by 219	*Modius Julius (Brit. Inf.)*
220	*Tiberius Claudius Paulinus (Brit. Inf.)*
221–2	*Marius Valerianus (Brit. Inf.)*
222/35	*Calvisius Rufus (Brit. Inf.), Valerius Crescens Fulvianus (Brit. Inf.)*
223	*Claudius Xenophon (Brit. Inf.)*
by 225	*Maximus (Brit. Inf.)*
c.235	*Claudius Apellinus (Brit. Inf.)*
235–70s	Civil wars and invasions in East and West of empire
by 237	*(T)uccianus (Brit. Inf.)*
by 237	York receives title of *colonia*
238/44	*Maecilius Fuscus (Brit. Inf.), Egnatius Lucilianus (Brit. Inf.)*
by 242	*Nonius Philippus (Brit. Inf.)*
?after 244	*Aemilianus (Brit. Inf.)*
253/5	*Titus Desticius Juba (Brit. Sup.)*
255/70	Riverside wall of London built
259/60	Revolt of Postumus in Gaul: Gallic Empire (*Imperium Galliarum*) formed
259/60–74	Britain under rule of Gallic emperors
263/8	*Octavius Sabinus (Brit. Inf.)*
270s	Renewed growth in Britain
274	Surrender of Tetricus, end of Gallic Empire
after 274	*Lucius Septimius? (Brit. Sup.)*
275–6	Germanic invasions of Gaul
c.277	Probus repeals restrictions on viticulture in Gaul and Britain
277/9	Burgundian and Vandal troops settled in Britain used in suppression of a governor's revolt
282–5	Britain under control of Carinus
284	Accession of Diocletian
286	Maximian's campaign in Gaul
287	Carausius seizes Britain
287–93	Britain under rule of Carausius; last certain record of Twentieth Legion (coinage of Carausius)
293	Tetrarchy formed; Carausius' forces expelled from Boulogne, Carausius assassinated by Allectus
293–6	Britain under rule of Allectus
294	Palatial building work in London
296	Britain retaken by Constantius I as *Caesar*

after 296	Britain becomes a civil diocese of four provinces
296/305	*Aurelius Arpagius (Brit. Inf. or Brit. Secunda)*
late 3rd/ early 4th c.	*Hierocles Perpetuus (province unknown)*
297/8	Constantius I sends skilled tradesmen from Britain to restore Autun
before 305	Reconstruction work begins on the northern frontier
306	Campaign of Constantius I in Scotland, Constantine the Great proclaimed at York
311	Persecutions of Christians end
312	Battle of the Milvian Bridge (defeat of Maxentius by Constantine)
313	Edict of Milan, Peace of the Church confirmed
314	British bishops at Council of Arles
by 319	*Lucius Papius Pacatianus (vicarius)*
324	Constantine sole emperor, foundation of Constantinople
340	Defeat of north-western Roman armies at Aquileia in civil war
340–69	Period of severe stress in Britain, internal troubles, harassment by barbarians
342/3	Visit of Constans to Britain in winter
?c.350	*Flavius Sanctus (province unknown)*
350	Proclamation of Magnentius in Gaul
350–3	Britain under rule of Magnentius
353	Suicide of Magnentius
353/4	*Martinus (vicarius)*, purge by Paul the Chain, suicide of Martinus
355	Julian appointed *Caesar*, in charge of Britain and Gaul
356–9	Victories of Julian on German frontier
357/8–60	*Alypius (vicarius)*
358/9	Julian ships grain from Britain
359	British bishops at Council of Rimini
360	Picts and Scots attack frontier region of Britain, expedition of Lupicinus
360–3	Julian as sole emperor, official revival of paganism in empire
367–9	*Barbarica Conspiratio*, Picts, Attacotti, and Scots attack Britain, Franks and Saxons raid Gaul; recovery and restoration of Britain by the elder Theodosius, revolt by exiles suppressed
367	*Civilis (vicarius)*

378	Battle of Adrianople, massive defeat of eastern section of Roman army by Goths
382	Theodosius the Great settles Goths in Thrace
383	Proclamation of Magnus Maximus in Britain; victory over Picts
383–8	Britain under rule of Magnus Maximus
388	Defeat and execution of Magnus Maximus
391	Theodosius bans all pagan worship
392–4	Western half of empire under control of Arbogast and Eugenius, paganism again tolerated in West
394	Battle of the Frigidus, Theodosius the Great regains control of whole empire with forces that include high proportion of barbarian allies
394–408	Stilicho commander-in-chief of western armies (*magister utriusque militiae praesentalis*)
395	Death of Theodosius the Great, effective division of empire between East and West
?395/400	Mobile army established in Britain under *comes Britanniarum*
?395/406	Chrysanthus (*vicarius*), Victorinus (*vicarius*)
?395/425	Last record (*Not. Dign.*) of Sixth Legion (at York) and Second Legion *Aug.* (Richborough, also in field army in Gaul)
*c.*396	Visit to Britain of Victricius, bishop of Rouen
398/400	Victories over Picts, Scots, and Saxons
400/2	Possible troop withdrawals from Britain by Stilicho
402	Official import of new bronze coinage to Britain ceases
404	Western imperial court withdrawn from Milan to Ravenna
405/6	Proclamation of usurper Marcus in Britain, Germans cross Rhine
407	Gratian and Constantine III successively proclaimed in Britain
407–11	Constantine III rules from Arles
409	Britain revolts from Constantine III, end of Roman rule in Britain
410	Sack of Rome by Alaric; 'Rescript of Honorius'
411	Fall of Constantine III
416	Pelagianism officially condemned as heresy
417	First recorded exercise of Roman authority in northern Gaul since end of Constantine III's rule

418	Visigothic kingdom of Toulouse established
by **420/30**	Regular use of coinage ceases in Britain, factory-made pottery no longer available
425–9	Aetius in Gaul as *magister militum per Gallias*
429	Visit of St Germanus to Britain
431	Episcopate of Palladius in Ireland
432	Episcopate of St Patrick in Ireland begins (traditional date)
440s/50s	Traditional dates for Saxon takeover in Britain, probable final end of recognizable Romano-British society
446/54	Appeal of Britons to Aetius (Gildas)
451	Battle of Catalaunian Plains, advance of Attila halted by Aetius
454	Murder of Aetius, regular Roman army in West subsequently run down
460s	Britons recorded in Brittany
476	Romulus 'Augustulus' deposed by Odoacer at Ravenna
480	Julius Nepos, last western emperor, murdered in Dalmatia

List of Roman Emperors

This list gives the dates of reigns down to the death of the last western emperor. The dates are those of the effective reign (many emperors designated their sons or other intended successors as co-emperors, but these are only shown when there was a real sharing of the supreme power). The list does not attempt to differentiate between 'legitimate' emperors and 'usurpers', or to list every minor usurper, particularly after the end of Roman rule in Britain. Appointments to the Late Roman junior imperial rank of *Caesar* are only shown where they are relevant to Britain. Names are given in the forms in which they are commonly encountered in modern works in English.

Julio-Claudians

Augustus (Octavian)	27 BC–AD 14 (sole ruler from 30 BC)
Tiberius	14–37
Gaius ('Caligula')	37–41
Claudius	41–54
Nero	54–68

'Year of the Four Emperors'

Galba	68–9
Otho	69
Vitellius	69
Vespasian	69–79 (see also below)

Flavians

Vespasian	69–79
Titus	79–81
Domitian	81–96
Nerva	96–8
Trajan	98–117
Hadrian	117–38

Antonines

Antoninus Pius	138–61
Marcus Aurelius	161–80
Lucius Verus	161–9 (with M. Aurelius)

Commodus	180–92
Pertinax	193
Didius Julianus	193

Severans and their rivals

Septimius Severus	193–211
Pescennius Niger	193–4
Clodius Albinus	193–7
Caracalla	211–17
Geta	211–12
Macrinus	217–18
Elagabalus	218–22
Severus Alexander	222–35
Maximinus ('Thrax')	235–8
Gordian I	238
Gordian II	238
Pupienus	238
Balbinus	238 (with Pupienus)
Gordian III	238–44
Philip I ('the Arab')	244–9
Pacatian	248
Jotapian	249
Decius	249–51
Gallus	251–3
Aemilian	253
Valerian	253–59/60
Gallienus	253–68
Macrianus	260–1
Quietus	260–1
Regalianus	260/1
Aemilianus ('Aegippius')	261–2
Aureolus	267–8
Laelianus	268

Gallic Empire

Postumus	260–9
Marius	268
Victorinus	269–71
Tetricus	271–3
Claudius II ('Gothicus')	268–69/70
Quintillus	269/70
Aurelian	269/70–5

Vaballathus	270–1
Tacitus	275–6
Florian	276
Probus	276–82
Saturninus	280
Carus	282–3
Julian I	283
Carinus	283–5 (*Caesar* 282–3)
Numerian	283–4

The Tetrarchy

Diocletian	284–305
Maximian	286–305, 307–8 (*Caesar* 285–6)
Constantius I ('Chlorus')	(*Caesar* 293–305, *Augustus,* see below)
Galerius	305–11 (*Caesar* 293–305)
Carausius	287–93 (in Britain and Gaul)
Allectus	293–6 (in Britain and Gaul)
Domitius Domitianus	297 (in Egypt)
Flavius Severus	306–7 (*Caesar* 305–6)
Maximin Daia	309–13
Maxentius	307/8–12
Alexander	308–9/10 (in Africa)
Licinius	308–24
Valens I	316

House of Constantius and their rivals

Constantius I (*Augustus*)	305–6
Constantius I ('the Great')	306–37
Constantine II	337–40
Constans	337–50
Constantius II	337–61
Nepotian	350
Vetranio	350
Magnentius	350–3
Silvanus	355 (in Gaul)
Julian II ('the Apostate')	360–3 (*Caesar* 355–60)
Jovian	363–4

House of Valentinian and their rivals

Valentinian I	364–75
Valens II	364–78
Procopius	365–6
Gratian	375–83
Valentinian II	375–92

House of Theodosius and their rivals

Theodosius I ('the Great')	379–95
Magnus Maximus	383–8
Eugenius	392–4

In the West		*In the East*	
Honorius	395–423	Arcadius	395–408
Marcus (in Britain)	406		
Gratian II (in Britain)	407		
Constantine III	407–11	Theodosius II	408–50
Maximus (in Spain)	409–11		
Jovinus (in Gaul)	411–13		
Constantius III	421		
(Flavius Constantius)			
Johannes (John)	423–5		
Valentinian III	425–55		
		Marcian	450–7
Petronius Maximus	455		
Avitus	455–6		
Majorian	457–61	Leo I	457–74
Libius Severus	461–5		
Anthemius	467–72		
Olybrius	472		
Glycerius	473		
Julius Nepos	473–80	Leo II	474
Romulus			
('Augustulus')	475–6	Zeno	474–91

(etc. to 1453)

Maps

Map A Topography of Britain and Ireland: in the context of Roman Britain it is customary to point to a broad correspondence between the 'highland' and 'lowland' zones of mainland Britain and 'military' and 'civil' occupation, though there are many local anomalies. Recent research on later periods has, however, suggested an alternative way of looking at rural settlement in England and Wales which does not divide on the traditional lines (see Figures 18 and 19 above).

Map B The principal tribes of the British Isles in the Roman Era.

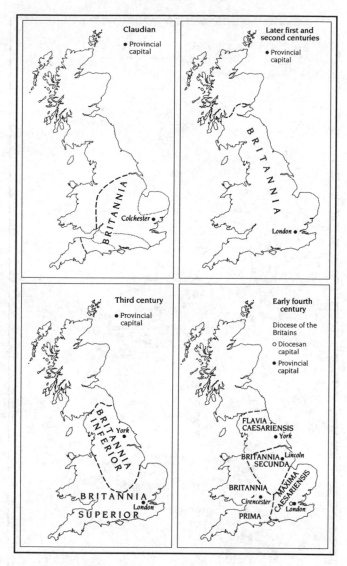

Map C The changing arrangement of provinces down to the early fourth century (details likely but not certain).

Map D Britain in the second century AD.

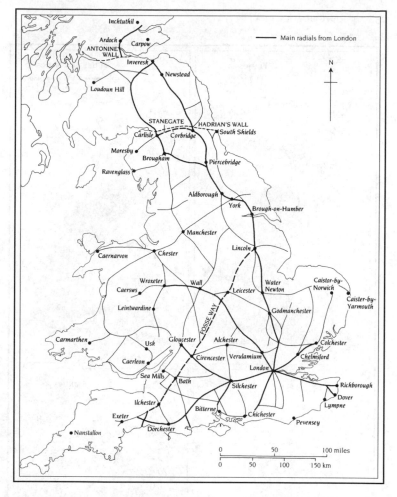

Map E The communications system of Roman Britain. This map shows the major roads (some lesser roads have been omitted for the sake of clarity). Water transport (inland and by sea) complemented road, but too little is known of routes to permit reliable mapping. It is reasonably certain that the roads inland from Richborough and Chichester represent the earliest thrusts of the Claudian Conquest, but the position of London at the hub of the network makes it clear that it was recognized as the natural strategic centre at a very early stage thereafter. By AD 50 the main section of the Fosse Way had been laid out, and the legion originally occupying Colchester had been moved westwards. The latter permitted the foundation of the *colonia* at Colchester, but the road system laid out originally for military/governmental purposes—'reducing Britain into regular provincial form'—was not centred there but on the new port at London. Other subsidiary networks and further ports were developed as the province expanded (e.g. the military port at South Shields to serve the northern frontier), but the major lines of campaign still stand out as the great roads from London to Exeter, London to Wroxeter, and London to Scotland.

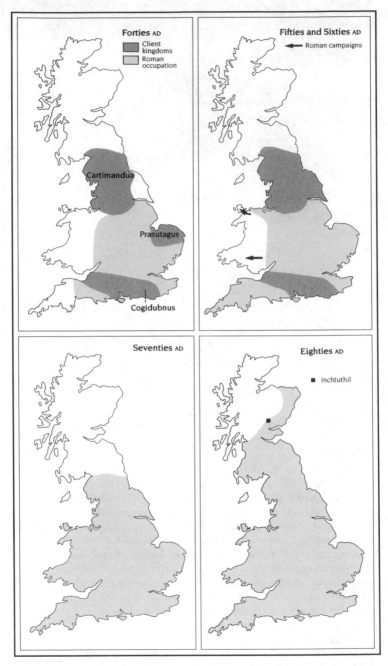

Map F Britain: the ebb and flow of Roman military occupation.

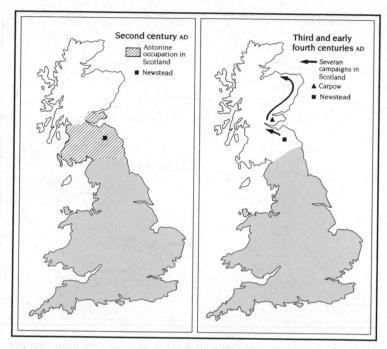

Map F Britain: the ebb and flow of Roman military occupation.

Map G In the early years of Roman rule the main units of the army were not stationed in fortresses large enough to take a whole legion except—significantly—at Colchester, the former centre of British power and the scene of the Emperor Claudius' personal victory: there seems to have been no general expectation of trouble.

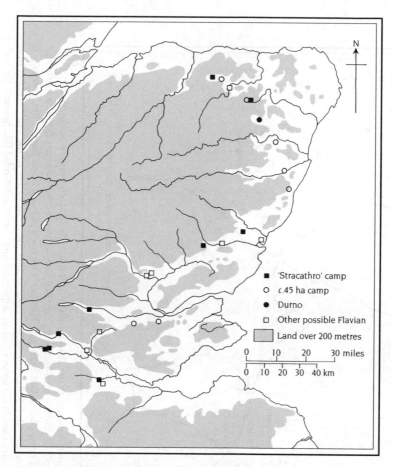

Map H Roman campaigns in north-east Scotland. The marching camps are of various sizes and designs: the huge camp at Durno (58 hectares: 143 acres) perhaps held Agricola's army before the Battle of Mons Graupius (83). However, being capable of accommodating a much larger force than described by Tacitus, it may date from one of the later expeditions led by emperors in person, accompanied by their personal troops and retinues: the nature of the imperial government meant that much of the administration of the empire had to travel with them, not to mention those prominent persons whom it was politically prudent to keep within reach.

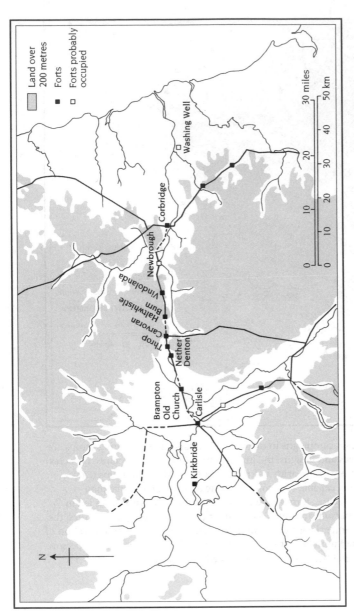

Map I The 'Stanegate Frontier'. Under Trajan, after the abandonment of the already reduced military occupation of southern Scotland, the garrisons furthest north were those along the road now known as the Stanegate between Corbridge and Carlisle, and to east and west of those places. The 'Stanegate Frontier' was not a physical linear barrier but a series of fortified points that could monitor and control movement. It is possible that the construction of the road was later than some of the posts, but from that point onwards the system had an important function as a defended link between the two main highways into Scotland.

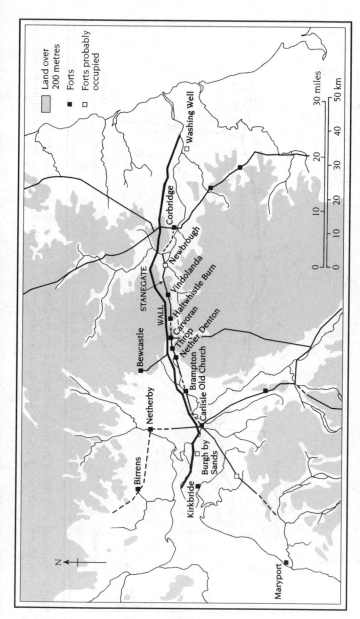

Map J Hadrian's Wall: establishment of a linear barrier. Originally it was intended to house most of the troops in existing forts on the Stanegate, with the Wall itself only lightly held. Outpost forts at the western end, however, suggest that difficulties were already anticipated there, and the system was continued down the Cumbrian coast, with sea taking the place of curtain wall.

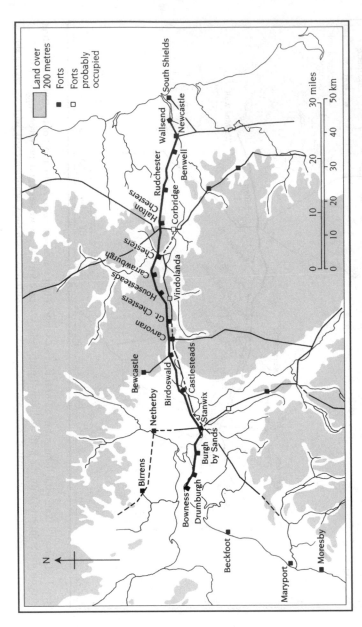

Map K Hadrian's Wall: Before the end of Hadrian's reign the linear wall had received both its first permanent garrisons and a supplementary series of forts, while some garrisons remained to secure the Stanegate and territory further southwards.

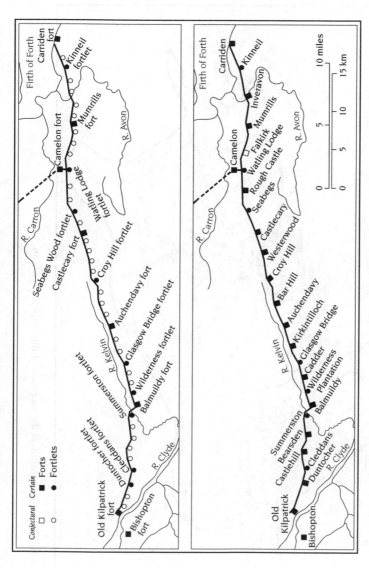

Map 1 The Antonine Wall: The original scheme (*above*) was a simplified version of Hadrian's Wall—a linear turf rampart (instead of stone) with mile-fortlets, and a small number of garrison forts on the line itself. The final version (*below*) added extra forts, reducing the intervals from around 8 miles to around 2.

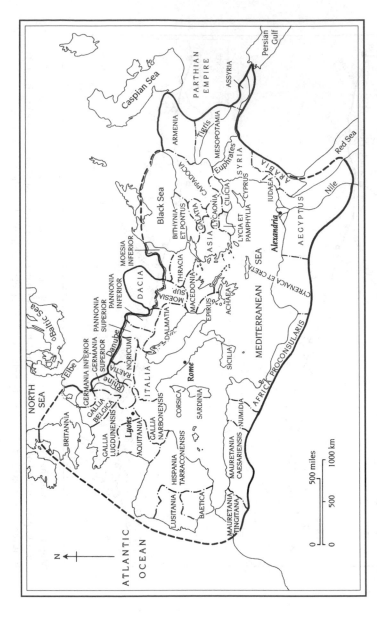

Map M The Roman empire at the accession of the Emperor Hadrian.

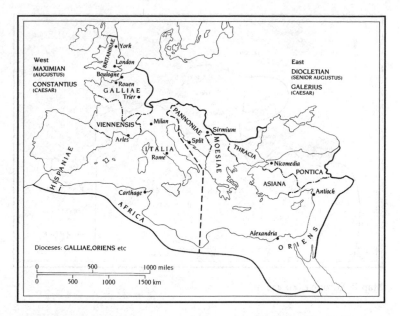

Map N The Roman empire *c.* AD 300: the reorganization under the Emperor Diocletian (the Tetrarchy).

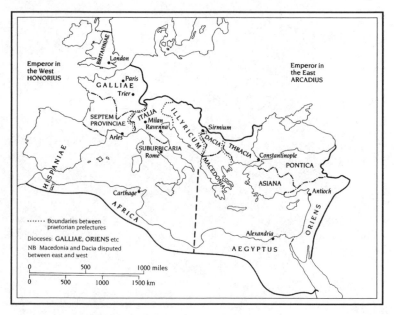

Map O The Roman empire *c.* AD 400.

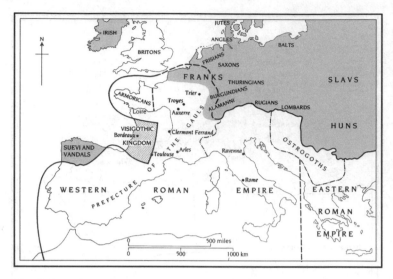

Map P Europe *c.* AD 420.

Index

Notes: 1. Page numbers referring to maps are shown in **bold**. 2. As is customary, the names of Roman citizens in the period before AD 284 are entered under the second element of the three-name system (*tria nomina*) that was a mark of citizenship, except for those otherwise very familiar under another name. 3. The qualification 'emperor' after a name includes usurpers as well as legitimate emperors.